Cyber Warfare

Recent Titles in
The Changing Face of War

Mismanaging Mayhem: How Washington Responds to Crisis
James Jay Carafano and Richard Weitz, editors

Private Sector, Public Wars: Contractors in Combat—Afghanistan, Iraq, and Future Conflicts
James Jay Carafano

Fighting Identity: Sacred War and World Change
Michael Vlahos

The Three Images of Ethnic War
Querine Hanlon

Spying in America in the Post 9/11 World: Domestic Threat and the Need for Change
Ronald A. Marks

The Future Faces of War: Population and National Security
Jennifer Dabbs Sciubba

War and Governance: International Security in a Changing World Order
Richard Weitz

Cyber Warfare

How Conflicts in Cyberspace Are Challenging America and Changing the World

Paul Rosenzweig

The Changing Face of War
James Jay Carafano, Series Editor

 PRAEGER

AN IMPRINT OF ABC-CLIO, LLC
Santa Barbara, California • Denver, Colorado • Oxford, England

Library of Congress Cataloging-in-Publication Data

Rosenzweig, Paul, 1959–
    Cyber warfare : how conflicts in cyberspace are challenging America and changing the world / Paul Rosenzweig.
        p. cm. — (Changing face of war)
    Includes bibliographical references and index.
    ISBN 978-0-313-39895-7 (hbk. : alk. paper) — ISBN 978-0-313-39896-4 (ebook)   1. Information warfare.   2. Cyberterrorism—Prevention.
3. Cyberspace—Security measures.   4. Computer security—Government policy—United States.   5. Computer crimes—Prevention—Government policy.   I. Title.
    U163.R68   2012
    355.4—dc23   2012027448

ISBN: 978-0-313-39895-7
EISBN: 978-0-313-39896-4

17 16 15 14 13   2 3 4 5

This book is also available on the World Wide Web as an eBook.
Visit www.abc-clio.com for details.

Praeger
An Imprint of ABC-CLIO, LLC

ABC-CLIO, LLC
130 Cremona Drive, P.O. Box 1911
Santa Barbara, California 93116-1911

This book is printed on acid-free paper ∞

Manufactured in the United States of America

For Katy:

"I love thee to the depth and breadth
and height my soul can reach . . ."

Contents

Acknowledgments

There are a number of people to thank for their help in making this book possible. Certainly, if victory has many parents, then a successful book can only be seen as a victory, with many who deserve thanks for its success.

To begin with, I offer my thanks to Jack Goldsmith of Harvard for the idea for this book. We were talking one day at a seminar in Montana and he suggested the need for a comprehensive survey of this sort. Thanks, too, to Greg Maggs and Peter Raven-Hansen of George Washington University School of Law. They hired me to develop and teach a course on cybersecurity law and policy and the research that went into the course formed the basis of much of this book. I owe them, along with Dean Paul Berman, a deep debt of gratitude for giving me an intellectual home at George Washington.

Thanks, also, to Angie Chen who teaches a technology and policy course at George Mason University—she loaned me her syllabus from that course and that was my starter material for the course I eventually taught.

I owe a special debt of gratitude to my friend, James Carafano, of The Heritage Foundation. Jim and I wrote a book together a few years ago and he is the series editor of this Praeger series. It was at Jim's urging that I first tried to pull the syllabus into a book proposal format and submit it. Heritage, as well, has been an intellectual home for me over the years and I am deeply grateful to the foundation for its support. Thanks, as well, to Steve Catalano, the acquisitions editor at Praeger, who saw something in the proposal and helped me shepherd it through the approval process. Without either of them, this book would not exist.

Particular thanks must go to the Medill School of Journalism, at Northwestern University, and my colleagues Tim McNulty, Ellen Shearer, Scott Anderson, Josh Meyers, Janice Castro, and Mary Nesbitt. I spent a joyous six months there as a Carnegie Visiting Fellow during 2011. Much of the research for this volume was done while I was in residence there, and I am grateful to them for giving me an academic home from which to work. My especial gratitude to the Carnegie Corporation which funded my Fellowship.

Thanks, as well, to my students at George Washington and Northwestern, who suffered through my development of the seminar and whose own research papers and interests have contributed to my education. One of my students, Brock Dahl, provided helpful comments on some of the early chapters.

There are a number of colleagues (other than those already mentioned) from whom, over the years, I have learned a great deal. Some of the best ideas in this book are ones I first had the chance to discuss with one of them, and I have benefited from innumerable conversations. In alphabetical order, I express an intellectual debt to: Michael Aisenberg, Ken Anderson, William Banks, M.E. "Spike" Bowman, Steve Bucci, Robert Chesney, Paul Clark, Raphael Cohen-Almagor, Jim Dempsey, Steven Dycus, Jayson Healey, Lance Hoffman, Adam Isles, Jeff Jonas, Orin Kerr, John Kropf, Harvey Rishikof, Marcus Sachs, Nathan Sales, Daniel Solove, Jay Stanley, K.A. Taipale, Matthew Waxman, and Benjamin Wittes.

I must also specifically mention a nonattribution e-mail group of which I am a member—The Cyber Loop—and thank my fellow Loopers for all they've done to add to my education. Many of the books in the bibliography were first recommended to me by some of them.

Stewart Baker was my boss at the Department of Homeland Security and, in this field, a philosophical guide. Whenever I wonder what the right answer is, I simply ask myself what Stewart will say? And, that usually proves the right answer. And, on those rare occasions when I disagree with him, I always suspect that I'm missing something.

I owe a quick shout-out, as well, to my grandson Aaron Kunzer, who showed me the T-shirt from Think Geek with the binary quote on it that serves as the epigraph of this book. And, I need to thank my parents, Bobbie and Irving Rosenzweig, and my brother Jim for all their love and support over the years. My mother and brother will read this book; I regret that my father did not have the chance to do so before he died.

I have had the opportunity to work with a number of publishers and journal editors over the past two years. Portions of this work have previously appeared in some of those other publications. Grateful acknowledgement is made to the various publications where these works first appeared and, where necessary, for permission to reuse that material in this volume, as follows:

• "Making Good Cybersecurity Law and Policy: How Can We Get Tasty Sausage?," 8 *Journal of Law and Policy for the Information Society* (2012);

- "Privacy and Counterterrorism: The Pervasiveness of Data," 42 *Case Western Reserve Journal of International Law* 625 (2010);
- "The Organization of the United States Government and Private Sector for Achieving Cyber Deterrence" in Proceedings of a Workshop on Deterring Cyber Attacks: Informing Strategies and Developing Options for U.S. Policy (National Academy of Sciences, 2010), reprinted by the courtesy of the National Academies Press, Washington, DC;
- *The Evolution of Wiretapping,* Engage (Federalist Society, 2011);
- *Cybersecurity: An Introduction, from Worms to Cyberwar* and *Beware of Cyber China,* Defining Ideas (Hoover Institution, 2011 & 2012);
- *Cybersecurity and Public Goods: The Public/Private "Partnership"* (Hoover Institution, 2011);
- *National Security Threats in Cyberspace* (American Bar Association & National Strategy Forum 2009), reprinted with permission;
- *Einstein 3.0* in Baker & Horowitz, eds., *Patriots Debate: Contemporary Issues in National Security Law* (ABA Publishing, 2012);
- "10 Conservative Principles for Cybersecurity Policy," The Heritage Foundation, *Backgrounder* No. 2513 (January 2011);
- "Lessons of WikiLeaks: The U.S. Needs a Counterinsurgency Strategy for Cyberspace," The Heritage Foundation, *Backgrounder* No. 2560 (May 2011); and
- "The International Governance Framework for Cybersecurity," 37 *Canada-United States Law Journal* (2012).

And, finally, of course, I owe a deep debt of gratitude to my wife, Katy Kunzer, who read the entire manuscript and offered her insights throughout. More importantly, her support and love are the foundation of my life and are the true parents of this successful volume.

1

Chapter

The Transformation of Cyberspace and Cyber Conflict

There are only 10 types of people in the world: Those who understand binary and those who don't.[1]

The binary system of counting, which uses only 1s and 0s, lies at the heart of computational algorithms. Every number, every bit of data, every voice communication, and every video can, in essence, be expressed as a string of 1s and 0s. In physical terms, deep within the innards of the computer, silicon chips create those 1s and 0s through a series of switches whose structure is etched onto wafer-thin silicon integrated circuits.[2]

The beauty of cyberspace and its genius lies in recognizing the universal power of these simple 1s and 0s. The rapidity with which they can be manipulated has, over the past decades, increased exponentially. And that explosion in computing power has fostered a wild explosion of new technology. Hardly a day goes by without the development of some new computer application that is intended to enhance our lives; indeed, they have become so ubiquitous that we now have a shorthand word for them—we call them "apps." America's increasing utilization of, reliance on, and dependence on technology for our social infrastructure is changing how we live our lives. The pervasiveness of technological advances has significant implications for how individuals interact, for how the economy functions, for how the government and the private sector conduct business, and—ultimately—for how we protect our national interests and provide for our common defense.

This book is about those changes. It is about how cyberspace has come to pervade our everyday activities. More importantly, it is about the vulnerabilities that arise from how we use cyberspace; and it is about what America, and the world, are doing (or could do) to respond to those vulnerabilities. If you want a shorthand way of thinking about this book, it is about our struggle to have our cake and eat it too—about how we try to reap the benefits in productivity and information sharing that come from a globalized web of cyber connections while somehow managing to avoid (or at least reduce) the damage done by malfeasant actors who seek to take advantage of that globalized web for their own reasons.

Like most efforts to eat cake without gaining weight, our labors cannot reasonably be expected to be fully successful. Our struggle can only be to minimize the threats as best as we can, while maximizing the benefits. That struggle is, in a phrase, the great conflict of the current generation. The nature of that conflict changes on a daily basis, but unless something deeply surprising happens, the specter of cyber warfare and the reality of a broader cyber conflict (including espionage, terrorism, and crime) are with us for the foreseeable future.

* * *

A symbol of the new era is a malicious software worm dubbed "Stuxnet." Malicious software has been with us for 25 years—but Stuxnet is different. Discovered in July 2010, it is the first demonstration, in the real world, of the capability of software to have a malicious physical effect. Up until the Stuxnet software was developed, the mantra of many experts in cyber conflict was that "cyber war only kills a bunch of little baby electrons." Stuxnet showed the world that cyber war could potentially kill real babies.

What Stuxnet did was infect a physical manufacturing plant—in this case, an Iranian uranium enrichment facility—and make it malfunction. Using only a cyber virus, Iran's adversary (and nobody yet is sure who it was, though the press has reported that it was the United States and Israel) made machines break down. That's scary. While Stuxnet only disrupted a uranium purification system, there is nothing at all that limits a cyber assault to uranium purification. If the Iranian facility at Natanz is vulnerable, so is the electric grid in New York.

And, that puts us at the brink of a transformative time—one that will be highly destabilizing. Settled assumptions and frameworks for resolving conflict will dissolve, almost overnight. The ways of war will have to be rethought, as will our definitions of espionage, terrorism, and even crime. The last time the settled geopolitical worldview was so disrupted, a nuclear explosion devastated Hiroshima. The physical effects of Stuxnet are nowhere near that severe, thankfully. But, the cognitive disruptions that will come are just as great. Stuxnet was, figuratively, the first explosion of a cyber atomic bomb.

* * *

To see why that is so, we need to understand exactly what cyberspace is and how it creates both opportunities and vulnerabilities. The power of binary computing lies at the heart of huge increases in productivity and improvements in human welfare and happiness. Amazon, WalMart, and Facebook would all be impossible without the power of the Internet. Today, America's real physical infrastructure has become deeply intertwined with the less corporeal world of cyberspace. Cyberspace is bound up in virtually every sector of our economy. It pervades our transportation system, our power and energy grids, our communications networks, our financial and banking programs, our emergency systems, and our military programs. The linking of these systems through cyberspace has created significant opportunities for business, trade, convenience, and efficiency. The Internet makes our lives better. Exploitation of these opportunities and emergent technologies has helped America to be a world-leading technological innovator.

And yet, as with every new technology, there is also a dark side. The same facility for manipulating data in binary code also lies at the heart of many powerful new negative influences; identity theft, distributed denial of service attacks, cyber espionage, and cyber warfare are powered by the same technological miracles that power Google. These are the dimensions of cyber conflict and our dependence on cyberspace makes conflict inevitable. Worse yet, it means that the effects of these conflicts are more pervasive than the conflicts we have previously seen in history. Physical conflicts, in the "real" world, are bounded in time and space. Conflicts in cyberspace are not, however, and can spin wildly out of control.

> According to Internet World Stats (a company that compiles this data), in 1995 there were roughly 16 million Internet users. In December 2011, the number of Internet users exceeded 2.2 billion, more than 30 percent of the world's population.

As Nassim Taleb, the author of *Black Swan*, recently put it, "connectivity and operational leverage are making cultural and economic events cascade faster and deeper."[3] This cascade effect has particular force in cyberspace because disruptions in cyber systems propagate much more rapidly, and to a wider extent, than disruptions have in the past—precisely because cyberspace connects the world so comprehensively.[4] To be fair, the interconnectivity of the world is not solely because of cyberspace. Advances in the speed of air travel and other factors of globalization also contribute to the phenomenon that Taleb has identified. But, it is undeniable that the globalization of cyberspace is a predominant factor in the globalization of international codependence.

As a result, in our post-9/11 world, we face a new type of threat to both our national economy and our national security. Deliberate attacks on our national infrastructure could crash key computer-dependent control networks, such as electrical power grids, telecommunications systems and networks, transportation systems, and financial institutions. These systems and structures are vital to America; their incapacitation or destruction would have an immediate and debilitating impact on national security, economy, public health, and safety.

The pervasiveness of cyberspace connectivity has also changed how we approach the gathering of intelligence and even economic espionage. Today, the theft of critical information can occur at a distance and with much greater ease than in the past. The wholesale degradation of secrecy threatens to erase our intellectual property, our competitive economic advantages, and our national security. Likewise, the same tools bid fair to strip average citizens of any privacy or anonymity they have in their private lives. When everything is connected to the Internet, adversaries can (and often will) destroy our secrecy and privacy almost at will.

* * *

These vulnerabilities call for a response. The actors who are responsible for meeting the challenges of cyber conflict range from the private sector, to the Federal government, to international institutions. When the Internet first came on the scene, our society paid little attention to the possibility of a cyber threat or conflict. We saw all the benefits of the technology, but none of the latent vulnerabilities.[5]

More recently, America has come to appreciate the threats and begun to react with much greater urgency. The last few years have seen a remarkable surge in the degree of concern publicly expressed by government officials regarding national security threats in cyberspace. The Bush Administration began the development of a Comprehensive National Cybersecurity Initiative (CNCI) in January 2008.[6] The Obama Administration followed, with a Cyberspace Policy Review and the appointment of a Cyber Czar to coordinate a federal government response.[7] Funding for initiatives to protect the cyber domain has been increased significantly.

Despite the surge of attention to cyber vulnerabilities, little consensus has emerged. Some question whether a cyber threat of any significance exists at all, while others deem the threat existential. Novel issues of policy and law surface on an almost daily basis as technological innovation runs headlong forward, leaving policy-makers and concerned legislators trailing in its wake.

The range of responses to our vulnerabilities includes technical fixes (like greater encryption) and a more active role for the Federal government in combating cybercrime and protecting the Internet. Concurrently, the United States has begun (as never before) to consider the cyber domain as an arena for offensive and defensive military actions. Just as American systems and information may be targeted, we have begun to look at how we can achieve and maintain dominance of the cyber domain when a conflict erupts.

In taking these steps, the United States does not (and cannot) act in isolation. It has begun attempts to coordinate our actions with other nations and global actors who face the same threats and dangers. Likewise, it is attempting to coordinate governmental efforts with those of the private commercial sector (who, after all, own more than 85 percent of the Internet infrastructure) to establish a comprehensive national cyber defense to protect the critical infrastructure of our nation.

* * *

The struggle—to benefit from fundamental scientific advances while avoiding the inevitable costs—is not a new one. It has recurred often in human history, whenever foundational changes in our capabilities have occurred. The policy upheaval wrought by the cyber revolution is, in some ways, no different than others we have experienced, most recently with the revolution of nuclear energy.

On the eve of World War II, just a month before it began, Albert Einstein wrote a cautionary note to President Franklin Delano Roosevelt. He told the president of advances in creating chain reactions involving uranium that might permit the construction of "extremely powerful bombs of a new type," a single one of which could destroy an entire city. He warned, as well, of possible German interest in uranium ores and, inferentially, in their war-making potential.[8]

With this, Einstein launched America's race to develop the atomic bomb (Einstein is sometimes reported to have thought this was the "greatest mistake" of his life).[9] The secret Manhattan Project proved Einstein's supposition correct. J. Robert Oppenheimer was the scientist in charge of the project. For more than two years, he, and hundreds of others, toiled in the desert outside Los Alamos, New Mexico. In the end, they proved that, by using a uranium isotope, it was possible to construct a massive bomb, capable of destroying an entire city.

When, in July 1945, the first experimental bomb was exploded, Oppenheimer immediately recognized the significance of the event. As he recounted some years later, in an interview:

> We knew the world would not be the same. A few people laughed. . . .
> A few people cried. . . . Most people were silent. I remembered the line
> from the Hindu scripture the Bhagavad Gita; Vishnu is trying to persuade the prince that he should do his duty, and to impress him takes
> on his multi-armed form, and says, "*Now I am become death, the destroyer of worlds.*" I suppose we all thought that, one way or another.[10]

But, even Oppenheimer barely understood the significance of the changes that arose from the first atomic bomb. At the time, he recognized its destructive power and the transformative effect it would have on war-making. But, no-body could, at the dawn of the nuclear age, anticipate its long-term effects.

Looking back now, with the perspective of more than 65 years, we can see some of those changes. From the first atomic bomb came nuclear power and cheaper electricity. But, it also brought us new ways of thinking about war, like the concept of Mutually Assured Destruction: the counterintuitive idea that world peace is better maintained through the hyperdevelopment of destructive capacity. This led to the equally counterintuitive view that defense is destabilizing and the effective banning of defensive technologies.

In the broader field of world geopolitics, nuclear weapons also wrought unexpected changes. In an extended sense, the existence of atomic weapons mandated a policy of containment, rather than confrontation, since nuclear war was too grave to risk. From a policy of containment came the Cold War, the Marshall Plan, NATO, and, ultimately, limited wars in Korea and Vietnam. At the beginning of the nuclear era, all of these developments were unanticipated glimmers on the far horizon, unseen by anyone who witnessed the first atomic explosion. Atomic weapons were utterly transformative.

* * *

Cyberspace is no different. We have had an easy (some would say, too easy) time exploiting the benefits of the Internet. Now, however, it seems as though the vulnerabilities threaten to overwhelm the benefits—the Internet is a bit of a wild and dangerous place, where our secrets, and even our identity, are increasingly at risk. Viruses, like Stuxnet, that threaten our critical infrastructure are but the most extreme example of those vulnerabilities. Like the explosion of the atom bomb, we can't even begin to predict what the future holds—but events like Stuxnet tell us that the changes will be very great indeed.

WHAT EXACTLY IS A "STUXNET?"

Stuxnet is a piece of software code. At its core, it was just a string of 1s and 0s, like any other program. But, this one was malevolent. Stuxnet was what is sometimes called a two phase attack—it had two parts. Its origins lay in malware that infected a Windows-based Microsoft operating system; call this the "delivery phase." From there, the malware jumped to infect what is known as a SCADA system—a Supervisory Control and Data Acquisition system—manufactured by Siemens, the German manufacturing giant.[11] Indeed, it targeted a very specific type of SCADA system software, the S7–400 PLC software (PLC stands for Programmable Logic Controller; it is the generic name for the type of software controller used to operate large-scale machinery operations worldwide). We can think of this as the attack phase of the program.

The entire program required two phases for its attack on the SCADA system because, not surprisingly, many SCADA systems that run sensitive or secret machinery are not directly connected to the Internet. Those connections are, rightly, thought to make a system more vulnerable to intrusion, so operators add an additional layer of security by creating an air gap (literally, when the operators of a system maintain a gap with nothing but air in between, which prevents a connection to the Internet) between their system and the wider world web of cyberspace.

The Iranian nuclear enrichment program was just such a sensitive program. It was almost certainly air-gapped from the broader Internet. Stuxnet entered the Iranian system (and other systems it infected) through some interaction between the SCADA system and an external Windows-based program. Nobody quite knows for sure how that happened. Perhaps, it was introduced into the control program when an engineer hooked up a Windows-based tablet to collect data for diagnostic purposes. Or perhaps, it was on a thumb drive mistakenly plugged into a Windows operating interface system. Or, more creatively, it might have been introduced on purpose by a human agent who infiltrated the facility for the purpose of introducing the worm into the system—we are likely to never know for sure.

Whatever the method of introduction, the second phase attack demonstrated a large degree of sophistication. It was designed to target only a single particular type of operating program (a bit like a fish seeking only a single type of bait). Unlike many malware programs, Stuxnet ran without any remote reference to an outside controller. Most programs look for instructions from the head office before acting, but Stuxnet was independent. And, in identifying two targets within the Iranian nuclear enrichment facility, Stuxnet's developers exhibited a significant degree of inside knowledge—they knew exactly what to attack and how to do so. That's why some have likened Stuxnet to a precision-guided smart missile.

The Stuxnet malware had two different targets within the Iranian enrichment facility. The smaller attack manipulated the speed of rotors in a nuclear enrichment centrifuge. The variations in speed were designed to slowly wear down and, ultimately, crack the rotors. The other digital attack was precisely configured to affect the centrifuge enrichment cascades at the facility. The precision was reflected in the match between the logic structure of the malware and the exact number of centrifuge cascades (164) operated at the Iranian facility in Natanz. At the risk of simplifying, the program operated by affecting the rate at which nuclear centrifuges spun. In order to produce uranium suitable for use in a nuclear bomb (or, for that matter, in a nuclear power plant), centrifuges must run at a constant speed. Stuxnet caused the centrifuges to run at a highly variable rate, causing the uranium it produced to be impure and unsuitable for use. Along the way, the worm also disabled and bypassed several digitally operated safety systems that were designed to make sure that the centrifuges ran at a fixed and safe speed.

Stuxnet was also a surreptitious piece of malware. Buried within the program was a pre-recorded series of data reports on the operation of the centrifuges. Of course, SCADA systems regularly provide reports to the operators about how the machinery is working. While Stuxnet was causing the centrifuges to operate poorly, it was using the pre-recorded data reports to falsely report to the operators that everything was in good working order. Think of the movie *Ocean's Eleven*, where the robber/heroes play a pre-recorded tape of what is happening in the vault they are robbing to cover their true activities, and you get an idea of how the Stuxnet worm covered its tracks.

Finally, Stuxnet used four separate zero-day exploits in order to achieve its objective. A zero-day exploit is one that works on the zeroth day. In cyberspace, most vulnerabilities are gaps in programming code that, when discovered, can be exploited by outsiders. But once the vulnerability is exposed and exploited, it can also be fixed by software designers. That's why software security firms are constantly shipping updates to your computer and software developers are constantly recommending users to download patches for their software; they are providing you with the fixes to vulnerabilities that have recently been discovered, most often because some malicious actor has abused them.

For this reason, new vulnerabilities—ones that have not been used before—are a valuable commodity for bad actors. The actors save them up and use them for important later attacks because they are unlikely to have been patched and will work. These zero-day exploits are the coin of the realm. Using one of them in an attack is standard; using two is a little profligate. To use four zero-day exploits (as Stuxnet did) is a sign of the importance that the developer put on the success of the attack.

In short, the use of four zero-day exploits and the amount of inside information and testing required for the worm to be developed make many observers believe that Stuxnet is the most advanced and effective malware ever to be released. Iran has, understandably, been unwilling to say much publicly about how badly it was affected by Stuxnet. At a minimum, confirmed reports suggest that the malware destroyed 1,000 centrifuges at the Natanz facility.[12] One Israeli analyst told the *Jerusalem Post* that Stuxnet may have set Iran's nuclear program back by at least two years.[13]

Of course, as in the real world, sometimes, even the most precise missiles cause some collateral damage. Though Stuxnet was probably targeted at the Iranian Natanz nuclear processing facility, according to Symantec (a computer security firm), by September 29, 2010, there were 100,000 infected hosts in the world, with approximately 60 percent of those residing in Iran. The next five countries to experience the most infections were Indonesia, India, the United States, Australia, and the United Kingdom, respectively.[14]

SO, WHO DID IT?

At least on the public record nobody (except, of course, those who designed Stuxnet in the first place) knows for sure who designed Stuxnet. There has been no successful or decisive demonstration of attribution of responsibility for the Stuxnet malware, although press reports have attributed it to U.S. and Israeli manufacture. And there has been a lot of educated (and maybe less than educated) speculation. For example, some analysts think that there are hints as to the authorship of the worm buried in the malicious code itself. There were two pieces of evidence found in the Stuxnet code that allegedly are signatures that demonstrate Israeli authorship of the worm—a conclusion that certainly would be consistent with Israel's geopolitical concern for the development of an Iranian nuclear capability.

One piece of evidence is the prominence within the code of the number 19790509. This is thought by some analysts to represent the date May 9, 1979 (though contrarians want to highlight the fact that 0509 is an Americanized representation of the month/day formulation and that an Israeli is more likely to have used the European date/month formulation, making the date represented here stand for September 5, 1979). But if this is a date (and the format certainly bears the weight of that suggestion) then it might be related to the execution of Habib Elghanian, a Jewish Iranian on, that's right, May 9, 1979.[15] Some historians suggest that the execution, shortly after Ayatollah Khomeni's ascension to power, was the impetus for a mass Jewish exodus from Iran. That, it seems, is a pretty thin reed on which to rest the attribution of so significant a cyber intrusion.

Likewise, the other code-based piece of evidence (the use of a file location name of "Myrtus") seems fairly thin. Myrtus is plausibly a reference to the Book of Esther in the Old Testament. And Esther was responsible for saving the Jews from the Persians. On the other hand, RTU stands for Remote Terminal Unit—a device commonly associated with a SCADA system. This location name may be nothing more than MyRTUs—a convenient mnemonic.

Still, if this were a mystery novel then the Israelis would have the means, motive, and opportunity to have committed the crime. As already noted, they have a powerful incentive to degrade Iranian nuclear progress. But so do others, including the United States. Indeed, the *New York Times* reported that the two cooperated in the production of Stuxnet—using American knowhow to build the worm and then test it at Israel's Dimona complex in the Negev desert. According to the *Times,* the Stuxnet worm was tested on P-1 centrifuges (possibly obtained from the United States, which, in turn, got them from Libya when that country dismantled its nuclear program) identical to those at the Natanz nuclear facility.[16] More recently, the *Times* reported on leaks from inside the Obama Administration, which seemed to confirm U.S. participation in the Stuxnet attack.[17] In addition, there have been some reports that the Israelis have been less than circumspect in taking quiet credit for the development of Stuxnet.[18]

But an equally interesting possibility has been advanced by at least one observer. Writing in *Forbes*, Jeffrey Carr (a well-known cyber observer) speculated that China might have been behind the Stuxnet worm.[19] He linked the advent of Stuxnet to the failure of one of India's communications satellites. As a result of that failure, Indian service providers of direct-to-home telecommunications were forced to switch their traffic to a Chinese satellite—one owned by Chinese government investors. Interestingly, Carr notes, the failed Indian satellite also runs a Siemens SCADA interface of the sort that Stuxnet targeted. The transfer was, of course, financially beneficial to China, which might have had a motive for inducing the change (and for concealing its own role). Indeed, if China (or any other country for that matter) were concerned about an Iranian nuclear enrichment program and developed malware to disrupt it, their natural instinct would be to conceal their own role in the effort—and who better to blame than the Israelis and Americans with their undeniable motive?

And so, Stuxnet also serves as an introduction to one of the fundamental properties of the Internet; it is a realm where attribution is often difficult, if not impossible. Though much of the evidence seems to point to Israeli and U.S. responsibility, in cyberspace it is easy to spoof the evidence. Things are not what they seem and evidence can be created or merely misinterpreted.

WAS THAT IT?

If all Stuxnet did was destroy 1,000 centrifuges and delay the Iranian nuclear program by two years, that would be significant indeed. But in truth Stuxnet was transformative. As designed, the program simply made small changes to the operation of certain centrifuges to degrade their performance and, over the long run, make them inoperable. But once inside the SCADA system, an attacker can do almost anything. In theory, there is little difference between a code that makes centrifuges run out of synch and a code that causes all of the graphite control rods (which keep a nuclear reactor from overheating) to withdraw from the reactor, allowing it to overheat, or one that causes a chemical plant to mix two hazardous chemicals.

Whatever its source, Stuxnet's significance is the demonstration that incorporeal software can have real world, physical effects. Stuxnet was proof of the concept that cyber war can be real. And, as the Department of Homeland Security recently noted: "attackers could use the increasingly public information about the [Stuxnet] code to develop variants targeted at broader installations of programmable equipment in control systems."[20] Because SCADA systems are pervasive and generic, the Stuxnet worm is, essentially, a blueprint for a host of infrastructure attacks with catastrophic real world effects. Much as the American demonstration that nuclear weapons were capable of being manufactured assured the Soviets that their efforts would eventually succeed, the demonstration of a kinetic capability in Stuxnet has opened up a whole world of possibilities for malware designers—many of them potentially catastrophic. If you doubt this last proposition, consider that the largest SCADA system in the world is run by Gazprom, the massive Russian gas and oil producer.[21] That ought to give anyone pause for reflection.

Indeed, we may have already seen the first copy cat of Stuxnet. In October 2011, security experts discovered a variant of the Stuxnet worm, nicknamed "Duqu." Duqu uses much of the same code as Stuxnet, which may mean that it was written by the same individual or group, or that Stuxnet has already been successfully reverse engineered. Duqu is different from Stuxnet in that it does not have a malicious payload. Instead, it infiltrates a system and then logs all of the inputs from a keyboard (a program known as a keylogger). So, Duqu appears designed to steal sensitive data from infected systems and relay it back to the attackers. It hides the stolen keystroke logs in an image file to make it look like innocuous Internet traffic.[22]

Or, think of this possibility: maybe Stuxnet wasn't really intended to have that great an effect. Maybe the damage to Iran's nuclear program was just a useful collateral benefit to a larger purpose—that of sending a message to the Iranians that even their most sensitive programs were vulnerable. This is sometimes called an info hack, where the purpose is more to let your opponent know that he is vulnerable (and therefore should be cautious and circumspect in his actions) than it is to achieve any particular result.

Indeed, some strategic cyber analysts are convinced (albeit without any direct evidence) that Stuxnet was not the only payload delivered into the Iranian systems. After all, having gone to the significant effort of exploiting a vulnerability and having burned four very valuable zero-day exploits, why stop at disrupting the uranium enrichment centrifuges? A sensible adversary may have left behind at least one other (if not more!) payload with the capability of other far more significant disruptions—payloads that are virtually impossible to detect and scrub from an existing control system.

This sea-change in cyber vulnerability is reminiscent of the transformative changes that attended the explosion of the first atomic bomb. Of course, there are substantial differences as well; nobody would, today, argue that the destructive power of a Stuxnet-type attack equates to the destruction that an atomic bomb would cause. And, perhaps more importantly, even at the dawn of the nuclear age, we were confident that we could identify anyone who used atomic weapons and that they would all be peer nation-state actors. In the cyber realm, we have much greater difficulty identifying who fired the weapon and it might well be fired by a nonstate actor, like the cyber hacktivist group Anonymous or the patriotic hackers who supported Russia in its war against Georgia.

The similarities between atomic weapons and cyber threats, however, lie in the disruptive nature of the event. Imagine what it must have been like the day after the first atomic bomb was exploded. Around the globe, settled assumptions about war, policy, foreign affairs, and law had, in an instant, all come unglued. Even 17 years after the atomic bomb was first exploded, the uncertainty about their use and the threat they posed was so great that the Cuban Missile Crisis nearly engulfed the world in nuclear war. We're about to experience that same sort of tumultuous time and almost nobody in America, except a few very concerned senior policy makers, knows it.

We struggle, for example, to decide what a theory of cyber deterrence might look like. Is there an equivalent to the nuclear policy of Mutually Assured Destruction? How can we build a policy of containment (as we did with the Soviet Union) when we don't even know who we are trying to contain? And, in a cyber world without borders, how do national sovereigns react to nonstate threats? In short, we stand on the threshold of a new world, much like we did in 1945. From this vantage point, nobody can really say where the future might lead.

* * *

Conflict and warfare in cyberspace are a complex and challenging business. Every initiative has its own set of technical, legal, and policy problems. To put this in context with a single example, consider the issue of data encryption (a topic we will explore more fully in chapter 12). Encryption is fundamentally good in many ways: it protects privacy and personal data, and if used appropriately it reduces vulnerabilities in cyber systems. But, it also allows enemies, criminals, and terrorists to conceal their actions in cyberspace from effective counteraction. It is not at all obvious how we should best strike the balance between those competing concerns.

Time and again, we will see in this book that effective action on cyber conflicts requires us to assess the most effective means of protecting the American economy and society, while at the same time, recognizing and preserving the individual civil liberties that underpin our way of life. The convergence of the real and perceived threats from terrorists, cyber hacktivists, and foreign states, the advancement of sophisticated and readily available technologies, and America's dedication to preserving the civil liberties of its citizens alongside the obligation to ensure our country's national security gives rise to a mind-numbing array of legal and policy issues of first impression.

Worse yet, even when we think we find the right answers to these difficult questions, the questions have a disturbing tendency to change. Cyberspace is a dynamic environment where innovation is the only constant. As technology develops rapidly, the ability of law and policy to keep pace or anticipate dynamic situations has been overwhelmed. This book is a snapshot in time at the frontiers of evolving cyber conflicts. It explores the existing laws, equities, and variables in this compelling, new, multidisciplinary area, along with the tensions that are created as a result of the various competing concerns. Though some of the specifics may be dated as soon as this book is published, the principles and policy questions identified will, undoubtedly, endure.

Part I

The Nature of Conflict
in Cyberspace

Our exploration of cyber conflict begins with an attempt to understand its true nature. After all, one cannot truly solve a problem unless one has first defined exactly what the problem is. We must attempt to answer some of the questions that lie at the foundations of cyberspace conflict and define a baseline of knowledge. How significant, for example, is cyber conflict and how prevalent? Who are the major participants or, should we say, combatants? What are their motives? In the end, we may find that there are fundamental limits to our understanding and thus to our solution set, but any effort must begin with an attempt to know precisely where we are.

Broadly speaking, conflict in cyberspace is structured something like a pyramid. At the base of the pyramid, most frequently occurring but least harmful, are the all-too-common instances of cybercrime—cyber scams and fraud that typically involve the theft of money or of identity. We can think of this as the daily churn of conflict, which is certainly annoying and, to those affected, sometimes quite catastrophic. In the end, however, cybercrime is a lot like crime in the real world—endemic and disruptive but not overwhelming or an existential threat.

Higher on the pyramid, we find instances of cyber espionage. Here, we see less frequent, but far more sophisticated and systematic, attacks by nation states and nonstate actors bent on stealing national security secrets or valuable intellectual property. This is where most of the conflict today occurs as giga- or terabyte loads of information are being compromised. It seems, at times, as if America's peer-competitors have backed a series of trucks up to the Pentagon and are loading secret information continuously. Here, the losses are serious and disturbing, with significant adverse effects on national security.

The next higher level is what we may come to think of as cyber insurgency. Here is where we begin to see true conflict in cyberspace (akin to what the military calls a low-intensity conflict), as competing factions begin to wage something close to a war, but at a much lower level of destruction than any full-scale conflict would create. When cyber insurgents (or hacktivists), like Anonymous and LulzSec, attack websites or when patriotic hackers assist Russia in its conflict against Georgia, they are evoking the first forms of true cyber war. But, often their weapons limited to common cyber tools and the principal result from their actions is the defacement of a website or the denial of access.

Finally, at the highest level, we can imagine a cyber war between peer nation-states, that is, countries with sophisticated cyber capabilities. We've yet to see this sort of conflict, and perhaps we never will. More likely, this type of conflict will emerge as a collateral part of a true kinetic war. When and if a full-on cyber war begins, its destructive capacity will likely rival that of a physical conflict, but we cannot be sure of its true scope until we experience one.

And so, in Part I, we lay the groundwork for our consideration of cyber conflicts. We begin our exploration and our efforts to define the nature of the conflict by first exploring the true nature of the Internet and how it operates. We then conduct a tour de horizon of the pyramid of cyber conflict today, beginning at the top and working our way down, to the level of cyber espionage, leaving our discussion of cyber crime to Part II.

2

Chapter

Of Viruses and Vulnerabilities

The first known virus ever to infect a personal computer was named "Brain.A." It was developed (dare we say invented?) by two Pakistani brothers, Basit and Amjad Alvi. We know this because, amusingly, they signed their work and included contact information in the code of the virus. Brain.A was first detected in January 1986, just over 25 years ago. In its initial form, the virus did no significant harm. It renamed a volume label (in effect a file name) to "Brain" and could freeze a computer. Basit and Amjad say they meant no harm from their creation. Last year, a Scandinavian cybersecurity expert, Mikko Hypponen, went to Pakistan to look them up and found the brothers still living at the same address.[1] In a bit of poetic justice, they complained to him that they were constantly suffering from virus infections on their own computers.

How the world has changed! In just a single generation, we have gone from novelty to very real threats to cyberspace. Hardly a day goes by without news of some new cyber attack or intrusion that causes widespread consternation. Simply by way of example, on the day this chapter was first drafted, the hacker group Anonymous announced what it called Military Meltdown Monday,[2] a large-scale hack of the IT system of Booz Allen, a major federal military contractor. The next day, it was a malware attack targeted at Frenchmen celebrating Bastille Day.[3] Just a few days earlier, it had been Syrian security forces using social media to support President Bashar al-Assad against protesters.[4] Still more frequently, it is a simple invasion of privacy, whether through the theft of identity or hacking a voicemail system.[5] And the list goes on. Vulnerability in cyberspace is an everyday reality.

But, why is security in cyberspace such a challenge? And, what does that vulnerability mean for our national security?

WHAT IS THE WEB ANYWAY?

It is hard to understand cyber vulnerabilities, cybersecurity, and cyber warfare if you don't understand how the web is built and why it works the way it does. To a very real degree, much of what we consider a vulnerability in the system is inherent it its design. Indeed, the Internet is so effective precisely because it is designed to be an open system, and while that makes the network readily accessible, it also makes it highly vulnerable.

As David Post explained in his wonderful book, *In Search of Jefferson's Moose*,[6] the networks that make up cyberspace were built for ease of communication and expansion, not for security. At its core, the logic layer of the Internet (about which, more later) is fundamentally dumb. It is designed to do nothing more than transfer information from one place to another—very quickly and very efficiently. So, even though most users tend to think of Internet connections as nothing more than a glorified telephone network, the two are, in fact, fundamentally different.

The telephone networks are hub and spoke systems with the intelligent operation at the central switching points. Sophisticated switches route calls from one end to the other (indeed, at their inception, the intelligence at the hub of the telephone networks was human—operators making the required physical connections). In the world of telephone communications, for example, intercepting a communication was as simple as attaching two alligator clips to the right wire—hence the word "wiretapping."

Communications through the Internet are wholly different. The information being transmitted is broken up into small packets that are separately transmitted along different routes and then reassembled when they arrive at their destination. This disassembly of the data makes effective interception appreciably more difficult; there is no single route that the entire message follows. Thus, by contrast, the Internet is truly a world wide web of interconnected servers that do nothing more than switch packets of information around the globe.

Doing that requires very little intelligent design. All that is needed (to simplify matters somewhat) is an addressing system so that everyone has an address on the web, and a protocol that everyone agrees to, about how to move information from one address to the other. The addressing system is known as the Domain Name System (or DNS) and the transmission protocol is known as Internet Protocol Suite or, more commonly, the TCP/IP, which derives its name from two of the most important protocols in it: the Transmission Control Protocol (TCP) and the Internet Protocol (IP).

But, that's really it, for the innards of the working of the network. The real intelligent operations occur at the edges (in our mobile devices and laptops running various "apps"). And, that's what makes the Internet so successful. Access to it is not controlled at a central switching point. You don't need permission to add a new functionality (unlike, say, the phone system, where the telephone company has to hook you up and give you your new phone number). The way the Internet is built, anyone with a new idea can design it and add it to the network by simply purchasing a domain name and renting server space. The addressing directory (the DNS) that allows information to be correctly routed is operated on a distributed basis that no one person really controls. And, as long as you use the commonly accepted addressing protocols, virtually any function can be hooked up to the web—a store, a virtual world game site, or a government database. This flexibility is precisely what has driven the explosive growth of the Internet (today, there are more than 2.2 billion users worldwide) because everyone and anyone can use the network however they want to.

Let's consider the structure that this wild growth has given us. When we talk colloquially of the Internet, almost everyone is talking about the logical network layer where all of the information gets exchanged. If you tried to map all of those connections, it would look like a star burst pattern of colorful electronic veins going this way and that. A map today would look very similar to, but also completely different from a map created earlier in the timeline of the Internet, since the connections on the network are ever-changing. The Internet is a vast switching system for the distribution of information at near instantaneous speeds across great distances. There are no borders on the Internet and its structure makes action at a distance the norm rather than the exception.

But, this logic layer is only a piece of the puzzle. While most people think of cyberspace as the web of connections between computers, its full structure is really more complex. The graphic in Figure 2.1 gives you some idea of the

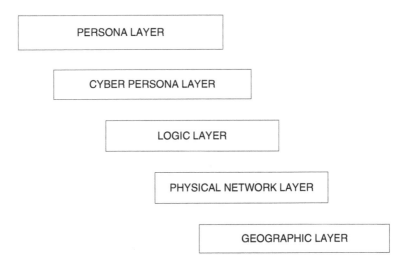

Figure 2.1 The five layers of the cyber domain.

scope of the entire cyber domain: in essence, a five-layer cake of connections, each of which presents its own set of cyber warfare challenges and issues.

At the bottom is what we might call the geographic layer, that is, the physical location of elements of the network. Though cyberspace itself has no physical existence, every piece of equipment that creates it is physically located somewhere in the world. One consequence of this is that the physical pieces of the network are subject to the control of many different political and legal systems.

Next is the physical network layer. This is the place where all of the hardware and infrastructure exists and is connected together. The components of this layer include all of the wires, fiber optic cables, routers, servers, and computers linked together across geographic spaces (some of the links are through wireless connections with physical endpoints). If we need a reminder that cyberspace is firmly grounded in the real world of geography and a physical network, we need only recall the December 2006 earthquake off the coast of Taiwan. In addition to the human tragedy it caused, the quake also cut six of seven undersea telecommunications cables, disrupting Internet traffic to Japan, Taiwan, South Korea, the Philippines, and China. Another cable break in Asia, which occurred in August 2009, had a similar effect. So did a pair of accidents at sea in February 2012, which inadvertently cut the East African Marine Systems fiber optic cable, setting off widespread telecom outages.[7]

In short, we should never forget that though the cyber domain is an artificial one created by man, it exists only in the context of the fundamental natural domain of the world.

Above these two real world layers is the middle layer, which is the heart of the network, the logic network layer that we've already seen. This is the virtual space of the cyber network, where the information resides and is transmitted and routed by servers. It is all of the 1s and 0s of binary code.

The logic layer in turn needs to be connected to the users. So, above the network layer is the cyber persona layer. In this layer, we see how a user is identified in the network. It includes details like his e-mail address, computer IP address, or cell phone number. Most individuals have many different cyber persona. Just think of how many different e-mail addresses and phone numbers you have. Here, too, are other items connected to the network, like the pieces of an electric grid or a smart house. It is also in this layer that the 1s and 0s get translated into an intelligible output—a webpage on your computer, for example. Among other things, it is at this level (and the next) that the true sources of Internet activities like cybercrime can be concealed.

Finally, there is the persona layer. This is where we talk about the actual people using the network, and who has their fingers on the keyboard, so to speak. While an individual can have multiple cyber personas (and, conversely a single cyber persona can have multiple users), in the end, we can also think about resolving the identity of individuals in a way that uniquely identifies a particular person connected to the network. And, of course, the true maliciousness of the network is at this level—where people chose to act in malevolent ways.

In short, as then deputy secretary of defense, William Lynn, put it in a speech announcing the Obama Administration's military Strategy for Operating in Cyberspace: "The Internet was designed to be open, transparent, and interoperable. Security and identity management were secondary objectives in system design. This lower emphasis on security in the Internet's initial design . . . gives attackers a built-in advantage."[8] And, it gives rise to significant vulnerabilities in at least four ways.

THE NATURE OF CYBER VULNERABILITY

The first vulnerability is the problem of anonymity. Given the vastness of the web, it is quite possible for those who seek to do harm to do so at a distance, cloaked in the veil of anonymity behind a false or ever changing cyber persona. While anonymity can be overcome, doing so requires a very great investment of time and resources. It also often requires the good guys to use bad guy techniques to track the malefactors. In effect, this makes many malfeasant actors immune, for all practical purposes, from swift and sure response or retaliation.

The second vulnerability lies in the difficulty of distinction between different types of cyberactivity. All the 1s and 0s in the logic layer look the same. But, that means that different types of activity in the logic layer are hard to distinguish. Thus, for those on the defensive end, it is virtually impossible to distinguish *ex ante* between espionage, and a full-scale cyberattack. They all look the same at the front end, and both also often look like authorized communications. The difference arises only when an intrusion has happened and the cyber payload "explodes" and the effects are felt. The closest physical world analogy would be something like never being able to tell whether the plane flying across your border was a friendly commercial aircraft, a spy plane, or a bomber.

Third, the ubiquity of the Internet creates enhanced asymmetries of power. Where, in the kinetic world, only nation-states and large-scale insurgencies could effectively compete against each other, in the cyber domain, small-size nonstate actors can challenge nation-states and poor Nigerian con artists can scam people on a global scale. One individual with multiple, complex relationships to other levels of the environment can send anything through the network to virtually any location worldwide. With that, we empower small groups like Anonymous (the cyber hacktivists who attacked PayPal, Amazon, and MasterCard) to, in effect, make all sorts of mischief.

Finally, the Internet is a globalized domain. There are no real borders on the network (though, as we shall see, countries are trying to erect them) and information is transmitted across the globe at the speed of light. This allows action at a distance, across national boundaries, in ways that are impossible in the physical world.

And that, in a nutshell, defines the problem: the very structures that make the Internet such a powerful engine for social activity and that have allowed its explosive, world-altering growth are also the factors that give rise to the vulnerabilities in the network. We could eliminate anonymity and resolve distinction, but only at the price of changing the ease with which one can use the Internet for novel commercial and social functions. Those who want both ubiquity and security are asking to have their cake and eat it too. So long as this Internet is "The Internet," vulnerability is here to stay. It can be managed, but it can't be eliminated.

ROBERT TAPPAN MORRIS AND THE TAXONOMY OF VULNERABILITY

Of course, it had to start somewhere. If Brain.A was the first virus, the first notable damaging attack on the web occurred by accident, though it was a purposeful accident, if that makes any sense. In late 1988, a Cornell graduate student, Robert Tappan Morris, released a worm intended to demonstrate flaws in the security protocols of the early Internet.[9] A worm, as its name implies, burrows through legitimate programs and hides in the dirt of computer code, so to speak. This worm was designed to enter through a security gap, replicate itself, and then move onward to infect more computers. Because of a design flaw in the worm, it spread like wildfire and caused significant damage, effectively clogging the entire Internet (which had limited bandwidth at the time) and preventing information from being transmitted (the Internet was much smaller back then). It was, in effect, a global denial of service on the network. In fact, when Morris realized that he had made a mistake, he tried to send out messages to other Internet users, telling them how to kill the worm, but his own messages of warning were blocked by the congestion his worm had caused.

Today, the Morris worm would be a mere pinprick. The cyber domain has not yet reached the state where interconnectedness is so great that a *Die Hard* IV scenario is plausible (for those who have not seen the movie, it imagines a mad cyberscientist who takes down all of the electric and transportation networks of the United States, only to be beat up by Bruce Willis).[10] But, the vulnerabilities to both intrusion and attack are real. Criminal theft and espionage occur at the billion dollar/terabyte level. And, cyber-hacktivists have waged proxy wars on behalf of Russia against Estonia and Georgia.

Given the widespread nature of vulnerability in cyberspace, it is at least moderately useful to have a taxonomy of the nature of the many types of exploitations that can occur. Given how wide a variety of intrusions there are, any taxonomy is in some sense arbitrary, and minor differences in definition are often important. A working taxonomy would look something like this:

- *Cyber intrusion*—A broad term comprising any instance of unauthorized access to a computer system (or access in excess of authorization). Intrusions may sometimes have no effect at all, as a hacker enters a system just to demonstrate the possibility (think of this as sort of like joyriding the Internet). Indeed, ethical hackers (those who intrude but do no harm) call their more malfeasant brethren "crackers" in order to distinguish them.
- *Cyber exploitation*—Unauthorized access to a computer system where the vulnerability is exploited in some fashion. The exploitation might be the removal of data (and, thus, espionage or theft, depending on what the data is), the insertion of a delayed action logic bomb, or an outright attack. An example might be the Anonymous intrusion into Booz Allen and the release of their e-mails publicly.
- *Cyber espionage*—Exploitation of a system for the purpose of securing data and information that is intended to be kept confidential. Espionage can come in two distinct flavors, just as in the physical world: industrial espionage for the purpose of commercial gain or governmental espionage to uncover secret or classified information. At the margins, of course, these two flavors can blend into one another.
- *Cyber theft*—Exploitation of a system for the purpose of stealing money or goods or intellectual property. The category includes cyber intrusions, but is also sometimes used to refer to any criminal theft, where a computer system or the Internet is used as a means of perpetrating the crime (as, for example, when Nigerian scam artists ask you to send them money).
- *Cyber operations*—Not all intrusions by a malevolent opponent are intended to have immediate effect. Many operations involve what the military would call "preparation of the battlefield." In the physical world, this might involve the surreptitious laying of mines or the creation of a base of operations behind enemy lines. In the cyber realm, it might involve the placement of a logic bomb or other Trojan horse program that does not activate immediately, but rather activates at a fixed time or signal.
- *Cyber defense*—Not all cyber defense is pure defense, though much of effective cyber defense involves the operation of firewalls and intrusion detection systems within your own network. But, many effective defensive

techniques involve active defenses (somewhat like having scouts on patrol near the base) where your own exploitations intrude on an opponent's system for the purpose of gauging his activities and thwarting them.

- *Cyber attack*—Though the phrase almost needs no explanation, cyber attack is when the a cyber payload is activated (or, executes) and causes some adverse consequence to an opponent.

THE INCREDIBLE SCALE OF THE INTERNET

One of the greatest cognitive difficulties in coming to grips with vulnerabilities in the network is that policy makers, legislators, and citizens simply don't have a good understanding of just how *big* the Internet really is.[11] The statistics are so sizable that they sometimes overwhelm human conception. Consider this: Today, there are more than 2.2 billion Internet users. That's more than 30 percent of the world's entire population connected to each other. No other human endeavor has ever been this big.

And those users are busy. Every single minute of every day, they conduct 700,000 Google searches, 11 million IM (Instant Message) conversations, and post one million Facebook status updates. In every single minute, they create more than 1,800 terabytes of new information and data.[12] How big is a terabyte? According to the Library of Congress, the approximate amount of its collections that are digitized and freely and publicly available on the Internet is roughly 74 terabytes.[13] So, every minute of every day, we add 24 new digital Libraries of Congress to the world's storehouse of information (granted some of it isn't worth adding, but that's another story).

Here's another way of thinking of it: More than 25 (and possibly as much as 48) hours of video are uploaded on Youtube every minute. That's 5–8 years of video to watch added every day. In other words, more content is posted to YouTube every month than the combined output of all US television networks since their inception in the 1940s. Or, consider this: According to Google's CEO "[e]very two days, we now create as much information as we did from the dawn of civilization up until 2003."[14] That's daunting.

And, with the growth of information also comes a growing threat to our security. Every minute, more than 168 million e-mail messages are sent. That's 88 quadrillion messages every year, and each and every one of them is a potential threat vector and source of a malware intrusion. The scale of the vulnerability is exactly as great as the scale of the Internet.

Perhaps, even more significantly, the scale of the vulnerability comes with an immense governance problem: how in the world can any human institution manage and regulate so large an enterprise? In many ways, that is the fundamental question posed in this book and the fundamental problem for the challenges of cybersecurity.

CYBERSECURITY EFFECTIVENESS—IS IT WORKING TODAY?

So, just how bad is it? Today, it is commonplace to say that effective cybersecurity is more of a dream than a reality. In general, cyber attacks defeat cyber defenses and that situation is likely to prevail for the foreseeable future. In short, life in the cyber domain is thought of as Hobbesian in nature—often "solitary, poor, nasty, brutish and short."[15] But, how accurate is this portrayal? What, if anything, can we say about the delivery of cybersecurity as an empirical matter? How effective are our efforts?

Sadly, though the question is a vital one, there is little data to support effective policy making. Typical is the US-Computer Emergency Readiness Team (US-CERT) Monthly Activity Report for April 2011, which reports not (as one might expect) activity involving cyber intrusions, attacks, and thefts, but, rather, the activities of US-CERT itself, that is, how many reports it has issued.[16] Given that US-CERT is "charged with providing response support and defense against cyber attacks for the '.gov' network and information sharing and collaboration with state and local government, industry and international partners," the lack of data on the necessity of its efforts (much less their efficacy) is troubling.

The problem is not limited to the intrusion detection realm. It also pervades efforts to measure actual effects. As three authors from PayPal recently noted, "estimates of the magnitude and scope of Cybercrime vary widely, making it difficult for policymakers and others to determine the level of effort to exert in combating the problem."[17] While individuals, companies, and trade associations have disparate pieces of the information puzzle, the data on cybercrime has never been convincingly aggregated. And, what is true of cybercrime is true, to an even greater degree, of instances of cyber espionage (of both the industrial and sovereign variety).

To be sure, some reports are more substantive than the US-CERT data, but they provide limited insight. For example, in 2010, the Internet Criminal Complaint Center (IC3) received 303,809 complaints of Internet crime.[18] Likewise, the Department of Homeland Security (DHS) reported 5,499 intrusions into U.S. government computer systems in 2008.[19] Neither of these numbers is terribly informative about the scope of the problem; the unreported and undetected instances of crime or intrusion are, by definition, unknowable. Indeed, these modest numbers pale next to other more apocalyptic estimates of malfeasant activity on the Internet: former deputy secretary of defense William Lynn said in 2010, for example, that military systems are "probed thousands of times and scanned millions of times" every day.[20]

More concrete estimates of the economic costs of cybercrime and cyber intrusions are available and offer some indication of the scope of the problem but are, in some views, highly conjectural. For example, the consulting firm

Detica has estimated the annual loss from cyber intrusions in the United Kingdom at £27 billion.[21] Two years earlier, McAfee Security estimated the annual cybercrime losses at $1 trillion globally.[22] Likewise, the annual cybercrime report from Symantec estimates that direct monetary losses in 2010 were $114 billion, while other losses (e.g., from lost time) amounted to $274 billion for a total of $388 billion globally.[23]

These estimates may be somewhat inflated by their methodology. The lion's share of these losses are estimated to flow from the theft of intellectual property (i.e., some form of industrial espionage), with direct monetary loss estimates running roughly an order of magnitude less (i.e., £3.7 billion annually in the United Kingdom, from fraud and identity theft).[24] If the same factor were applied to the McAfee global number, then the annualized monetary loss worldwide would be $100 billion—a significant number, but by no means astronomical. More notably, this data is a rough estimate at best, and they produce figures that are inherently suspect. At least one critic, for example, has characterized the Detica study as "nonsense" and "a grubby little piece of puffery."[25]

A CAUTIONARY NOTE

Given the relative paucity of data from official government sources, our best sources of information on the scope of cyber vulnerabilities comes from Internet security companies like Symantec and McAfee or security consultants like Detica.

While there is no reason a priori to doubt their reporting, many observers think that the authors have a conflict of interest of sorts—they are, after all, in the business of selling security and the worse the problem, the better their business. That said, we must use the data available—it is better than no data at all—while being mindful of its provenance.

Perhaps somewhat more authoritatively, the U.S. Government Accountability Office, repeating an estimate made by the Federal Bureau of Investigation (FBI), believes that in 2005 the annual loss due to computer crime was approximately $67.2 billion for U.S. organizations. The estimated losses associated with particular crimes include $49.3 billion in 2006 for identity theft and $1 billion annually due to phishing.[26]

One other way of trying to estimate the scope of the cybersecurity problem would be to examine how much is spent in preventing intrusions and theft. After all, nobody would expect rational businesses to spend more in prevention than they anticipate in losses. In 2011, the Ponemon Institute (a well-regarded Internet study group) conducted a survey study of 45 major American companies and found that the median amount lost annually because of cybersecurity breaches was $5.9 million, or $265.5 million for these companies in total.[27] No convincing extrapolation from this data has been (or, frankly, is likely to be), but a follow up study by Ponemon suggested that the amount being spent was less than 10 percent of what was necessary to stop 95 percent of all attacks.[28]

And clearly, there does seem to be a lot of churn on the network. One massive study of Internet traffic conducted for Bell Canada both demonstrates the scope of the problem and the difficulty of definitively assessing its severity. The study reviewed 839 petabytes of data,[29] containing more than four billion e-mails each month, carrying more than $174 billion (in Canadian dollars) of commerce every day. Within this flood of data, more than 53 gigabytes per second (!) contained malicious code of some sort. The investigators observed on the order of 80,000 zero-day exploits per day (a zero-day exploit is a vulnerability that has never before been discovered, and so there are no patches for it) and estimated that more than 1.5 million compromised computers attempted more than 21 million botnet connections each month.[30] This data is more or less consistent with estimates by large cybersecurity companies: Symantec, for example, discovered 286 million new unique malicious threats in 2010, or roughly nine new malware creations every second.[31] And yet, from all this, the most that can be said is that a large number of financial transactions are at risk—data about actual harm remains painfully elusive.

From the disparate data on cyber events, we can reach one firm conclusion and one tentative one. The firm conclusion is that governments worldwide need to undertake the difficult task of developing a useful data set on the scope and effect of cyber intrusions and cybercrime. No such metrics exist today and good policy is difficult to make in a data vacuum.

Both the United States and Europe seem to recognize this critical gap.[32] Each is, separately, moving toward a mandatory data reporting regime that would require private sector actors to report some intrusions into their systems. In the United States, the Obama Administration has proposed a mandatory data breach notification law that would, for significant breaches, require notification both to the individuals affected and to the federal government.[33] Likewise, in 2009, the European Union adopted a directive relating to the telecommunications industry. Article 13a of the directive required all electronic communications providers to report on security breaches to the European Network and Information Security Agency (ENISA).[34] While neither proposal has yet been implemented (the EU directive requires enactment by each member state and the Obama proposal is, as of September 2012, still nothing more than a proposal), both would, if ultimately developed, provide a better factual understanding of the nature of actual security breaches. Notably, however, even under these proposals, the data collected would be about breaches and intrusions; there would still be only limited data collected about the actual consequences of any security breach.

The second, more tentative conclusion, is that the broad overall economic impact of cyber intrusions and cybercrime is likely significant but not insurmountable. The inference is inescapable that some harm is occurring (otherwise, actors would not engage in the profitless conduct), but the magnitude of the actual harm seems, on current estimates, modest. In a global economy, even actual losses of $100 billion per year are significant, to be sure, but not beyond comprehension.

CYBERSECURITY AS NATIONAL SECURITY

One important caveat to the foregoing discussion of the lack of data is in order: We should understand that this data (and the attendant conclusions) are only relevant to the extent that the analysis is generally limited to assessing the economic impacts of cybercrime and cyber espionage. No fair estimate can be made about the impact on national security of a singular or significant cyber event.

To cite one incident, consider the recently analyzed Gh0stNet malware.[35] That malware imported a Trojan horse program onto infected computers, which allowed a remote user to, effectively, control the computer. The remote user could activate a keystroke logger, turn on the computer's video camera or microphone, and, of course, copy and steal any data stored on the computer. First observed on computers operated by the Dalai Lama, the malware was found in dozens of other computers including some located in the embassies of India, Malaysia, and Indonesia, ministries of foreign affairs, and even NATO headquarters (albeit on an unclassified system). Extended analysis eventually traced the malware to a set of Internet Protocol addresses and a server on Hainan Island, off the coast of China, an island that, perhaps coincidentally, is home to the headquarters of China's signals intelligence agency.

Or, consider the cyber war waged by Russian hacktivists against first Estonia and then Georgia. In August 2008, for example, when Russian troops conducted a land war against Georgia, Russian cyber patriots waged a cyber campaign against Georgia. The campaign was powered by the botnet world and involved mostly denial of service attacks against Georgian websites (like the website for Georgia's Ministry of Foreign Affairs) as well as website defacement. According to the U.S. Cyber-Consequences Unit (a study group set up to assess cyber events), the attacks were the work of civilians who, though not directed by the Russian military, had advance knowledge of the attack so that they were able to pre-plan and organize the cyber effort.[36] The civilian hacktivists used social media to organize their efforts.

It is difficult to assess how significant such incidents might have been. It is even more difficult to conduct a realistic assessment of the risks of further espionage activity, much less the risks that are associated with infiltrations into networks that might have physical effects, such as Stuxnet. Considerations of policy in regard to these sorts of national security vulnerabilities turn, not on a review of data about ongoing criminal intrusions, but rather on a reasonable risk assessment of the likelihood of such an event, measuring aspects of threat, vulnerability, and consequence. The little data we have addresses, inferentially, the vulnerability aspect of that question; from intrusions, we can learn where the loopholes are. We may also collect some data about consequence, especially when the effect on the infrastructure can be measured, but that data is difficult to quantify. What, for example, were the consequences to society of the Anonymous attack on PayPal, Mastercard, and Amazon? And, in the end, no solid data on the threat exists; we measure only capabilities, and then only by educated guesswork. We have no clear sense of true intent. As a result, we lack a solid quantifiable risk assessment of the cyber threat to national security and this leaves policymakers only with a speculative guess as to the extent of our risk from a cyber attack by a willful cyber opponent.

3

Chapter   **Nations in Conflict**

In December 2009 more than 200 computers belonging to top-ranking Indian government officials, including three service chiefs and former national security advisor M.K. Narayanan, were compromised in a hacking operation that probably originated in China.[1] In 2011, the United States contemplated, but did not launch, a cyber attack on Libyan anti-aircraft defenses in conjunction with its close air support of the anti-Gadhafi resistance.[2] Some say that when Israel destroyed the Syrian nuclear power plant in 2007, their planes used sophisticated cyber tactics to defeat Syrian air defenses.[3] And, a series of successful systematic cyber attacks in 2008 appear to have been aimed at al-Qaeda websites, by persons or entities unknown (though if motive is any indicator, likely to be a Western nation-state).[4]

All of these events reflect the growing reliance of nation-states on cyber weapons and tactics of varying degrees and kinds. Sometimes, the intrusions seem more in the nature of whole-sale espionage (as with the attack on Indian cyber systems). In other cases, the weapons used seem more intended to cause harm and disruption, either to an opponents' command and control systems (as with the Israeli attack) or, possibly, to hard targets within the country (as happened to Iran with the Stuxnet intrusion). Though the prospects for a full-scale cyber war remain somewhat difficult to assess, there can be little doubt that, increasingly, nations are coming into conflict through the medium of cyberspace.

Indeed, the judgment of the threat by American leaders is harsh, bordering on the extreme. James Clapper, the Director of National Intelligence, testified in January 2012 that state actors in China and Russia were responsible for multiple intrusions into American cyber systems.[5] At the same hearing, FBI director Robert Mueller testified that "threats from cyber-espionage, computer crime, and attacks on critical infrastructure will surpass terrorism as the number one threat facing the United States."[6] With such a pessimistic assessment, it is no wonder that American leaders are preparing for cyber war.

DEFINING CYBER WAR

But, this proliferation of means of conflict in cyberspace raises an interesting and challenging question: Are all of them weapons of war? Or, are some of them of dual character, such that their use is not equivalent to an armed conflict in the physical world. Put more fundamentally, we know what war looks like in the real world—things get blown up. But, what would be an "act of war" in cyberspace? Consider the following hypotheticals (all of which are reasonably realistic). An adversary of the United States (known or unknown):

- disrupts the stock exchanges for two days, preventing any trading;
- uses cyber weapons to take offline an early warning radar system;
- introduces a logic bomb (i.e., a piece of malicious software that can be activated at a later date) into a radar station that can disable the station when triggered, but doesn't trigger it just yet;
- makes a nuclear centrifuge run poorly in an nuclear production plant;
- implants a worm that slowly corrupts and degrades data on which certain military applications rely (say, for example, by degrading GPS location data);
- adds a back door to a piece of hardware that is built into a computer system, allowing the potential for the implantation of a worm or virus that would disrupt or destroy the system;
- takes the U.S. command and control systems offline temporarily;
- probes a Pentagon computer to map its structure and identify its vulnerabilities;
- blockades another country's access to the Internet; or
- disables an industry (say, part of the electric grid).

Some of these, like probing the Pentagon computer, are clearly analogous to espionage in the physical or kinetic world and won't be considered acts of war. Others, like disrupting our military command and control systems, look just like acts of war in the kinetic world. But, what about the middle ground? Is leaving a logic bomb behind in a radar station similar to espionage, or is it similar to planting a mine in another country's harbor as a preparation for war? Is the blockade of Internet access like a military blockade in time of war? Is causing a brown out by degrading the electric grid an attack?

We have only just begun to answer these questions. The new Department of Defense *Strategy for Operating in Cyberspace*, in its unclassified public version, focuses on the legitimacy of active defenses, which will authorize real time counter-attacks against incoming efforts to penetrate the Pentagon's systems.[7] Meanwhile, the classified version of the strategy is reported to conclude that the traditional laws of armed conflict apply in cyberspace just as they do in the physical world.[8] Though unsurprising (if not the traditional rules then which ones?), it is by no means clear this decision will work out.

This choice means that traditional rules of war will apply, including rules against the targeting of civilians and respecting the rights of neutrals that are of problematic application in cyberspace. Does, for example, the rule on neutrality mean that the United States cannot, if it abides by the laws of armed conflict, route its cyber attacks through neutral servers? That would be a significant self-limitation. Likewise, is the battlefield of cyberspace limited to geographic areas of military conflict or does U.S. CyberCommand have authority to execute military operations against all adversaries, wherever they may be?

More fundamentally, the strategy builds on the laws of armed conflict to define an act of war as any act that is equivalent in kinetic effect to a military attack. Under this definition, an attack on the electric grid *would* be a military attack if the cyber assault has the same effect as a missile attack might have. The logical consequence of this analysis, also said to be part of the Pentagon's policy, is to authorize the United States military to use any weapon in its arsenal in response.[9] In other words, we reserve the right to answer a cyber weapon with a real world weapon of proportional effect, which seems like the right policy.[10]

If we use this sort of definition then, today, the world has not seen a true cyber war. The Russian attack on Georgia (already briefly mentioned in the previous chapter) is a close approximation, however. In August 2008, Russian troops came into conflict with Georgian troops regarding a disputed border area between the two countries. During the course of that conflict, a number of cyber attacks were also made on Georgian Internet services. Among many collateral cyber effects of those attacks, a "Distributed Denial of Service" or DDoS attack (i.e., one that uses multiple computers and accounts to flood a computer server with messages and overload it, preventing any legitimate efforts to connect to the server) prevented the Georgian ministry of foreign affairs and other official Georgian sites from using the Internet to convey information about the attack to interested third parties. In other instances, cyber intruders corrupted the code for various official Georgian websites, defacing them with pro-Russian messages. In this particular conflict, the website of the Georgian president was attacked from 500 Internet Protocol (IP) addresses.[11]

According to the U.S. Cyber-Consequences Unit,[12] these attacks were actually carried out by Russian civilians (so-called patriotic hackers) who had advance notice of Russia's military intentions and were aware of the timing of Russia's military operations. The civilians were, in turn, aided by elements of Russian organized crime in their efforts. In particular, the Russian criminal networks provided access to their own network of controlled computers (known as botnets) for use in the attacks. In addition, the main social media chatroom (stopgeorgia.ru) that was used to organize the attacks was registered to an address located just blocks from the headquarters of the GRU, the Main Intelligence Directorate of the Russian Armed Forces, suggesting strongly (but not proving) the possibility that Russian intelligence agents may have coordinated the attacks.[13]

The attacks were effective, not only in preventing Georgia from getting its own message out to the world, but also in preventing the Georgian government from communicating with its own people in order to respond to the Russian military invasion. Thus, in some ways, the cyber attacks on Georgia represent the first use of cyber weapons in a combined operation with military forces. But, notwithstanding their effectiveness, it is not clear whether the attacks met the traditional definition of an armed conflict; though highly disruptive, it is difficult to say that their effect was equivalent to that of a kinetic attack.

But, the Russian–Georgian war demonstrates the limits of our practical knowledge about cyber conflict between nation states. First, in the cyber domain, unlike in the real world, the attacker may not be so readily identified. In the end, the critical question in a cyber war may well be: "who attacked us?" For, even though we have grave suspicions about Russian intent in the Georgian war, the reality is that the Internet is not designed to allow for conclusive identification of the source of an attack. As the DoD strategy puts it, in designing the Internet, "identity authentication was less important than connectivity."[14] But, if you don't know who the attacker is, how can you respond? Imagine if a nuclear missile landed in Chicago, but we didn't know who launched it.

Here, the quasi-links between the patriotic Russian hackers and the Russian military make it difficult to draw firm conclusions about the modalities of a true cyber war. In the absence of experience, no solid predictions can be made about the threat of future cyber wars. We can only assess the potential for cyber war by measuring the capabilities of our potential adversaries, and then only, by educated guess work. We have no clear sense of true intent. As a result, we lack a solid quantifiable risk assessment of the cyber threat to national security and this leaves policymakers only with speculation as to the extent of our risk from a cyber attack by a willful cyber opponent.

Finally, the challenge is compounded by our peer-opponents' own, sometimes divergent judgments. After all, what is sauce for the goose is also, inevitably, sauce for the gander. If America takes an expansive view of the applicable laws of armed conflict, others may as well. Some, for example, have argued that the failed Iranian assassination attempt against the Saudi Arabian ambassador was motivated, in part, by the Iranian conclusion that America was complicit in the Stuxnet virus attack.[15] This may, or may not, be factually accurate, but by some potential measures Iran might view Stuxnet as an armed attack, which permits it to use military means in self-defense. Or, perhaps its judgment is ill-founded; there is precious little in the public domain connecting Saudi Arabia to the Stuxnet virus, suggesting that the Iranian response (if, in fact, it was a response) was disproportionate.[16]

The uncertainty in resolving these questions does not, however, prevent us from thinking about the problem. Even while national security lawyers and scholars seek to define cyber war, the national security apparatus must move forward in developing an understanding around key related issues. We struggle today with two interrelated questions: How will we fight in cyberspace? And who are we likely to fight?

CYBER "FIRES"

In military doctrine, our warfighters define the tools they use with the concept of "fires." According to doctrine, fires are the use of weapon systems that have a lethal or nonlethal effect on a target.[17] In its traditional, kinetic form, the types of fires available can range from direct fires (like a tank shell) to indirect ones (like a standoff artillery shell). The systems can include missiles and bullets and can be delivered from a variety of platforms, including planes and ships. Moving forward, we must translate that concept of fires to the cyber domain.

As conflict in cyber space expands, the military concept of fires has grown to include the use of cyber tools of all sorts to conduct offensive and defensive operations. Many of the tools are widely known (e.g., DDoS attacks like the one in Georgia that flood an opponent's system with attempts to connect, preventing it from operating normally). Others, like the Stuxnet intrusion into the Iranian SCADA system, are initially developed in secret, though they are capable of deconstruction once they are used.

Perhaps, most importantly, cyber fires will be very complex tools—often, far more complex than kinetic fires that have an equivalent effect. Consider, for example, this description of a fairly typical intrusion (taken from a McAfee study of a compromise known as Operation Shady RAT):

> The compromises themselves were standard procedure for these types of targeted intrusions: a spear-phishing e-mail containing an exploit is sent to an individual with the right level of access at the company, and the exploit when opened on an unpatched system will trigger a download of the implant malware. That malware will execute and initiate a backdoor communication channel to the Command & Control web server and interpret the instructions encoded in the hidden comments embedded in the webpage code. This will be quickly followed

by live intruders jumping on to the infected machine and proceeding to quickly escalate privileges and move laterally within the organization to establish new persistent footholds via additional compromised machines running implant malware, as well as targeting for quick exfiltration of the key data they came for.[18]

The technical description is a bit complex, reflecting the intricacy of these types of attacks, so let's unpack the jargon. Shady RAT began with a simple e-mail to someone in the target company. It was called a spear-phishing e-mail because it was designed to target a specific individual or recipient, much like a spear used to catch a particular fish. In other words, the e-mail was designed to appear as though it had come from an innocent source, but it had a malicious program hidden within—either in the e-mail itself or quite possibly in an attachment. When the unsuspecting recipient clicked on the attachment, the malware began the automated download of a controller program. This program then opened up a back door communications channel, allowing individuals from outside of the target company to access the target's command and control system. When the communications opened up, the attackers flooded the system (much like an army moving through the breach in a defensive line). Some of the attackers created new breaches; others used their position to promote themselves within the system to access all of the data available, and began removing information from the target system. In short, the simple e-mail cracked open the security of the target and then a team of cyber specialists exploited the defensive gap.

The complexity of these tools makes the development of cyber weapons very difficult. One reason no such weapon was used in Libya is that the military estimated it might take more than a year to develop the precise weapon needed.[19] That's an exceedingly slow pace given the prospects of war. And, the complexity is compounded by the difficulty of inserting malware into systems disconnected from the broader network. That's why a critical research project for the American military (and presumably others too) is exploring the use of radio signals or other "at a distance" methods for inserting code into military systems that are offline.[20] All of which suggests that, at least for now, true targeted cyber weapons, like Stuxnet, will likely be used at a strategic level against known targets (such as an electric grid) rather than at tactical targets of opportunity—only the former are sufficiently static in nature to be subject to the requisite analysis.

The Shady RAT attack also demonstrates another truism of the cyber conflict: often, though not always, the target of the first part of the exploit is a human error, rather than a flaw in the software code. Here, the defensive lapse was in the thoughtless clicking on the attachment of a seemingly innocent e-mail. These types of human frailties are all too common.

Consider, as another example, the results of a recent study in which the testers left USB thumb drives on the ground in a parking lot outside of a federal office building. One would have hoped (indeed, expected) that federal employees, well-schooled in cybersecurity, would know better than to plug an unknown USB drive into a government computer system. On the contrary, "[i]t seems that of those who picked them up, 60 percent plugged the devices into computers in their office. [Even worse, i]f the drive or CD case had an official logo, our well trained, cyber-savvy government employees and contractors plugged in 90 percent of the bogus mobile media. Does that mean that official logos make mobile media that much safer? It would seem so, at least to some."[21] Indeed, as we've already seen, some speculate that the Stuxnet virus was introduced to the Iranian system through a human agent—either through the deliberate act of a spy or through a form of trickery.

Of course, not all attacks or intrusions will rely on social engineering and the human factor for their success. Some, indeed many, of our cyber fires operate wholly external to the target system and derive their power and effectiveness from gaps in the underlying code or the power of the attacking system. One of the most virulent forms of malevolent activity on the net these days is the botnet, a network of infected, zombie computers, whose operations can be controlled by someone other than the true owner. When a botnet worm infects a computer, it plants controlling software that allows the botnet controller to give orders to the computer, and then moves on, looking for other computers to infect. And, all of the infected computers with a particular botnet infection can, when linked together, be given a collective order. There are thousands of botnets in the world, and they are so easy to create and maintain that members of the Russian Business Network (a criminal computer cartel) rent out botnets for a fee. But, most botnets are small; only a few hundred or thousand computers are linked at a time. The largest known botnet, named Conficker, links upward of 10 million computers, and though we've identified it, nobody knows how to defuse it or what its ultimate purpose is.

Why are botnets a risk? They can be used to pass around more malware or steal information. They can be used for a denial of service attack—where a server is overwhelmed by spam messages so that legitimate messages are unable to get through. That's the tactic that the hacktivist group Anonymous used to target Amazon and PayPal in 2010. Once created, botnets are valuable tools for criminal enterprise. But, botnets can also be weapons of war; working together they can crack codes and passwords and attack critical infrastructure systems, like the banking system or the electric grid. What's particularly scary about Conficker, for example, is that nobody knows who owns or operates it or what they plan to do with it.

And, of course, this is just a sampling of cyber techniques available as fires for operations in cyberspace. Often, they go by technical names like "SQL injections" or "BIOS-based Rootkit" attacks that reflect their operational methodology. In many ways, however, that methodology is irrelevant to the broader question of cyber war. It is enough, for now, to know that multiple means of intrusion and compromise exist and that once the vulnerability has been identified it can be exploited in several ways, ranging from theft or degradation of data to the disruption of communications or the destruction of systems.

CHINA RISING

The second key question with which national security experts must currently deal requires an awareness of and preparedness for who, specifically, we may be required to fight. So, who are we afraid of? In recent years, we've seen intrusions from Russia and Iran.[22] We expect that some of our traditional allies, like Germany and Israel, have significant capabilities. But, by all reports, American military strategists see China as the most likely peer-opponent in cyberspace.

As the Department of Defense's 2010 report to Congress, *Military and Security Developments Involving the People's Republic of China,* concluded:

> numerous computer systems around the world, including those owned by the U.S. government, continued to be the target of intrusions that appear to have originated within the [People's Republic of China]. These intrusions focused on exfiltrating information, some of which could be of strategic or military utility. The accesses and skills required for these intrusions are similar to those necessary to conduct computer network attacks. It remains unclear if these intrusions were conducted by, or with the endorsement of, the [People's Liberation Army] or other elements of the [People's Republic of China] government. However, developing capabilities for cyberwarfare is consistent with authoritative [People's Liberation Army] military writings.[23]

China has demonstrated significant cyber capabilities in recent years. Consider the following sampling of events and incidents from the last few years.

Operation Aurora

In early 2010 Google announced that it had been the subject of a "highly sophisticated and targeted attack" that had originated in China, resulting in the "theft of intellectual property" from Google. The attacks seemed to be targeted at Chinese human rights activists.[24] And, Google was not alone. At least 20 other major companies spanning sectors including the Internet, finance, and the chemical industry were also targeted. At its core, the attack apparently attempted to corrupt some of Google's source code.

China, naturally, denied responsibility for the attacks and even claimed that evidence of their complicity had been falsified. But, according to one classified State Department cable (released by WikiLeaks), the operation was authorized by the Politburo Standing Committee, the rough equivalent in authority of America's National Security Council.[25] And, later analysis by Google (assisted by NSA) traced the source of IP addresses and servers used to facilitate the exploitation to a single foreign entity, consisting either of "agents of the Chinese state or proxies thereof."

Titan Rain/Byzantine Hades

Titan Rain and Byzantine Hades are the formerly classified code names given by the U.S. government to a series of coordinated attacks on American government and industrial computer systems. The attacks began in roughly 2003 and have, in some form, continued to this day. Analysis has convinced most observers that the intrusions originate in China, though it has never quite been established whether they are merely random hacker attacks, industrial espionage, or espionage sponsored by the Chinese sovereign. The true identities of the intruders have, generally, been concealed by the use of proxy servers and zombie/botnet computer systems. On the other hand, several Chinese websites that were portals for Byzantine Hades intrusions were registered in China using the same postal code used by the People's Liberation Army Chengdu Province First Technical Reconnaissance Bureau, an electronic espionage unit of the Chinese military.[26]

According to American investigators, these programs have stolen terabytes of data. They have intruded on many military systems, even being found on Defense Secretary Gates' unclassified computer.[27] Indeed, the Byzantine Hades attack may have stolen the designs of the F-35, America's newest fighter jet, from the defense contractor who is building the plane.[28]

Operation Shady RAT

Shady RAT, described earlier, was identified by McAfee Security in 2011.[29] (RAT is an acronym for Remote Access Tool.) The malware intrusion infected several hundred agencies, companies, and institutions around the world, including several systems operated by the federal government and American defense contractors. In many ways, it had the same signature as the Gh0stRat intrusion discussed in the previous chapter, indicating its Chinese origin.

Perhaps, more significantly, there were indications from the patterns of intrusions, suggesting that a state-actor was behind the attack. Several of the targets were Asian and Western national Olympic Committees, as well as the International Olympic Committee (IOC), and the World Anti-Doping

Agency. Most of these were compromised just before, during, and after the 2008 Beijing Olympics. Clearly, there was little or no economic benefit to be gained from these targets. In addition, some of the targets were political nonprofits (including one private western organization focused on the promotion of democracy around the globe and an American think tank focused on national security issues). And, as a final indicator, intrusions of Shady RAT were detected at the United Nations and the Association of Southeast Asian Nations (ASEAN) Secretariat. In the absence of the potential for commercial gain, some other motivation, likely political, must have animated this attack.

Operation Night Dragon

In 2008 and 2009, a systematic series of intrusions of American and European oil and gas companies was discovered. The focus of the intrusion seemed to be confidential internal bidding information regarding proposals to purchase offshore oil leases. The companies that were exploited were all in competition with Chinese companies for the leases and the methodology used (innocent e-mail as the attack vector, followed by an exfiltration piece of malware) had the hallmarks of similar programs that had been attributed to China. This led many observers to surmise that the Night Dragon attacks were also derived from Chinese sources.[30]

Internet Hijacking

Another display of Chinese capabilities occurred in April 2010, when the Internet was hijacked. Traffic on the Internet is, typically, routed through the most efficient route. Servers calculate that route based on a call-and-response interaction with other servers; in effect, downstream servers advertise their own carrying capacity and current load, thereby soliciting traffic.

On April 8, 2010, China Telecom began broadcasting erroneous network traffic routes. As a result, American and other foreign servers were instructed to send Internet traffic through Chinese servers. In the end, according to the United States–China Economic and Security Review Commission, roughly 15 percent of the world's traffic was routed to China.[31] This included official U.S. government traffic, as well as the traffic from any number of commercial websites.

Electric Grid

Even more chillingly, some reports have suggested that our electronic grid and telecommunications systems have already been infiltrated by logic bombs (malicious code inserted in a system that will be set off only on instruction or when certain conditions are met). In 2009, the *Wall Street Journal* reported that software had been placed into our system, so that it could be detonated at a later date, presumably during the time of war. Doing so could cripple our economy and military capabilities at a time of crisis.[32] Richard Clarke, the former cybersecurity czar, likens these cyber logic bombs to mines, and blames China for their placement.[33]

U.S. Chamber of Commerce

In December 2011, the FBI told the U.S. Chamber of Commerce that its servers had been penetrated by intrusions from China.[34] Until the FBI told them, the Chamber apparently had no idea that security had been compromised. Not normally thought of as a repository for classified information, most people think that the Chamber was attacked as a stepping stone to other major American companies. Using the e-mail addresses and other personal information harvested from the Chamber of Commerce, the intruders would, presumably, be better able to craft a sophisticated spearphishing attack.

Hacking the Patches

One of the more unusual efforts appears to be an attempt to get inside the turning radius of the defending side. Typically, Microsoft (and other companies) release patches to known vulnerabilities on a fixed schedule. The schedule is so common that some call the first Tuesday of every month "patch Tuesday" because Windows users can expect a routine monthly patch of vulnerabilities as a download that day.

To make the patches that they ship work more effectively, Microsoft gives advance notice of the patches to a select group of security companies. With proof-of-concept code that they receive in advance, these companies can prioritize and test the fixes before installing them to provide protection to their customers. But, what if the hackers had advance notice of the patches? Since even the patches can be reverse engineered, hackers who were inside the system and had advance notice of what patches were coming out would be well-positioned to develop their own offensive countermeasures that get around the patch—before it is even installed.

Something like that seems to have happened to the March 2012 Microsoft patch.[35] The proof of concept code for the patches was found on a website in China before Microsoft's official patches shipped. It may have been an error, or an insider leaking the data, or a hack from the outside. Nobody knows. Once again, however, a sophisticated operational plan that seems to have originated in China created a vulnerability in America.

NASA

In testimony before the House of Representatives in February 2012, the NASA Inspector General, Paul K. Martin, painted a distressing picture of the vulnerability of NASA's data system.[36] At least one of the attacks was reasonably attributable to China:

> Our ongoing investigation of another such attack at JPL [the Jet Propulsion Laboratory, one of America's premier space science labs] involving Chinese-based Internet protocol (IP) addresses has confirmed that the intruders gained full access to key JPL systems and sensitive user accounts. With full system access the intruders could: (1) modify, copy, or delete sensitive files; (2) add, modify, or delete user accounts for mission-critical JPL systems; (3) upload hacking tools to steal user credentials and compromise other NASA systems; and (4) modify system logs to conceal their actions. In other words, the attackers had full functional control over these networks.

Thus, Chinese hackers gained complete control over NASA's JPL. With that control, they could, for example, delete sensitive files, add user accounts to mission-critical systems, upload hacking tools, and more—all at a lab that is a central repository of U.S. space technology. Here, again, conclusive proof of Chinese involvement cannot be found, but the inference of deliberate espionage is strong.

Byzantine Candor

In July 2012 public reports identified another Chinese infiltration program code-named Byzantine Candor. This program was the concerted work of a Chinese hacker group known as the "Comment Group" because its trademark method involved the use of hidden web-page code, known as "comments." Investigators identified more than 20 different targets, ranging from the European Union, to energy companies, to lawyers who were representing clients adverse to China.[37]

Most notably, counter-espionage researchers were able to exploit a gap in the Comment Group's own security that enabled them to keep detailed logs of the group's activities. Based on those logs the investigators assert that they were able to link the Comment Group to elements of the People's Liberation Army. One of the most troubling targets of the group was the Diablo Canyon nuclear plant near Santa Barbara, which, apparently, was penetrated.

RSA

Finally, and perhaps most chillingly, the security firm RSA (manufacturer of the security tokens that many companies use to control access to secure systems) was penetrated by an intrusion that compromised the company's SecureID system. This SecureID system was, at the time, the single most common piece of security hardware; it was a little token that periodically generated random numbers and those numbers, in turn, were used with traditional user identification and passwords to authenticate an attempt to, say, login to a company's computer servers from a remote site. Though details remain very unclear even now, the intruders apparently compromised the random number generation algorithm so that they would be better able to infiltrate the companies that used the RSA SecureID token.

Just a few weeks later, Lockheed Martin was attacked by someone using the stolen RSA data who attempted remote access to their system. The attack is said to have been thwarted, but the focus on a defense contractor, rather than on a bank, seems a clear indication that the RSA hack was done by a sovereign peer-competitor, not by cybercriminals who would have used the data to break into bank accounts instead. Other companies compromised using the same command and control infrastructure as that which hacked into RSA include: Abbott Labs, the Alabama Supercomputer Network, Charles Schwabb & Co., Cisco Systems, eBay, the European Space Agency, Facebook, Freddie Mac, Google, the General Services Administration, the Inter-American Development Bank, IBM, Intel Corp., the Internal Revenue Service (IRS), the Massachusetts Institute of Technology, Motorola Inc., Northrop Grumman, Novell, Perot Systems, PriceWaterhouseCoopers LLP, Research in Motion (RIM) Ltd., Seagate Technology, Thomson Financial, Unisys Corp., USAA, Verisign, VMWare, Wachovia Corp., and Wells Fargo & Co.[38]

Again, China denied any responsibility for the attack but, as Richard Clarke said, "this attack [has] all the hallmarks of Chinese government operations." Indeed, recently, RSA completed its own analysis of the intrusion. At a conference in London in October 2011, their Chairman said: "There were two individual groups from one nation state, one supporting the other. One was very visible and one less so. We've not attributed it to a particular nation state although we're very confident that with the skill, sophistication and resources involved it could only have been a nation state."[39] And, of the 334 command and control servers used by the malware, 299 were located in China.[40]

* * *

In the end, what are we to make of these Chinese activities? How should we assess them? Should we credit the routine denials that China makes, disclaiming responsibility? Are they significant threats?

Here, opinion is very much divided. In some ways, the exploits we have discovered are rather mediocre. Though extensive in nature and highly successful, many of them have proven easy to decipher and the pattern of activity has left the West with a well-founded understanding of China's intentions. In short, they are sufficiently poorly executed and have stripped the Chinese government of all but the barest fig leaf of plausible deniability.

And, there really is little basis for accepting Chinese denials of awareness and responsibility. A recent propaganda error by the government was instructive. Chinese news broadcast a story about China's military system. In the midst of the story was a segment on cyber war and that segment included footage of a computer screen where the military were logging cyber attack commands against a server in the United States.[41] Shortly after Western news outlets noticed and remarked on the apparent admission, the government recognized its mistake and the video was pulled from Chinese websites.[42]

While it is certainly plausible to believe that some of the hacks from China are done without the government's knowledge, the frequency and persistence of the attacks, along with their political focus, seem to implicate Chinese involvement. As one analyst put it: "The Chinese government has employed this same tactic in numerous intrusions. Because their internal police and military have such a respected or feared voice among the hacking community, they can make use of the hackers' research with their knowledge and still keep the hackers tight-lipped about it. The hackers know that if they step out of line they will find themselves quickly in a very unpleasant prison in western China, turning large rocks into smaller rocks."[43] Indeed, the degree of intrusion has gotten so bad that corporate travelers heading to China these days, routinely, take blank computers and never let their cellphones out of their possession; the Chinese reputation for routine hacking has become, in a word, legendary.[44]

Indeed, some of the exploits, like the intrusion into RSA, are remarkably sophisticated. This is not unexpected. After all, the top 1 percent of China's programmers are greater in number than the entire profession in the United States. With so many at work, we might expect the average programmer to be, well, average. But, the very best are likely to be exceptional.

And, what is true for the Chinese is true of other nations and nonstate organizations who have demonstrated equally threatening capabilities. Russia's prowess has been discussed earlier. International organized crime syndicates have shown sophisticated capabilities that may be used to steal critical information and align with anti-American elements to pose security threats that are both kinetic and economic in nature. In short, there is no lack of potential enemies on the horizon.

Which leaves us with one final question: If these exploits are the ones we are identifying (typically, after the fact), what about the ones we are missing? By definition, we can't know what they are. To paraphrase former Secretary of Defense Donald Rumsfeld, they are known unknowns—but the thought is certainly a daunting one.

AN AMERICAN RESPONSE

In the face of so much uncertainty, America is, of necessity, preparing to deal with new strategic threats. It is in the nature of strategic planners to always think of the worst case scenario. From that perspective, the espionage intrusions attributable to China tell only part of the story.

It appears, as well, that China is preparing for a conflict in cyberspace. And, China sees the United States as its principal cyber-competitor. A recent report in the Chinese-language, *Liberation Army Daily* (an unofficial but well-vetted source), put it this way: "The U.S. military is hastening to seize the commanding military heights on the Internet, and another Internet war is being pushed to a stormy peak. . . . Their actions remind us that to protect the nation's Internet security, we must accelerate Internet defense development and accelerate steps to make a strong Internet army. . . . Although our country has developed into an Internet great power, our Internet security defenses are still very weak. So we must accelerate development of Internet battle technology and armament."[45]

And so, it is not surprising that, in late May 2011, China announced the formation of a cyber Blue Army, with two stated purposes: defending the nation against cyber attacks and leading cyber offensives, in case of war.[46] A recent report to Congress gives a flavor of Chinese military activity:[47] the military has begun testing attack capabilities during exercises, most recently during an exercise in October 2011 involving "joint information offensive and defensive operations." According to the report, the People's Liberation Army (PLA) is likely to focus its cyber targeting in a tactical way rather than a strategic one. Thus, they estimate that an initial focus would be on transportation and logistics networks or command-and-control systems just before an actual conflict to try to delay or disrupt the United States' ability to fight.

The capabilities being developed are significant. In short, as the report concludes: "Chinese capabilities in computer network operations have advanced sufficiently to pose genuine risk to U.S. military operations in the event of a conflict." Though a full cyber war has yet to be fought, the Chinese appear to be preparing to use cyber weapons as a part of any future conflict.

Whether America's actions are a response to these activities or their cause is debatable, but they were, in either event, inevitable. The Department of Defense has now created its own cyberspace war-fighting unit, U.S. Cyber

Command. The goal of this reorganization was to centralize a relatively de-centralized military cyber effort and provide a unified operation command for both offensive and defensive operations. On the defensive side, Cyber Command is responsible for actions designed to "protect, monitor, analyze, detect, and respond to unauthorized activity within DOD information systems and computer networks."[48] Notably, though formally restricted to DOD systems, the Department has begun partnering with private sector manufacturers in the Defense Industrial Base, to assure the security of its supply chain.

Offensive cyber operations can involve both information gathering (sometimes also called "computer network exploitation") and computer network attack. When an intrusion is for exploitation and information gathering purposes, the boundary between military operations and the espionage of the intelligence community gets blurred. Recognizing how espionage activities can blend into military operations that prepare the battlefield and involve reconnaissance, the first commander of Cyber Command, General Keith Alexander, is also dual-hatted as the Director of the National Security Administration (NSA), our electronic intelligence gathering agency. Computer network attacks involve military operations through computer networks that are designed to "disrupt, deny, degrade, or destroy information residing in computers and computer networks or the computers and networks themselves."[49] It may even involve exploitations that are intended to have destructive kinetic effects on hard military or civilian infrastructure targets. All these fall within the purview of the new command.

Consider, as a final example of the complexity of warfare in cyberspace, the operation reported to have been conducted by the United States in Iraq against al-Qaeda at the time of Iraqi elections in March 2010.[50] The elections were critical to a successful transition of responsibility in Iraq and an important milestone in the reduction of American forces there. To foster the election, at least two insurgent websites were disabled by a cyber attack (including one site that was posting operational instructions for physical attacks to disrupt the elections).

Earlier, in 2008, then-president Bush had broadly authorized cyber operations in Iraq, declaring it a war zone for cyber purposes. Particular operations are said to be reviewed and approved by an inter-agency task force comprised of representatives from the Departments of Defense, and Justice, and the intelligence agencies. Tactics used by the military go by names like "overloading," "webspoofing," and "false band replacement." Al-Qaeda's own web watermarks are carefully replicated so that false messages appear to be official communications. We reportedly could even penetrate the insurgents' computer networks and send false text messages to mislead them and sow discord.

* * *

In short, the prospect of cyber war looms ahead of us. Nation-states that now do battle on the air, sea, and land may soon come in conflict on the man-made cyber domain. Already, the major nations of the world are developing cyber capabilities and organizing their military efforts. They have begun flexing their muscles with espionage operations, and limited military attacks. Broader efforts (like the use of cyber weapons against Libya) have been considered but have not yet come to fruition.

All of this development of new cyber weaponry comes against a backdrop of legal and political uncertainty. We are developing new methods of attack without a clear understanding of when they can or should lawfully be used. This uncertainty is likely to endure for a substantial period of time as technological developments outstrip international law and policy.

As we prepare for cyber war, one is reminded of the uncertainty faced by medieval mapmakers. As they reached the edge of the known world on their maps, they would carefully inscribe on the edge "hoc est dracones" ("here be dragons"). That's just as true of cyberspace today, in more ways than one.

4

Chapter

Cyber War and the Law

We have seen how confusing some of the issues are regarding cyber war and how difficult it is to decide when something is an attack. But, of course, that sort of judgment is not everything. Lurking behind every question of fact is a question of law. In this case, both domestic American law and a branch of law known as International Humanitarian Law, and the related doctrine, sometimes called the Law of Armed Conflict (LOAC). Indeed, often our knowledge of facts (we are "pretty sure" it was a Russian hack) outstrips the legal constraints of the laws of armed conflict (i.e., to respond, we must be more than "pretty sure").[1]

In this chapter, we take a slight detour to illustrate the difficulties of taking a settled body of international law—the law of armed conflict—and applying it to a putative cyber attack. We look, as well, at aspects of American law. The results can be counter-intuitive and also deeply mystifying.

Put briefly (and with some risk of oversimplification), there are two international law aspects to any question of armed conflict: the first relates to *when* a country can respond to an armed attack and the second relates to *how* it can respond. Think of it this way: not all intrusions are attacks that justify an armed response under international law. And, even when an armed response is permitted, some types of armed response (think of deliberately targeting civilians or a hospital) are still out of bounds. The first of these questions goes by the Latin phrase *Jus Ad Bellum*, which translated means "the right to wage war." The second is called *Jus In Bello* or "justice in war" and defines acceptable wartime conduct.

ARMED ATTACKS AND SELF-DEFENSE

To begin an examination of this question, we first need to define the appropriate conflict principles for assessing whether and when a nation-state can use force. The paradigm, of course, is that aggressive armed conflict is generally prohibited by international law unless authorized by an action of the Security Council of the United Nations. This does not, however, disable states from responding when attacked. On the contrary, states may legitimately act in their own self-defense under Article 51 of the UN Charter when confronted with an armed attack.

The first question, then, is how does one assess whether a cyber attack, in some form, may be characterized as an armed attack? This is especially difficult, because there is no international consensus on the definition of what constitutes an armed attack, even in the physical realm. Generally, however, such an assessment looks to the scope, duration, and intensity of the use of force in question. A single shot, for example, fired across the DMZ by a North Korean soldier does not mean that a state of war now exists between South Korea and the North.

This ambiguity in the physical arena has carried over into the cyber domain. In this domain, there are three schools of thought regarding when a cyber attack might be viewed as tantamount to an armed attack (assuming always that we have been able to determine that the event was, in fact, an attack using cyber means).

One school looks at whether the damage caused by such an attack could previously have been achieved only by a kinetic attack. For example, using this model, a cyber attack conducted for the purpose of shutting down a power grid would be deemed an armed attack, inasmuch as, prior to the development of cyber capabilities, the destruction of a power grid would typically have required using some form of kinetic force.

A second school looks only at the scope and magnitude of the effects of a cyber attack on a victim-state, rather than attempting to compare these effects to any form of kinetic attack. Here, for example, consider the disablement of a financial network. With real effects, but no physical harm, this would be seen as equivalent to an armed attack, despite the fact that nothing was broken or destroyed—only some digital financial records were disrupted.

A third view is akin to a strict liability rule: any attack on a state's critical national infrastructure, even if unsuccessful, would be deemed an armed attack per se (and, thus, would cover attempted intrusions that had no consequences). It might also include any preparatory intrusions that fell short of an armed attack but could be viewed as "preparing the battlefield" for later success.

By and large, U.S. policy makers have adopted the middle view—focusing on the overall effects of a particular cyber attack. But, even here, there is no consensus. There are, of course, some relatively easy cases. Data exploitation without damage is almost certainly not a use of force. When Operation Titan Rain (which we discussed in the previous chapter) stole design secrets for the F-35, it was a problem, but we aren't at war with China because of it (any more than they are at war with the United States when, hypothetically, the design for their new aircraft carrier is stolen through cyber or any other kind of espionage).

By contrast, a cyber attack causing physical damage is a use of force. Were China to take down the electric grid, the United States would be within its rights to view that as an armed attack if it persisted in scope and duration. Indeed, it is an interesting question (as only lawyers can define "interesting") to consider whether the Stuxnet intrusion on Iran's nuclear program met the definition of an armed attack. It certainly had the requisite physical effect. But, its scope and duration were relatively narrow, modest, and short-lived. Nevertheless, Iran could make a plausible argument that it was entitled to respond with armed force against the Stuxnet attacker . . . if it knew for sure who the attacker was, of course.

The hard questions lie in the grey area. If, for example, cyber agents were introduced into a system for exploitation and attack, but not yet activated, should that be considered a use of force? Or, to identify another issue, is the mere destruction of data, a use of force? Some in the intelligence community might even deem aggressive phishing (i.e., acquiring sensitive information through fraud) to be a use of force. Here, we have no settled doctrine.

The consequence of this determination is critical: if we conclude as a matter of law that an armed attack has occurred, then in law the United States is entitled to respond with its own use of force. This could include offensive cyber operations[2] against those who are deemed responsible for the attack, but it could also include the full panoply of other military options. As one wag put it, this means that "Obama Reserves Right to Nuke Hackers."[3] Such a response is unlikely in the extreme—at least in part because it would violate other rules of armed conflict that require proportionality in a response—but it does emphasize the significance of the determination. When an armed attack occurs, nations are entitled to go to war.

WHO IS IT?

Even if it can be determined that a cyber attack is an armed attack, one must then resolve whether the attack can be attributed to a nation-state. In the cyber world, attribution will often require crossing several sovereign boundaries, and if responsive force is to be used, the actions taken will occur within some other state's territory. But, in the cyber realm, a state is often not directly involved in the cyber attack; the attack is the product of independent or semi-independent actors. Under what rules can we attribute their actions to a state (assuming, of course, that, forensically, we can even identify these independent actors)? Put more concretely, we saw how Russian hacktivists supported the Russian invasion of Georgia through cyber attacks on Georgian websites. What degree of coordination and/or control is necessary in order for Georgia to lawfully attribute those attacks to Russia?

The doctrine of "state responsibility" has long been an established international law concept, but it has become particularly relevant in terms of assessing responsibility for cyber attacks. Simply put, this doctrine stands for the proposition that that every state has an affirmative legal obligation to prevent its territory from being used for attacks on other states. If a state is unable or unwilling to prevent such attacks, it can (if self-help is unavailing) be held responsible for these attacks. A common example of this might be when a country, like Pakistan, doesn't take steps to prevent an insurgency from conducting attacks in Afghanistan and allows them to use Pakistani territory as a safe haven.

Again, however, the practical assessment of state responsibility is contextual in nature. One asks whether the state has effective control of the actors, that is, the capacity to direct their actions. Failing this, does it exercise overall control of the actors, that is, while not directing their actions, does the state, nevertheless, affect the overall coordination and planning of their actions? In both these situations, it is likely that state responsibility is implicated.

Finally, and most frequently, however, one asks whether the state is indirectly responsible for certain acts in issue, that is, does its failure to act constitute a basis for deeming it responsible for a cyber attack, or a series of such attacks. Here, the questions become even more indefinite. One asks whether the state has effective laws on cybercrime on its books; whether it has aggressively enforced these laws; whether it cooperates with victims in the investigation of cyber incidents; and whether the state has a long history of serving as a haven for cyber attacks. We might, for example, look at the recent history of Chinese intrusions and be justified in concluding that at a minimum China has not exercised its obligation to control activity within its borders (or, at a maximum, that it is affirmatively fostering such activity). Were the acts to rise to the level of an armed attack (as, we must hasten to add, Chinese activity to date has *not*), then they would be attributable to the Chinese government.

Attribution will, however, likely be exceedingly difficult. The reality is that some attacks (for example, by botnets) truly have no geographic source. They are transnational in nature, straddle multiple borders, and are derived from the acts of coalitions of individuals residing in multiple jurisdictions. The web group Anonymous has no home. As this discussion makes clear, application of the state responsibility doctrine to cyber attacks is likely to be both highly contextual and controversial on the international stage.

This will especially be so when one adds a political overlay to any incident (as will inevitably be the case). Imagine, for example, a cyber attack on the Federal Aviation Administration and/or the New York Stock Exchange that results in significant disruption of public services. Even if attribution is uncertain, the public dynamic will pressure U.S. leadership to respond. A realistic appraisal is that they will be willing to do so with significantly less than 100 percent certainty of attribution, with the concomitant danger of incorrectly attributing the source of the attack. The first cyber war might well start by mistake.

LAWFUL USES OF CYBER FIRES

Only if one answers the armed attack and attribution questions satisfactorily can you then turn to determining whether a particular use of force in response is appropriate under the LOAC. The LOAC provides that a state may use a justified, proportionate amount of force.

To determine proportionality, we (yet again) turn to a multi-factored analysis. Those advising on this matter will be obliged to determine whether a use of force response is militarily necessary or whether the incident at issue could be resolved in another manner. Is a planned use of force response proportional in nature? That is, is the degree of force to be used excessive, when balanced against the value of the military objective sought to be gained? Does it adequately distinguish between military objectives and civilian property? Questions like these, about proportionality, are why the nuclear response to a hack is simply infeasible—nobody would think that it was a proportionate response.

These questions are particularly indeterminate in the cyber context. Nobody can definitively say, in most situations, what an appropriate cyber response might be. And, those responses we can imagine (hacking back into an adversary's systems, for example) might cause collateral damage to civilian property or systems that is disproportionate in nature (often because, in the cyber realm, they are inextricably intertwined).

We can see the tension these uncertainties cause in the Department of Defense's most recent report to Congress.[4] In some ways, the report is revolutionary. For the first time ever, it announces that the United States will use cyber offensive weapons (a policy that was conspicuously absent from earlier Defense Department policy pronouncements). But, as Jack Goldsmith of Harvard has pointed out,[5] this policy is limited to retaliation for significant or crippling cyber attacks. Small-scale insurgency attacks or other forms of espionage are immune from retaliation. This might be proportionate but it also means that those forms of intrusion (which are, recall, indistinguishable from large-scale attacks before execution) are not capable of being deterred. More plausibly (as we will see in the next chapter), a comprehensive strategy should also address ways of dealing with these more frequent forms of cyber conflict.

In addition, since the laws of armed conflict require a nation to avoid collateral damage where possible and to minimize it where it is unavoidable, the uncertainty of cyber effects from an attack make offensive cyber weapons particularly problematic. It was precisely considerations of this sort that caused the Bush Administration to shelve plans to launch a cyber attack on Iraq; they had no idea what the collateral consequences of the attack might be.[6] Likewise, the same sort of concerns were part of the calculus that let the United States to eschew a cyber attack against Libya in connection with the NATO-led military operation in 2011.[7]

As if those complexities were not enough, the lack of distinction in cyber fires and the borderless nature of the Internet can lead to a host of other almost insoluble legal issues regarding the use of cyber force. Consider the following sample of questions:

- International law allows the targeting of combatants who are participants in the war. Killing armed combatants is a lawful act and is not murder. But, who is a cyber combatant? Is a civilian hacker an armed combatant? How about a civilian employee with cyber responsibilities in a nonmilitary government agency (like the CIA or its Russian equivalent)? If they are combatants, then, in effect, the domain of lawful warfare is as broad and wide as the Internet itself.
- Certain targets, like hospitals, are immune from attack under international law. But, IP addresses don't come with labels that say "I am a hospital system" and most server systems are inextricably intertwined with one another. How can a military attack ensure that it avoids damage to privileged targets? And, if it cannot, does that mean that any cyber attack is, *de jure,* illegal?
- Under the laws of war, combatants must carry their arms openly and be readily identified as combatants by the uniforms they wear. The main purpose of this is to allow opposing military forces to distinguish between combatants and noncombatant civilians, and target only lawful combatants. Yet, almost no cyber warrior wears a uniform. Nor are they readily distinguishable from noncombatant civilians. Indeed, one of the principal tactics of a cyber warrior is to hide his actions behind the veneer of seemingly innocent civilian activity (an innocuous e-mail, for example). Since these cyber soldiers don't abide by the laws of war, does that mean that they, like terrorists, are not entitled to the protections of those laws when identified and/or captured?
- One of the gravest violations of the laws of armed conflict is the act of perfidy, that is, falsely surrendering or seeking a truce under a white flag and then using the cover to wage war. Yet, one of the most effective tactics used in cyber conflict is the false flag—appearing to surrender or

be an innocent while using that opportunity to intrude malware into an opponent's system.

- The laws of armed conflict respect the right of neutrals. World War I was, at least in part, exacerbated by the German violation of Belgium's neutrality. In the cyber domain, however, successful attacks will almost always violate neutrality by using servers and computers that are located in a noncombatant country, as a means of masking an attack. Only a fool would, for example, make a direct attack from a U.S. server to, say, one in China. Yet, due respect for the principle of neutrality suggests that this is precisely what is required by international law. At least one news report indicates that lawyers in the Department of Justice believe that network attacks on servers outside of a formal war zone require the host country's permission and that, absent the permission, the attacks are unlawful.[8]

INTELLIGENCE OR WAR? TITLE 10 AND TITLE 50

To all of this, one must add another dimension of legal confusion: one that has a bearing on cyber war both under international law and under domestic American law. The problem arises, as do so many such problems, from the fundamental nature of the Internet; in this case, the lack of any ability to distinguish between cyber espionage intrusions and cyber attacks. Our laws, however, traditionally rely on and define that distinction. Spying is spying and fighting is fighting. So much so that the actual laws that control the two activities are contained in completely different parts of the United States Code of laws. Military matters are all regulated by Title 10 of the U.S. Code, while intelligence matters are all regulated by Title 50.[9]

Which law applies makes a great deal of difference. Domestically, it defines who is in control—a matter of both operational importance and (in the real world of Washington) a matter of some concern to those who are protecting their bureaucratic turf. It also makes a difference in determining who in Congress gets told about an operation and when; covert intelligence operations are reported to different committees than military operations and secret military operations sometimes never get reported at all. On the other hand, covert operations can be, and sometimes are, publicly denied and never intended to become known, while military operations almost invariably become public at some point.

A recent example of the importance of this distinction (from the noncyber realm) was the killing of Osama bin Laden. Though the operation was carried out by Navy Seals using military helicopters and even though it was not intended to remain secret once the operation was completed, the entire project was officially an intelligence operation—run by then CIA director Leon Panetta.[10]

The line between the two types of activity is often indistinct (and growing more so by the day). Yet, we do attempt to define the line (albeit in a rococo way, typical of how Washington writes law). We first define covert activities to be those secret operations that are intended "to influence political, economic, or military conditions abroad, where it is intended that the role of the United States Government will not be apparent or acknowledged publicly." We then say, however, that the definition does not include "traditional military activities,"[11] involving operational planning or execution and using military personnel.

In some ways this line is clear, but in the cyber realm it becomes impossibly complex. Think, for example, of the simple idea of communications. It has long been a traditional military activity to disrupt an opponent's communications. We shot down carrier pigeons and we bombed radio relay stations. Today, when the opponent will rely on Internet communications, the military sees those operations as within its zone of responsibility. But, the CIA, not unreasonably, sees cyber operations that are intended to be covert as part of its own domain. That's why the CIA and the military are in a turf war over who should carry out certain types of Internet operations.[12]

It also makes a difference that the cyber realm has no geographic borders. The CIA asserts that classic covert operations can occur worldwide and that traditional military activities are confined to a relatively well-defined battle space (say, the area near Afghanistan). The military sees cyber operations against al-Qaeda as a form of traditional military activity, because it is a lawful military opponent. And, they argue, their activities need to be worldwide precisely because the al-Qaeda movement knows no geographic boundaries.

The distinction becomes even more complex when we consider that some of these activities might actually take place inside the United States. The Constitution and intelligence statutes delimit the nature of intelligence activity that U.S. officials may undertake, especially when operating domestically. In general, the purpose of the domestic law is to permit the exploitation of foreign intelligence sources while protecting American civil liberties. It also serves as a bedrock foundational source for the authorization of all national intelligence activity. Likewise, strict laws limit how the military may operate inside America's borders. And yet, inasmuch as cyber is borderless, it is difficult, if not impossible, to conduct an operation wholly outside American borders.

Finally, let us consider international law. We have already discussed the legal limitations on military activity that arise from international law. By contrast, in the context of foreign laws or international law, espionage is sometimes characterized as lawless. When exploiting sources overseas, the premise is that good work is all about breaking the law of some foreign jurisdiction. Without doubt, any cyber espionage done by U.S. assets in, say, China, violates domestic Chinese law, but it is of little concern to American law.

The question is slightly more complex when one considers applicable customary international law, that is, the part of international law that is defined by the customs of nations. Here, the uncertainties are greater—both as to the content of the law and as to its binding nature. While some international norms are absolute and accepted by the United States (e.g., the prohibition against assassination), most international legal questions about espionage activity have indefinite answers. When asked: "Can I do this?" the answer, most frequently, is "Maybe." Thus, for example, it may be that if a cyber attack is a traditional military activity, it will need to respect the neutrality of other countries and not use their servers to assist in the attack, but that if we characterize the action as a covert intelligence action, it is lawful under international law to use neutral countries as a transit point surreptitiously.

Perhaps the best example of how this uncertainty plays out in the real world lies in one person—General Keith Alexander. He is, in effect, America's top cyber warrior, but also our top cyber spy. General Alexander is at the same time head of U.S. Cyber Command (a Title 10 organization) and of the National Security Agency (a Title 50 organization). Giving him both roles makes it easier for him to assure that there is less in-fighting and more coordination between those two groups, but it has to be awfully confusing for his lawyers.

THE ASSUMPTION OF RAPIDITY AND THE NEED FOR HUMAN CONTROL

The application of law to cyber conflict is also confounded by what we might call the assumption of rapidity, that is, the predominant belief that things in cyberspace all happen at lightning quick speed. If that is true, then the necessity for a legal determination can be a huge problem.

We have seen that, for issues relating to the laws of armed conflict, no consensus exists among international law practitioners. Creating more law may not help, however, as such decisions will always involve subjective judgments often based on ambiguous facts.

What is certain, however, is that these decisions applying law to cyber operations are fraught with national importance. It is likely, therefore, that as a matter of policy, we will want them to be made at the highest levels of government, and not at the level of, say, a Defense Department systems administrator. But, even the identity of the appropriate decision maker is uncertain. The Commander of Strategic Command has said that he believes he can make the decision to respond to a cyber attack degrading U.S. defense capabilities. Some in the Air Force, focusing on the speed of cyber events, have suggested that there is a need to develop an automated response for certain cyber scenarios. Many observers are of the view, however, that because there currently exist no definitive rules of engagement for cyber war, at least as a first approximation, all decision-making will have to be conducted at the level of the president.

This impulse for centralized control conflicts with another of the unique aspects of cyberspace that will particularly affect our organizational structures and processes—the rapidity with which cyber activities occur. When a cyber domain attack is perceived to occur at the pace of milliseconds, it may be that the deterrent or defensive response will need to occur with equal rapidity. As General Alexander, wearing his military hat as the first Commander of U.S. Cyber Command, told the Senate, "[A] commander's right to general self-defense is clearly established in both U.S. and international law. Although this right has not been specifically established by legal precedent to apply to attacks in cyberspace, it is reasonable to assume that returning fire in cyberspace, as long as it complied with the law of war principles (e.g. proportionality), would be lawful."[13] We therefore face a situation where it is possible (indeed, likely) that some subordinate commanding officer may feel compelled (and authorized) to act without higher authorization if the commander perceives that a cyber attack has begun. And, what is true for the military may also be true of private actors who are protecting their own networks—they may feel the need to act instantaneously without the benefit of reflection.

This perception of the need for rapidity reflects a sea-change in conception. The physics of the Internet, it is believed, destroys time and space.[14] Even in the nuclear domain, the imminence of the threat was measured in minutes, allowing the development of processes (like the classic nuclear code, "football") that permitted a considered, albeit hurried, human response. As General Alexander put it, some believe that the cyber domain is best characterized as one in which a near-instantaneous response is necessary.

That characterization may not, however, be accurate and its prevalence may actually be pernicious. A counter-response may be essential immediately as a purely defensive measure, but it is likely that a deterrence-based cyber response can be delayed without significant cost. As Martin Libicki pointed out in a 2009 RAND study, a cyber response is unlikely to be able to disable a cyber attacker completely. As a consequence, for deterrence policy, "[m]ore important than [the] speed [of the response] is the ability to convince the attacker not to try again. Ironically, for a medium that supposedly conducts its business at warp speed, *the urgency of retaliation is governed by the capacity of the human mind to be convinced, not the need to disable the attacking computer before it strikes again.*"[15]

The problem for cyber response is, in some ways, the same organizational challenge faced in other domains. The issue is "how to sustain human control [that is, maintain a] man-in-the-loop. . . . For example, control structures can have human control to unlock weapons systems, or automatic system unlock with human intervention required to override. An example of the former is the control of nuclear weapons and of the later, the control of a nuclear power reactor. This may be high tech, but the big questions are political and organizational."[16] Indeed, the problems associated with automated responses were demonstrated, in a more prosaic fashion, in 2010 when automated trading rules caused a 1,000 point decline in the Dow Jones Industrial Average in less than 10 minutes of trading on the New York Stock Exchange.[17]

Our organizational structures and processes have not yet matured sufficiently in the cyber domain to understand this distinction, much less to enable the implementation of policies that maximize the sustainment of human control at senior policy levels. On the contrary, it would appear today that the default in response to a cyber attack is to permit critical decisions to be made at an operational level, informed only by system assurance necessity.

Such a structure is problematic. The governing rule should be, wherever possible, to go slow and permit human control. We have already seen how easy it is for automated systems to create a flash crash; we want to make sure that they don't start a flash war.

LAW AT THE FRONT

Turning this issue on its head, the conduct of cyber operations may actually yield an increasing centralization of command and control. For analogies of this trend, we need not look far. One of the least-well-kept secrets in America is the CIA's operation of a covert drone campaign in the borderland between Pakistan and Afghanistan. If press reports are to be believed, the program has been successful in steadily constraining action by the core al-Qaeda leadership and slowly whittling down their numbers. Perhaps as few as two of the original leadership are still alive (at least as of the time of the writing of this book—by the time you read it, the number may be fewer). By all accounts, the drone program has been one of the most effective means of projecting force developed by the United States in the past quarter century.

One little recognized consequence of this new practical reality has been a restructuring and centralization of command and control. Because the drone program acts at a distance, and because it is mostly operated from inside the United States, we have seen the development of a system where key targeting decisions are being taken by increasingly more responsible and senior officials. Indeed, as Professor Gregory McNeal, of Pepperdine University describes it,[18] when any significant chance of collateral damage from an attack exists, the "go/no-go" decision is typically made by a General officer and is sometimes even made by the Secretary of Defense or the President.

The new norm of cyber conflict will, like the atomic bomb, create surprising new policies, new practical realities and, in the end, new law. One area in which we can already see this is the same centralization effect that we can observe with respect to armed drone attacks. Cyber weapons, just like drones, act at a distance. They are often deployed with forethought and are part of a pre-planned series of military actions. As such, they are, like drones, far more likely to be controlled by more senior authority than is typical for a military engagement.

It is difficult to overstress how significant this change truly is. In war, as we know it in the physical world, decisions are typically made by a commander on the scene in relatively close geographic proximity to events. One consequence of that situation is that legal judgments about proposed courses of action will be made by attorneys who are attached to combat units at the front and who have situational awareness of the conflict.

By contrast, with the centralization of control here at home (a policy we might well approve for other reasons), we necessarily bring with that policy an increasingly important role for lawyers. Where there is time for reflection, lawyers are far more likely to intervene. Many, of course, will see this as a good thing, but it is likely to produce some odd results. It is no surprise that, as we noted earlier in this chapter, Department of Justice lawyers have tentatively concluded that as a matter of law U.S. cyber attacks must respect the neutrality of other countries, and that, therefore, they cannot transit through servers in neutral countries.[19] To nonlawyer technologists, this seems to elevate form over substance; we might as well say that the United States will disarm and not conduct cyber offensive operations, for no successful operation is likely where neutrality is strictly respected. Thus, while there are benefits to centralizing command and control, the proximity to unwieldy bureaucracy also poses challenges for the management of military operations.

* * *

And so, we are on the horns of a dilemma, or more accurately more than one. First, the laws of armed conflict are not readily translated to cyber space. They were built for warfare involving armies and munitions and are, in the cyber domain, inherently ambiguous. Second, given the lack of distinction in cyberspace, the line between intelligence and war is ill-defined, at best. Third, lawyers love ambiguity. So much so that our uncertainty may be crippling our possible cyber responses. And yet, finally, the nature of cyber conflict is such that we really do *want* to have a considered centralized decision-making process. We don't want to go to cyber war by mistake. All of this vagueness leaves us deeply unsettled; we know that cyber war is possible and we have no idea what rules, if any, will apply. That is not a formula for a stable international regime where the rule of law prevails. It is, instead, a formula for the Hobbesian law of nature.

5

Chapter   Cyber-Insurgency

Cyber war between nation-states is, in the end, as likely (or unlikely) as a kinetic war. While the possibility exists for a cyber attack by a foreign nation to occur independent of a military operation, the far more likely scenario is for a cyber assault to occur in the context of a shooting war. If, hypothetically, tensions were rising between Taiwan and China and the United States moved to intervene, we could imagine situations in which the Chinese might engage in cyber activity as a way of influencing, deterring, or defeating American actions (and vice versa). Seen in this light, the risks of a full-scale cyber war, though substantial in terms of consequence, are relatively modest in terms of likelihood. It is, in effect, a low probability/high consequence event.[1]

The same cannot, unfortunately, be said of cyber intrusions by nonstate actors. Unconstrained by the limits of sovereignty, devoid of any territory to protect, and practically immune from retaliation, these groups pose a significant danger to stability. We might think of them as cyber terrorists, but perhaps a better conception is that of a cyber insurgent.

A good way to look at this is through the prism of the challenge to social and governmental authority by WikiLeaks and its founder, Julian Assange, and its support by the hacktivist group Anonymous. Their story is one of both enhanced information transparency and, more significantly for our purposes, the ability to wage combat in cyberspace.

The transparency aspect of the story is well known and widely remarked on (and we will address it in Chapter 11); WikiLeaks is now a brand name for the disclosure of government secrets. But, the more interesting (and less widely remarked on) part of the story revolves around the reaction to Mr. Assange's arrest in Great Britain and the decision of many companies (such as PayPal, MasterCard, and Amazon) to sever financial relationships with WikiLeaks.

Their response turned the WikiLeaks fiasco into a kind of cyber war involving nonstate actors. The important decisions, however, had nothing do with technology. They were decisions that undermined WikiLeaks's finances and likely played a larger role in hindering access to its website than any other effort.

THE WIKILEAKS WAR

With the disclosure of classified information, WikiLeaks appeared to be launching an assault on state authority (and, more particularly, that of the United States, though other governments were also identified). Confronted with WikiLeaks' anti-sovereign slant, the institutions of traditional commerce soon responded. There is no evidence that any of the governments ordered any actions, but the combination of governmental displeasure and clear public disdain for Mr. Assange soon led a number of major Western corporations (MasterCard, PayPal, and Amazon, to name three) to withhold services from WikiLeaks. Amazon reclaimed rented server space that WikiLeaks had used and the two financial institutions stopped processing donations made to WikiLeaks.[2]

What soon followed might well be described as the first cyber battle between nonstate actors. Supporters of WikiLeaks, loosely organized in a group under the name Anonymous (naturally), began a series of distributed denial-of-service (DDoS) attacks on the websites of the major corporations that they thought had taken an anti-WikiLeaks stand, in order to flood the websites and prevent legitimate access to them.[3] The website of the Swedish prosecuting authority (who was seeking Mr. Assange's extradition to Sweden to face criminal charges) was also hacked. Some of the coordination for the DDoS attacks was done through social media, such as Facebook or Twitter.[4] Meanwhile, other supporters created hundreds of mirror sites, replicating WikiLeaks content, so that it couldn't be effectively shut down.[5] The hackers even adopted a military-style nomenclature, dubbing their efforts Operation Payback.

And, when Anonymous attacked, the other side fought back. The major sites used defensive cyber protocols to oppose Anonymous. Most attacks were relatively unsuccessful. The announced attack on Amazon, for example, was abandoned shortly after it began because the assault was ineffective. Perhaps, even more tellingly, someone (no group has, to my knowledge, publicly claimed credit) began an offensive cyber operation against Anonymous itself. Anonymous ran its operations through a website, AnonOps.net, and that website was subject to DDoS counterattacks, which took it offline for a number of hours.[6] In short, a conflict readily recognizable as a battle between competing forces took place in cyberspace, waged almost exclusively between nonstate actors.[7]

The failure of Anonymous to effectively target corporate websites and its relative vulnerability to counter-attack are, likely, only temporary circumstances. Anonymous (and its opponents) will learn from this battle and approach the next one with a greater degree of skill and a better perspective on how to achieve their ends. Indeed, many of Anonymous' more recent attacks—such as the effort to shut down the Vatican website—show a great deal more sophistication and effectiveness.[8]

Moreover, Anonymous has demonstrated that even with its limited capacity it can do significant damage to individuals and companies. When Aaron Barr, the corporate head of a security firm HB Gary, announced that his firm was investigating the identity of Anonymous participants, Anonymous retaliated. They hacked the HB Gary network (itself a significantly embarrassing development for a cybersecurity company) and took possession of internal e-mails that, in turn, suggested that HB Gary was engaged in some questionable business practices. As a result, Barr was forced to resign from his post— exactly the type of individual consequence that is sure to deter an effective counter-insurgent response.

Anonymous has made quite clear that it intends to continue the cyber wars against, among others, the United States. "It's a guerrilla cyberwar—that's what I call it," says Barrett Brown, 29, a self-described senior strategist and propagandist for Anonymous.[9] "It's sort of an unconventional asymmetrical act of warfare that we're involved in, and we didn't necessarily start it. I mean, this fire has been burning." Or, consider the manifesto posted by Anonymous, declaring cyberspace independence from world governments: "I declare the global social space we are building together to be naturally independent of the tyrannies and injustices you seek to impose on us. You have no moral right to rule us nor do you possess any real methods of enforcement we have true reason to fear."[10] In February 2012, Anonymous went further—formally declaring war against the United States and calling on its citizens to rise and revolt.[11]

Indeed, in many ways, Anonymous conducts itself in some of the same manner that an opposing military organization might. Also, in February 2012, for example, it was disclosed that Anonymous had hacked into a telephone conversation between the FBI and Scotland Yard, the subject of which was the development of a prosecution case against Anonymous.[12] That sort of tactic—intercepting the enemy's communications—is exactly the type of tactic an insurgency might use. And, by disclosing the capability, Anonymous has successfully sown uncertainty about how much *else* it might be intercepting.

In advancing their agenda, the members of Anonymous look somewhat like the anarchists who led movements in the late 19th and early 20th centuries—albeit anarchists with a vastly greater network and far more ability to advance their nihilistic agenda through individual action.[13] And, like the anarchists of old, they have their own internal disputes; recently another group called "Black Hat" effectively declared war on Anonymous because it disagreed with the Anonymous agenda.[14] But, even more, Anonymous and its imitators look like the nonstate insurgencies we have faced in Iraq and

Afghanistan—small groups of nonstate actors using asymmetric means of warfare to destabilize and disrupt existing political authority.

BEYOND ANONYMOUS

Anonymous is not the only group that looks like an anarchist/insurgency hybrid. In the months since the initial Anonymous–PayPal conflict burst onto the scene, a number of other organizations have surfaced that are intent on disrupting Internet traffic as a means of expressing some political viewpoint (though precisely what viewpoint is often unclear).

One of the most notorious is/was a splinter group known as LulzSec (the "Lulz" part of the name is a play on the common text message "LOLs," which stands for Laugh Out Loud (plural), and the "Sec" is a shortened form of security—all of which indicates that the group laughs at cybersecurity measures). The group has claimed responsibility for a number of significant intrusions in 2011, including the compromise of user accounts at Sony, affecting the millions of PlayStation3 users. They also claimed that they were responsible for taking a CIA website offline. By many accounts, LulzSec had no more than six core members who caused all the disruption and, unlike Anonymous, some of their public posts suggest they were motivated by a childish enthusiasm (best captured in the phrase "just for laughs") for creating chaos rather than by a more anarchic worldview akin to that of Anonymous. Recently, LulzSec announced that it was quitting.

Precisely why LulzSec is quitting is not known. It may, however, have been in possible reaction to the threats from other hackers (most notably "The Jester" who goes by the handle "th3j35t3r"[15] and whose identity was publicly disclosed in mid-2012) to track down and expose LulzSec members. It may also have been because of arrests of at least three suspected members of LulzSec by police in the United Kingdom and a fourth arrest by the FBI in America. Whatever the cause, LulzSec seems to be operating with diminished capacity at this point.

Or, consider a relatively new group, called "Inj3ct0r Team." This group recently claimed that they had compromised a server belonging to the North Atlantic Treaty Organization (NATO). The group announced that they had removed confidential data from a backup server and left behind a scatological message in a Notepad file. As with some other groups, it is suspected that Inj3ct0r began as an individual effort and became a team as that individual attracted a group of loyal followers.

One particularly vexing issue for many of these intrusions by Anonymous, LulzSec, and their hacking compatriots is the challenge of drawing a line between impermissible crime and activist protests. To be sure, many in the hacktivist community see themselves in the model of a latter-day civil rights movement. Indeed, many of the fringe participants who respond to requests and tasking orders from the leadership of the hacking collectives expressly see themselves as lineal descendants of that era, sometime likening their DNS attacks to the sit-ins of prior decades.[16] One lawyer, John Hamasaki of San Francisco, represents a defendant who allegedly participated in the Anonymous denial of service attack on PayPal. He contends that even if true, the most that can be said is that his client engaged in "political protest that caused a minor inconvenience."[17] Or, as Eugene H. Spafford, a computer security professor at Purdue, recently put it: "A whole bunch of people were angry, they didn't really think about whether it was legal or not. It never entered their minds. . . . This was kind of the equivalent of a spontaneous street protest, where they may have been throwing rocks through windows but never thought that was against the law or hurting anybody."[18]

In America (if not in other countries around the globe) that claim partially resonates—at least to the extent that the protests are nonviolent and don't amount to the virtual equivalent of rock throwing. We see the Internet as a global commons for political protest and watch with a large degree of approval as the modalities of Internet communication are used to foster debate and dissent (as in the Arab Spring movement stirring rebellion in the Middle East). There is reluctance, then, to apply law enforcement principles to some of the insurgents' less disruptive acts—a reluctance that is even greater when a more militarized response is contemplated.

In the end, however, the cyber insurgents also live in the real world. They cannot occupy only the cyber-persona layer without also occupying the true persona layer. And, therein lies the easiest means of response to their tactics. For some, like the LulzSec members, the response may be an arrest and criminal prosecution. Twenty-five members of Anonymous were, likewise, arrested in early 2012 by Interpol.[19] And, in March 2012, the FBI demonstrated the utility of human intelligence in combating the cyber insurgents when it arrested more members of LulzSec.[20] It turned out that one of the leaders, the infamous Sabu (real name, Hector Xavier Monsegur), had been identified earlier and had become an informant, cooperating with the government in identifying his colleagues.[21]

For other institutions, like WikiLeaks, the physical world response has been a concerted effort to bring to bear the levers of power that operate in that domain: when last WikiLeaks was heard from, the financial pressures from the cutoff of its traditional funding streams had led it to suspend operations entirely.[22] Though WikiLeaks had, arguably, changed the world, it may not survive to see what changes it had wrought.

IMPLICATIONS FOR CYBERSPACE CONFLICT

What these stories tell us is that the world today may be in the same place in cyberspace that American troops were in Iraq in 2005. In Iraq, the American military faced a small dedicated group of stateless actors (in that case, al-Qaeda operatives and their sympathizers) who were using asymmetric means of warfare (like Improvised Explosive Devices [IEDs]) to harass the troops and to create chaos for the Iraqi government. America, in turn, had no doctrine for dealing with or countering the influence of these insurgents. Our last counterinsurgency effort had been during the Vietnam War, and since that time the concepts for dealing with insurgent behavior have atrophied.

Recognizing that gap in doctrinal training, the Army conducted an extended examination of the problem, led by then-Lieutenant Generals David Petraeus and James Amos. The result was a new field manual on counterinsurgency (COIN).[23] The manual advanced the thesis of coordinated military-civilian effort against insurgents—a thesis that now forms the intellectual framework of all American efforts in Iraq and Afghanistan. In Iraq, weaning local leaders off support for al-Qaeda arguably had a greater impact in weakening the insurgency than tracking down and killing insurgents.

Neither the United States nor any other nation has yet to undertake the same doctrinal developmental effort in cyberspace. The real lesson of the WikiLeaks war is that cyber actors behave, in many respects, like insurgents do in a kinetic conflict. Indeed, that may well be the far more common form of conflict in the future and some indications exist that terrorists, like al-Qaeda, are looking to recruit hackers to work for them.[24] The methods for confronting these cyber insurgents will be different from those used to confront armed insurgents in the real world, so the current counterinsurgency manual won't suffice. Understanding the scope of the problem suggests that a new cyber insurgency doctrine is needed.

And, therein lies the beginning of a series of lessons that we can learn about the dynamics of conflict in cyberspace. The growth of cyber insurgency has significant implications for cyber conflict policy development. At the root, the enablement of nonstate actors in cyberspace has begun a challenge to the hegemony of nation-states that have been the foundation for international relations since the Peace of Westphalia.[25] The challenge is premised, at the bottom, on three interrelated aspects of the nature of conflict in cyberspace:

- *Asymmetric warfare is here to stay.* The Anonymous challenge to large corporations and to governments worldwide is, in the end, inherent in the structure of the Internet. That structure allows individuals and small groups to wield power in cyberspace that is disproportionate to their numbers. Similarly, states can use electrons to do their fighting for them rather than sending armies into battle. States can also use nonstate actors as proxies or mimic the activities of cyber insurgents to hide a government hand behind malicious activities. (It is suspected that China and Russia do precisely that.)

This description of the correlation of forces in cyberspace is, in many ways, congruent with similar analyses of the physical world. Terrorists enabled by asymmetric power (IEDs and box cutters) have likewise challenged traditional state authorities. And, just as Americans must learn to deal with these kinetic insurgent challenges, so too must they respond to cyber insurgency.

- *Current capabilities of nonstate actors are weak but improving.* The current capabilities of organized nonstate actors in cyberspace are relatively modest. While DDoS attacks can be a significant annoyance, they are not an existential threat. This state of affairs is unlikely to hold for long. As the Stuxnet computer virus demonstrates, significant real-world effects can already be achieved by sophisticated cyber actors. It is only a matter of time until less sophisticated nonstate actors achieve the same capability.
- *Attribution is always a challenge.* Determining the origin of an attack can be problematic. Sending a message from a digital device to a provider is akin to mailing a letter. The service provider acts as an electronic carrier that sends the message through routers and servers which deliver the message to the targeted computer. The attacking computers may have been hijacked and be under the control of a server in another country. An attacker may disguise its locations by circuitous routing or by masking the message's source identification, similar to fudging a letter's return address and postmark. A cyber insurgent may strike several countries, multiple Internet service providers, and various telecommunications linkages, all subject to varying legal requirements and reporting standards, which makes tracing the source extremely difficult.

Overcoming these difficulties by technical means alone is a vexing problem—and an unnecessary one. As the scope of conflicts in cyberspace develops, governments around the world will use *all* techniques in their arsenal to exploit the weaknesses of the nonstate actors who are part of the threat.

COUNTERINSURGENCY AND CYBERINSURGENCY

Though the problem of dealing with nonstate actors, like Anonymous, resembles in structure the problem of dealing with a nonstate insurgency on the ground in Iraq or Afghanistan (and before that in Vietnam and Malaysia), there will be very significant differences in the two domains—not the least of which being the borderless, global nature of cyberspace. Other distinctions also exist: in the kinetic world, the goal of an insurgency is often the overthrow of an existing government. As the COIN Field Manual puts it: "Joint doctrine defines an *insurgency* as an organized movement aimed at the overthrow of a constituted government through the use of subversion and armed conflict. Stated another way, an insurgency is an organized, protracted politico-military struggle designed to weaken the control and legitimacy of an established government, occupying power, or other political authority while increasing insurgent control."[26]

The Anonymous cyber insurgents and their compatriots seem to have a slightly different aim. Rather than the overthrow of a government, they seek, in their own words, independence from those governments. But, in truth, that independence is premised on weakening political authority over the cyber domain that Anonymous inhabits; as a consequence, the difference in goals may not be terribly germane. Conceptually, the challenge will pose many of the same problems—how to isolate fringe actors from the general populace and deny them support and refuge, for example.

In the last 10 years, the United States has devoted significant resources to the development of a counterinsurgency strategy for combating nontraditional warfare opponents on the ground. COIN requires a complex mix of offensive, defensive, and sustainment operations. In the context of a land-based operation, American doctrine has had to consider a range of issues including, by way of nonexclusive examples: integrating military and civilian activity, intelligence collection against insurgents, building up host nation security services, maintaining essential services in-country, strengthening local governance, offensive military operations, and economic development. Each counter-insurgency campaign is different and the building blocks will vary, but each of these aspects is likely to play some role in a counter-cyber insurgency strategy too.

ELEMENTS OF A CYBER INSURGENCY STRATEGY

No one has developed an equivalent COIN strategy for cyberspace. The American strategy must be much more expansive than treating cyber threats as primarily a technical challenge. Concepts that might find their way into a cyber insurgency approach to battling bad actors online include the following.

Collecting Intelligence

Dealing with cyber insurgents requires human intelligence (HUMINT) on the operation of nonstate actors in cyberspace. Rather than concentrating on technical intelligence, human intelligence focuses on information collected by human sources (such as through conversations and interrogations). HUMINT can provide all kinds of information on the cyber insurgents, not only the technical means of attack, but motivations, relationships, and finances—identifying weaknesses and vulnerabilities in their network that might not be available from merely deconstructing malicious software or looking through the files of an Internet service provider. Indeed, HUMINT and related intelligence tools may be the only means to positively attribute the source of an attack—one of the most critical tasks in combating cyber insurgents. Current U.S. strategies give short shrift to the critical role of a more comprehensive intelligence effort for cybersecurity. President Obama's National Security Strategy, for example, defines the mission of "securing cyberspace" exclusively in terms of designing "more secure technology" and investing in "cutting-edge research and development."[27] The strategy includes no discussion of the role of intelligence in cybersecurity.

Likewise, when Deputy Secretary of Defense William Lynn outlined the five pillars of the Department of Defense's cyber strategy, he emphasized the technical aspects of the threat and neglected the role of intelligence. Intelligence, however, could be crucial to identifying how to weaken the threat other than merely shutting down its servers. Good ground intelligence could be the precursor to other means at affecting the enemy (means that might range from a naming and shaming campaign, to an assault on his financial assets, to a direct attack).

Integrating Government and Civilian Action

As in the kinetic world, much of the U.S. effort will require coordination between military and civilian government assets. In cyberspace, the situation has the added layer of complexity posed by the need to coordinate with private-sector actors. President Obama's National Security Strategy rightly emphasizes the importance of public–private partnerships: "Neither government nor the private sector nor the individual citizen," the strategy notes, "can meet this challenge alone."[28]

When coordinated action is done well, it can have a demonstrative impact. In one recent instance, the FBI worked with companies that had been identified as being infected with a botnet program called Coreflood, malicious software that infects Microsoft Windows–based computers and is designed to steal usernames, passwords, and financial information. According to a court affidavit filed in the case:

> In one example, the chief information security officer of a hospital healthcare network reported that, after being notified of the Coreflood infection, a preliminary investigation revealed that approximately 2,000 of the hospital's 14,000 computers were infected by Coreflood. Because Coreflood had stopped running on the infected computers [as a result of FBI assistance], the hospital was able to focus on investigating and repairing the damage, instead of undertaking emergency efforts to stop the loss of data from the infected computers.[29]

The Coreflood case and cooperative public–private activities demonstrate that despite the myriad legal, cultural, and bureaucratic obstacles, effective cooperation is possible. Our goal should be to make it more routine.

For a cyber insurgency strategy to be effective, it is critical that the United States develop mechanisms for ensuring that successes and best practices are translated into a suitable doctrine and become part of the professional development of private-sector and public-sector leaders. Among other needs will be demands for education, training, and experience that qualify public and private actors to be real cyber leaders. A doctrine that addresses public–private cooperation must be a centerpiece of that strategy. No adequate effort to address this shortfall is currently underway.

Building Host Nation Cybersecurity

Strengthening the capacity of friends and allies for network security and resilience has to be an essential part of counter-cyber insurgency. The more that nations with common purpose and values work together, the more that can be done to shrink the cyberspace available to cyber insurgents. In the case of the recent Coreflood investigation, for example, in response to a request by the United States for assistance from the Estonia government under the Mutual Legal Assistance Treaty between the two countries, law enforcement authorities there advised the FBI of the seizure of several additional computer servers believed to be the predecessors to Coreflood command-and-control servers in the United States.[30] Estonia has undertaken some of the most innovative efforts to protect its nation's cyber infrastructure and deal with cybercrimes and cyber attacks. Estonia counts as a first-class cyber ally. Cooperative governments, principally in the West, are likely to band together in a common cause. Washington needs to encourage other nations to take similar steps to enhance their capabilities.

Resiliency

Just as a physical world insurgency can be frustrated by maintaining essential services to residents, a cyber insurgency can be opposed by promoting the resiliency of essential cyber services. In guerrilla war, one tactic of the insurgents is to destroy the infrastructure supporting the local community. We have come to recognize that these *in terrorem* tactics are intended to destroy the economy and erode loyalty to the existing order. Hence, the motto: "Always repair the road."

The same is true in cyberspace. Hacktivists attempt to control behavior by controlling people's access to the Internet and their experience. A DDoS attack that closes a website is functionally little different than an IED that destroys a road. And, the response has to be the same. In the cyber domain, resiliency of service (through backup servers and greater bandwidth) frustrates the insurgent's intent. In turn, providing for the continuity of service generates support and wins the loyalty of users.

Offensive Operations

One of the hardest questions we will have to address is to define when and how state actors can and should take offensive action against cyber insurgents like Anonymous. This will pose a number of challenges—both in defining when an attack by an insurgency justifies a military response (as opposed to a law enforcement response) and what tactics are permissible and proportionate. As we have already seen in Chapter 4, applying the laws of armed conflict to cyber conflict between nation-states is hard enough; the challenge becomes immeasurably greater when a nonstate actor is the source of the attack.

The fact that the insurgents are nonstate actors makes them less vulnerable to retaliation, less capable of diplomatic persuasion, and more ready and able to conceal themselves within the general population and hide behind neutral actors. Just as insurgent warfare needs to be exceedingly careful to avoid civilian casualties, so too must our offensive efforts in cyberspace be constrained by an appreciation for the negative consequences of collateral damage.

Cyber Militias and Letters of Marque and Reprisal

Finally, we will want to consider whether and how to engage civilian populations in the response to a cyber insurgency. One can imagine, for example, the development of cyber militias (somewhat akin to Russia's patriotic hackers) who are recruited by the American government to assist in responding to attacks by nonstate actors, like Anonymous. Those sorts of ready reserve militia might be available for defensive measures should an attack of significant proportions ever occur.

Perhaps, more creatively, we might even consider reviving the practice of Letters of Marque and Reprisal.[31] Authorized by the Constitution, but last issued in the 1800s, these letters were, in effect, a private license to an individual to go and wage war on behalf of the U.S. government against a specified target (the Barbary pirates are one example). As a thought experiment (more amusing than intended as a realistic proposal), we could imagine resuming this practice and giving patriotic American hackers a license to track down anonymous hacktivists who bedevil us.

* * *

America has already begun, slowly, to recognize the need to combat insurgency in cyberspace. One novel program, for example, aims at collecting intelligence while also countering the insurgent's use of the Internet as a method for mobilizing support. U.S. Central Command has created a Digital Engagement Team whose mission is to monitor social media in the Middle East and then counteract any information that is an inaccurate representation of American policy.[32] When, for example, doctored photographs of Osama bin Laden appeared online, purporting to show that he was still alive, the team responded with evidence to the contrary. And, when asked in one forum what Afghans had gained from 10 years of American intervention in Afghanistan, the team (which operates completely overtly, with official U.S. government approval) said simply: "The days of public stoning and the beating of women in the streets are over." Though this effort to win the hearts and minds of Islamic opponents has just begun, it is a good example of how thinking about the problem as one of insurgency leads the military to undertake a different set of tasks.

Of course, to simply list the many topics that require effort is to acknowledge the complexity of the task. However, just as the conceptualization of a counter-insurgency strategy and doctrine was a necessary precursor of success in Iraq, the development of a cyber insurgency strategy and doctrine is an important component of success in cyberspace. We can, as we did in Iraq, wait until the need for such a strategy is brought home by failures on the ground. Or, we can (more wisely) see the WikiLeaks war as a wake-up call and begin the necessary doctrinal thinking now.

ARE ALL "INSURGENTS" REALLY INSURGENTS?

At this juncture, it's worth stepping back a second and noting an important limitation on some of this analysis—that it presupposes that we know the nature of an insurgency. Our image, thus far, is of a group of hacktivist/ activists like Anonymous or, in a slightly more organized form, the patriotic Russian hackers who participated in the Russia–Georgia conflict. But, those aren't the only types of activists who exert control over the Internet. In fact, they may be comparatively less effective in their insurgent activities than another, more powerful group—the Internet service providers themselves.

Consider, by way of example, the day that portions of the Internet went dark: January 18, 2012. On that day, a worldwide protest by service providers shut down many portions of the web and modified many others—all in protest against a proposed set of online piracy laws under consideration by the U.S. Congress.[33] For example, Wikipedia's English language site went dark completely; Reddit (an Internet news accumulator) encouraged users to "take today as a day of focus and action to learn about these destructive bills and do what you can to prevent them from becoming reality"; and Google's iconic white search page featured a large black rectangle over the name (symbolizing the alleged censorship that was being protested). Other sites participating in the protest included craigslist, Mozilla, Imgur, Raw Story, Cheezburger, and the Consumer Electronics Association.

The subject of their protest (two bills directed at stopping the online piracy of intellectual content like movies and songs) hardly matters—what matters far more is the mechanism chosen to convey the message. These are not the acts of insurgents in any classical sense of the term; they don't seek to overthrow governments or start a revolution. But, in many ways, both their ideology (for a free Internet) and their tactics (of blocking or modifying Internet content access) are more than vaguely reminiscent of those adopted by some of the more radical Internet activists. It seems that even the most dynamic members of America's innovative corporate community can, when pressed, take advantage of their position at the center of all communications to advance their own interests.

And that, too, should give strategic thinkers pause. It demonstrates that, in a real way, the levers of control are now held by private sector actors. What if, to take a wild example, the owners of Verizon, Google, and Facebook were opposed to a war that an American administration proposed to wage against, say, Iran? What if they pulled the plug on Internet communications, not in support of the other side, but as an expression of their own views on peace? Would the result be any different than if patriotic Iranian hackers who supported the other country acted to achieve the same result? It seems not. Yet, the latter would be insurgents in our frame of reference, while the former would be what? Nobody quite knows.

Indeed, the quasi-insurgent nature of the overall conflict was confirmed, in an oddly reflective way, just the day after the organized protest/blackout. The federal government issued a 72-page indictment of the owners of a popular website, known as Megaupload.[34] If the allegations of the indictment are true, the operators of Megaupload caused more than $500 million of harm to companies and performers whose shows and songs they ripped off. According to the indictment, the entire business model of Megaupload was designed to promote the uploading of copyrighted material and they even paid users they knew were uploading illegal copyrighted content. In short, the indictment alleges theft, plain and simple—exactly the sort of activity the proposed laws were intended to stop.

In response to the indictment, Anonymous launched a DDoS attack on the U.S. Department of Justice website (along with attacks on the U.S. Copyright Office, the French Copyright Office, the Motion Picture Association of America, and the Recording Industry of America). For an extended period of time over the next two days, most of these sites were unavailable and offline because of the attack.

CYBER COUNTER INSURGENCY IN
ACTION—A CAUTIONARY TALE

As practiced by Western nations, counter-insurgency (whether conventional military or cyber) has certain rules. Though the rules can sometimes be violated (e.g., My Lai in Vietnam), those are the exceptions rather than the rule. One cautionary note we should sound is that in the cyber domain, there are *many* nonstate actors—and not all of them will feel bound by the conventions of war. When two nonstate actors go after each other, almost anything is possible.

Late in 2011, for example, the Anonymous hacker group announced that it had hacked into the database of the notorious Mexican drug cartel known as the Zetas. Inside the database, they had uncovered the names of those (presumably Mexican officials) who were on the Zetas' payroll and were collaborating with them. Anonymous released a video that conditioned the disclosure on the release of an Anonymous member who had been kidnapped in Veracruz.

The Zetas response was chilling, but effective. They warned Anonymous that if it published the names of the collaborators, Zetas would retaliate by conducting a mass killing of civilians—10 people for every collaborator named. Faced with that threat, Anonymous withdrew its threat and closed down its program, known as Operation Cartel.

All of which, in an oddly disturbing way, confirms that the cyber domain really can't be disassociated from the physical world. More fundamentally, it demonstrates that counter-insurgency tactics (even those of the most brutal variety) may be the right frame reference from which to think about opposing amorphous nonstate cyber actors. And, it also suggests that, like other insurgencies, the advantages held by cyber insurgents include their ability to rely on the nation-state's adherence to the rule of law.

Which is not to say that nation-states are disabled in their responses. Though nation-states can never threaten brutal tactics, such as those proposed by the Zetas, they can take steps to create real-world consequences—arrest, prosecution—for nonstate actors who otherwise would face none. But, it is to say that the range of tactics that might be available in response is different for the nation-state than for the insurgent. And, therein lies the challenge in a nutshell.

Part II

Protecting the Web

To live is to risk. There is no such thing as a risk-free environment—least of all, in cyberspace. Conflict on the Internet is endemic and pervasive. Some of the conflict is of modest import and effect; other aspects of it can be quite consequential. The ubiquity of these vulnerabilities has engaged policy makers, law makers, and technologists, intent on trying to ameliorate the problems in cyberspace, even if eliminating them is not feasible.

And, of course, elimination really isn't feasible. We can manage the risk of cyber conflict, but we are not likely to eliminate it short of simply killing the Internet altogether. The risks are inherent in the architecture of the environment and will continue so long as "evil lurks in the hearts of men and women."[1]

In Part II, we begin to look at some of the risk mitigation techniques available to us. Not all are equally effective. Some come with additional baggage that makes their implementation difficult and fraught with political challenges. In some cases, the problems to be addressed are so difficult that we have almost despaired of a solution.

We begin with one of those fundamental and nearly insoluble issues—the question of identity. At the core of almost every cyber conflict is the problem of anonymity: you cannot know who the intruder/attacker is and if you don't know, you cannot respond. There are strategies being developed to mitigate and manage the problem but, as we shall see, they are likely to be of limited effectiveness.

We, then, turn to another answer, perhaps the easiest to conceptualize—deploying the normal resources of law enforcement authorities and treating cyber conflict as a crime. After all, virtually all intrusions are violations of some criminal law. In Chapter 7, we look at the advantages and disadvantages of the cybercrime methodology.

Even our purely defensive efforts are also likely to present challenges. For example, when the federal government begins monitoring the Internet for malware (a process known as deep packet inspection), citizens fear that it will also be monitoring the content of their communication. And, that type of monitoring raises the specter of politicization and a threat to civil liberties. How little the Constitution constrains government action in the cyber domain is often a surprise to many.

Likewise, many will be surprised at how poorly the government now keeps its own secrets. Personal privacy and government secrecy are, after all, two sides of the same coin. The same tools that erode privacy destroy secrecy as well—all of which suggests that we need some new conceptions of how to protect privacy and secrecy in the context of the cyber conflict.

One such method is self-help. If the government and your friends want your secrets, one easy way to keep them is to put them in code, that is, to encrypt them. But, encryption, like so much else in the cyber conflict, is a two-edged sword. It allows me to keep my finances private, but it also allows criminals to hide their activities from law enforcement. It enables freedom aspirations in the Arab Spring by allowing activists to keep secrets from a repressive regime, but it also allows child pornographers to hide their tracks.

Finally, in the last chapter of Part II, we look at a unique subset of the cyber conflict—the problem of COTS (which stands for Commercial Off-The-Shelf technologies). Put simply, if we buy our computer chips from China or India, because it is cheaper to buy them overseas, how do we know that they will work the way they are supposed to? How do we know that they aren't hardwired to steal secrets or explode on command? The answer is . . . we don't.

6

The Fundamental Problem of Identity

Take this book and walk with it over to your computer. Open up your web browser and pick your favorite search engine (Google, Yahoo . . . it doesn't matter). Type into the search engine the word "WHOIS" (no spaces) and you will see at least a half-dozen links offering "who is" services—services that will, in theory, help you identify the people behind various domain names on the Internet. Seems like a wonderful service—almost like a Yellow Pages for Internet domain names. If only it were that simple.

DOMAIN NAMES

Domain names are familiar to everyone who uses the Internet. In any web address (for example, http://www.redbranchconsulting.com), it is the portion of the address after http://www. Domain names are familiar ways to identify the webpage you are seeking to access or the e-mail address you are trying to reach. We know them and recognize them readily—Microsoft.com takes you to Bill Gates' company and direct.gov.uk takes you to the front page of Her Majesty's Government in London.

Of course, computers don't use names like Microsoft or Her Majesty's Government to route traffic. They use numbers. The Domain Name System (DNS) is, in effect, a translation system; it takes a domain name and translates it to an Internet Protocol address (IP address). The IP address is a binary number inside the computer (that is, just a string of 1s and 0s), but it is usually written in a traditional format when put down for humans to read (for example 172.16.254.1). The IP address tells the Internet routing system where a particular server is on the Internet, and then the IP tells the system how to get the message from "here" to "there," wherever "there" may be.

IPV4 AND IPV6
Identifying a server is actually even more complex than knowing its IP address, because, unlike a physical street address in a city, a server's IP address doesn't remain constant.

The reason is simple. Right now there aren't enough IP addresses for all of the servers and other objects (cell phones, tablets, etc.) that are tied into the Internet. The current address system (Internet Protocol version 4 or IPv4) is limited by its configuration to roughly 4.3 billion addresses. The last unallocated blocks of addresses were given out in January 2011.

To alleviate the problem, the Internet is moving to IPv6, which will have more than 3.4×10^{38} available addresses. The transition to IPv6 is underway. When complete, every component on the Internet will have a single, unique, IP address.

So, the DNS link works in a three-stage process: an individual (Paul Rosenzweig) registers a domain name (redbranchconsulting.com), which is hosted on a server somewhere (as it happens Red Branch is hosted on a server owned and operated by a friend of mine, but you can buy your own server if you want, or rent space on a server farm operated by another company), and that server is identified by an IP address. When a potential client wants to access the Red Branch website by typing in that domain name, the DNS programming helps to route the request to the right server and return the webpage.

All of which means that the addressing function of the DNS is absolutely critical. If the DNS system were corrupted, hijacked, or broken, then communications across the Internet would break down. And, it also means that keeping a good registry of which domain names are in use is just as vital. If Microsoft.com is taken by Microsoft, the computer software giant, it can't be used by Microsoft, a (hypothetical) manufacturer of small soft wash cloths. Somebody needs to be in charge of keeping the books and making sure they are all straight.

That somebody is the Internet Corporation for Assigned Names and Numbers (ICANN). ICANN is a nonprofit organization that sets the rules for creating and distributing domain names. When the Internet was first turned on, the function for assigning names was actually done by a single man, John Postel, who helped create the first Internet as a project for the Advanced Research Projects Agency (ARPA). Since ARPA was a federal government funded agency this, in effect, meant that the naming function was handled by the U.S. government.

In the long run, of course, as the Internet grew to span the globe, a U.S.-run and -managed naming convention was considered too insular and unilateral. ICANN was chartered in 1998 as a means of transitioning control over

Internet naming from the U.S. government to a nonprofit, private sector organization. Today, ICANN operates from California but has a global constituency, registering new domain names every day.

In theory, the DNS system should be completely transparent—knowing a domain name (the cyber-persona of a person or company) you should be able to find out who the real person behind the domain name is. Unfortunately, the system doesn't work as effectively as it should.

If you are still at your computer with this book, let's continue the experiment. In WHOIS, try typing in "redbranchconsulting.com"—that's the domain name for the consulting company that the author operates. If you do that, however, you don't get my name. All you get is a notice that the domain name is registered with a domain name registry company called GoDaddy. com (that's a registry company who works with ICANN to organize the sale of domain names). Fortunately, they are a reputable company, so if you had a lawful reason to ask (if, say, you were the police conducting a criminal investigation and had the correct legal authorization), GoDaddy would tell you who was behind the domain. The same is true of cyberwarbook.com, which is a domain purchased to promote this book—it only resolves through the WHOIS lookup to "Wild West Domains." On the other hand, if you try to find WHOIS Heritage.org, you do get The Heritage Foundation (a thinktank in Washington), so the look up "who is" function has some utility. At least, you can find the Foundation's true address and the name of someone who works there.

Now, imagine that (unlike a book author) you actually wanted to hide your identity. The obscurity of the DNS system makes it easier. One can create a shell company registered just about anywhere in the world and hide behind the corporate structure to conceal the true persona behind the fictive cyber-persona.

In December 2011, ICANN completed a comprehensive review of the WHOIS functions.[1] The conclusion of the report is both chilling and accurate. The report "concisely present[s] in a balanced and fair manner the very real truth that the current [WHOIS] system is broken and needs to be repaired." Because domain registry companies (like GoDaddy or Wild West) accept identification that appears to be lawful and because they make no real attempt to verify the information they receive, the WHOIS registry is littered with errors, both accidental and deliberate.

SPOOFING

As if the inaccuracy of the addressing registry weren't enough, there are plenty of other techniques to hide on the Internet. Recall that messages that transit the net don't automatically come with authentication; they may purport to be from your friend, but almost everyone who uses the Internet has received at least one communication that's a fraud. "I'm stranded in London and need you to send me money" has become the modern day equivalent of "I've got a great bridge to sell you in Brooklyn." This kind of almost blatant fraud and misrepresentation is commonplace.

Perhaps even more troubling, many techniques exist to spoof any effort to backtrack a message to an original individual source. In the absence of a strong authentication rule, it is relatively easy as a technical matter to spoof an IP address so that a message purports to come from a location other than the one from which it was truly sent. Likewise, in a world where botnets allow a malicious actor to control computers other than his own, it is also technically feasible to originate a message from a computer that is not your own, but is under your control. As a result, the commonplace is that virtually every intrusion or attack on the network is obscured behind a farrago of false e-mail addresses, spoofed IPs, and botnets under the control of a third party. No attacker worth his salt would make any intrusion directly from his own IP address. They are always bounced through a number of false leads before arriving at their intended target.

ATTRIBUTION IS HARD; VERY HARD

One of my law professors at the University of Chicago, Bernard Meltzer, would sometime be challenged by young law students complaining about the unfairness or injustice of some counterintuitive legal result. His response was always the same: "Life is hard Mr. ____; very hard." What he meant by that became clear over the course of a semester. In an ideal world, we might have a different situation, but the real world is filled with problems and challenges that simply can't be wished away because they are unfair or unjust.

Attribution on the Internet is one of those issues. The difficulty of identification is perhaps the single most profound challenge for cybersecurity today. It is not just that it is hard (though, it is hard enough) to do attribution, it is that the converse of attribution—anonymity—is a fundamental part of our cyber consciousness. The anonymous Internet stems not just from the architecture of the communications protocols. It also stems from a quasi-libertarian streak that is, at its core, an ur-meme of Internet society. For some, Internet anonymity is part of their ideological commitment to a broad-based, diverse, individually empowered community.

But, let's leave the sociology of the Internet aside for a moment and focus on exactly where we are today. Attribution is deeply problematic in most applications, and that makes the network vulnerable to attack.

But, problematic doesn't mean impossible. The story of the GhostNet intrusion (previously discussed in Chapters 2 and 3) says something about the possibility of backtracking a hacker.[2] The Information Warfare Monitor group from Canada spent nearly a year on the effort, and broke into some of the hacker's own computers (as well as some of the computer transit points in between) to follow the trail, and in the end they were able to trace the origin of the intrusion to servers on Hainan Island, also the home of a Chinese military signals intelligence agency.

What the effort demonstrates is that, in the end, attribution is a question of resources and permissions. If you are willing to devote enough time, money, and personnel to the issue and if you have the requisite permission to do certain acts that, in other contexts, might be illegal, then in the end a good attribution can be achieved. The major problem with the effort, however, is that it takes a long time—of what value is an attribution six months after the attack?

In addition, this sort of effort has a significant blow-back potential. The types of techniques that are necessary to do attribution are quite sophisticated and ever-changing, as malicious actors and those who would track them engage in an ongoing game of cat and mouse. Whenever a defender makes the significant effort to do attribution, they run the risk that their actions will reveal their own methods and the scope of the signals intelligence they are collecting. As a result, attributors must act cautiously and only when they are reasonably confident of maintaining the integrity of their methods—or are willing to sacrifice their methods because identifying the attacker is critical in context.

As a result, though attribution is slow and cautious, it can be done—and that can provide us with better knowledge of the types of malicious actors who are at work. For example, it has been reported that the NSA has, through patient and diligent work, identified roughly 12 separate networks of hackers that are causing most of the damage experienced in America today.[3] The dozen groups are either tied to the Chinese military directly or tied to Chinese universities with ties to the government. Indeed, it is reported that the U.S. government now knows the names of specific individuals in some of these groups.

Which brings us to the final problem with direct attribution efforts: the "so what" question. For criminal intrusions (as we will see in the next chapter), most of the malicious actors are beyond the reach of the law. They cannot be extradited and prosecuted. Likewise, though attribution does give us a better sense of when and how cyber espionage is occurring, the degree of confidence we have attained does not make it any easier or likely that we can or will take concerted diplomatic action. We may now have better proof that China is behind some of the cyber espionage that is happening, but if our debt to China prevents us from taking effective counter-measures, what is the value of knowing? If the result of the expenditure of such resources is nothing more than the increase in our intellectual storehouse of knowledge, it is at least reasonable to ask whether or not the game is worth the candle.

TRUSTED IDENTITIES

And so, as a matter of policy, we have approached the question of identity and attribution from the other direction. Instead of working backwards from the intrusion to identify the attacker, our general policy proscription is to work forward, from the human–computer interface. What this means is that the policy solution of choice is to try and find a way to make access to the Internet available through trusted identities. Sometimes, this is caricatured as requiring a drivers' license to use the Internet. But, there is an element of truth to the caricature.

The *National Strategy for Trusted Identities in Cyberspace*,[4] envisions the creation of an entire identity ecosystem for creating trusted identities online. The ecosystem has three critical components to it (all of which will need to, more or less, be created from the ground up):

- An *identity provider* who is responsible for creating and maintaining a trusted online identity for an individual
- A *credential* that is a token authenticating an individual and linking him to the trusted digital identity. The credential can be physical (a smart card with a fingerprint on it) or logical (a password linked to a secure ID token) and
- *Attribute providers* (who may be but need not be the same as the identity providers) who, for example, attest that a particular identity belongs to someone who is over 21 years old or has a top secret security clearance.

The federal strategy recognizes that almost all of this infrastructure will have to be provided by the private sector. The federal role, such as it is, is one of encouragement and leading in the development of critical policy and legal regimes that would serve as enablers for the new ecosystem.

And, even at that, the ecosystem would, at least in America, have to be voluntary. It is almost impossible to imagine any system that would be politically acceptable that would call for mandatory participation in a trusted identity system. By contrast, in China the developing identification system is becoming mandatory. Chinese officials have, for example, expanded a program that requires users of microblog services to disclose their identities to the government in order to post comments online.[5] To be sure, if the equivalent of an Internet Drivers' License were ever required for access to the Internet, we would go a long way toward solving the attribution problem—but at great cost to Internet freedom.

Perhaps more saliently, even if a trusted identity system were developed and made politically viable in the United States, it is quite likely (though nothing is ever certain) that American courts would be very skeptical of the Constitutionality of a mandatory Internet trusted identity requirement. Anonymous and pseudonymous speech has a long history in the United States. Just think of the debates that occurred at the time of the adoption of the Constitution.

> **PRIVACY INVASIVE OR PROTECTIVE?**
> While most observers fear the privacy-invasive aspects of any identification program on the Internet, some note that there might actually be collateral privacy-enhancing benefits. A system of secure trusted identities would likely have the positive effect of reducing identity theft crime. Whether that is worth the attendant privacy risks is a significant policy question, but we should acknowledge that there are factors weighing on both sides of the privacy ledger.

Papers published essays by Brutus and Cato and the Federal Farmer. The most famous essays of all, *The Federalist Papers*, were published under the pseudonym Publius. Relying on this history, the Supreme Court has recognized a First Amendment right to anonymous political speech,[6] and that right will, almost certainly, trump any legislated identity requirement.

Still, even a voluntary system will have some utility. Those who are cautious can decline to do business with any identity that is not trustworthy. And, cautious companies and collections of individuals can create their own private networks comprised only of trusted users. In the end, however, these types of programs will only take you so far. In the absence of universality, the tendency will be to a fractioning of the network. But, the network's very universality is its strength.

Nor is that the end of the puzzling contradictions. We need to consider, as well, that broader American interests may not be best served by a system of trusted identification. To be sure, we would likely realize significant cybersecurity benefits from good attribution and identity authentication for our own security purposes. But, one man's security purpose is another man's political oppression. America's long-term interests might be better served by fostering Internet freedom of expression as a means, for example, of encouraging opposition to oppressive authoritarian systems.

And, for authoritarian countries, Internet identification may very well be a way of suppressing dissent. As Marc Rotenberg of the Electronic Privacy Information Center notes, Internet identification is a principal means by which China controls its citizens: "The Chinese government identifies users who access to the Internet in three ways: (1) mandatory registration requirements, (2) requirements on Internet Service Providers, and (3) regulation of Internet cafes."[7] Thus, America's best options remain, to some degree, an open question.

SECURING THE DNS

While individual identification and trusted identity remain, for now, just a vision, progress is being made at securing the next higher level—the authenticity of domain names.

Just as ICANN is the international organization the runs the program for assigning domain names, another non-governmental organization, the Internet Engineering Task Force (IETF), is responsible (in an indirect way) for developing the technical aspects of the computer code and protocols that drive the Internet. The IETF's self-described mission is to "make the Internet work better," but it quickly notes that it is an engineering group, so what it means by "better" is "more technically effective," not better in some metaphysical sense.

The IETF is a self-organized group of engineers who consider technical specifications for the Internet. Anyone may join and the group's proposals (or decision not to make a proposal) are the product of a rough consensus. The IETF has no enforcement function at all—anyone is free to disregard the technical standards it sets. But, they do so at their own peril. Because of the openness, inclusiveness, and nonpartisan nature of its endeavors, IETF standards have become the gold standard for Internet engineering. In addition to the standard setting function, IETF also identifies lesser standards, known as best current practices, that are more in the nature of good advice than of operative requirements. Given the near-universality of IETF standards and practices, anyone who chooses not to follow the standards set forth risks ineffective connections to the broader network. And so, even without a single means of forcing people to follow its dictates, the IETF in effect sets the rules of the road for Internet technical functions.[8]

One of the recent technical specifications adopted by the IETF is something known as DNSSEC, which stands for Domain Name System Security Extension. Under the general rubric of DNSSEC, the IETF has proposed a suite of security add-on functionalities that would become part of the accepted IP. The new security features would allow a user to confirm the origin authentication of DNS data, authenticate the denial or existence of a domain name, and assure the data integrity of the DNS. In other words, the DNSSEC protocols would allow users to be sure that when they attempt to connect to a domain name (say "whitehouse.gov"), they are reaching the true whitehouse.gov website and not some phony facsimile of that website.

Without that sort of security system, efforts to navigate the web are susceptible to man-in-the-middle attacks, that is, an attack where the malicious actor steps into the middle of a conversation and hijacks it by making independent connections with the victims. From the middle vantage point, he can relay messages between the victims, making them believe that they are talking directly to each other over a private connection, when in fact the entire conversation is controlled by the malicious actor.

DNSSEC will also prevent pure spoofing where your request to connect, say, to your bank at chase.com is maliciously redirected to a phony chase.com website and your bank password login information is collected. Once DNSSEC is deployed, a security resolver function will be able to check the registration of the chase.com website and return a message to the user confirming that the website was authentic.

The difficulties that have arisen in the deployment of DNSSEC demonstrate why attribution is so hard a problem to solve. First, DNSSEC has to be backward compatible. In other words, it has to work even with portions of the Internet that have not deployed the new security protocols. Otherwise, systems running the security suite would be disconnected from the broader web. Second, there is a substantial cost for upgrading and deploying DNSSEC across a global range of servers and systems: the process will take years to complete. To cite one of the most obvious examples, though the Office of Management and Budget has mandated that DNSSEC be deployed by all federal agencies across the .gov domain, that mandate is already two years past its 2009 deadline, without any prospect of near-term completion.

Finally, perhaps the greatest difficulty is establishing a chain of trust for domain name authentication. After all, how do you know that the chase.com webpage is authentic? Because a certificating authority (probably a company, like VeriSign, that is in the business of authentication) has distributed to Chase an authentication key. And, how do you know that VeriSign is, itself, authentic? At some point up the chain, there has to be an original root authentication that serves as a trust anchor to the chain of trust. Currently, the trust anchor is provided by ICANN, and some people don't trust ICANN because it is an American company and is thought to still be subservient to American interests.[9]

HACKING THE CHAIN OF TRUST

If you have a chain of trust to establish identity of domain names (or, for that matter, of individuals), you chain is only as strong as its weakest link. And, if your entire defense is based on establishing a chain of trust, we can be sure that malicious actors will seek to undermine that trust chain, if possible.

Just that sort of risk was demonstrated in July 2011 by an attack on a certificating authority in Holland, DigiNotar. DigiNotar was not issuing DNSSEC certificates but rather a different form of certificate known as an SSL (Secure Socket Layer) certificate. These certificates were intended to serve the same function as DNSSEC: give a user the assurance that he was accessing a legitimate website. They functioned, principally, through the mechanisms of your web browser, which is programmed to automatically consult a list of authenticated websites, including the list of authentications provided by DigiNotar.

An individual by the hacker name Comodohacker, who claims to be an Iranian student, penetrated DigiNotar.[10] He then used the penetration to issue more than 250 and possibly as many as 500 false certificates for real companies, like Google. What that means is that if a user typed in the address "mail.google.com" and were redirected to a captive malicious site, that site might appear authentic because the browser would look for, and find, a valid DigiNotar certificate.[11] Particularly because countries like Iran are interested in tracking dissent, some suspected that Comodohacker was an Iranian cyber spy. That impression became even more pronounced when it became clear that Comodohacker had also generated false digital certificates for the CIA, MI6, and the Mossad (Israel's secret service).[12]

In the end, the only way to combat this type of attack was for the web browser manufacturers (Apple's Safari, Google's Chrome, Mozilla Firefox, and Internet Explorer) to all issue death sentences for DigiNotar and revoke all of the certificates the company had ever issued. While that is lukewarm comfort for this particular attack, it also demonstrates the fundamental flaw in any plan that relies for authentication on a chain of trust—trust, it seems, can sometimes be forged.

* * *

When all is said and done, then, the promise of robust attribution and identification is a bit of a chimera. It seems absolutely clear that attribution is possible in many cases, but it is equally clear that creating a world of trusted and secure identities on the network is, ultimately, a nearly impossible dream. We can make a great deal of progress in some aspects of the effort, but in the long run, we have to recognize that anonymity is a feature of our current Internet architecture, not a bug.

As noted security expert Steve Belovin of Columbia University put it: "The fundamental premise of the proposed strategy [for *Trusted Identities*] is that our serious Internet security problems are due to lack of sufficient authentication. That is demonstrably false. The biggest problem was and is buggy code. All the authentication in the world won't stop a bad guy who goes around the authentication system, either by finding bugs exploitable before authentication is performed, finding bugs in the authentication system itself, or by hijacking your system and abusing the authenticated connection set up by the legitimate user."[13]

In short, there is no realistic way of creating a universal system of trusted identities. We can mitigate the consequences, but the fundamental problem of identity is here to stay.

7

Chapter   Cybercrime

In 2007, when the Estonian government removed a statute commemorating Russia's role in World War II, the entire governmental system in Estonia came under sustained attack from Russian patriotic hackers using DDoS tactics. Because Estonia had built an economy and a governmental system that was highly dependent on Internet access (Estonia is often said to be the first fully wired country in the world), the three-week effort was very debilitating.[1] Perhaps, this was a cyber war—but no shots were fired. The activists had no goal of bringing down the Estonian government. Though classification is, always, fraught with difficulty, this particular attack was as much a criminal act of intimidation as anything else.

Cyber war, if it ever comes about, will be a grave threat to national security. Our security interests may also be challenged by nonstate actors like Anonymous who are insurgents or hacktivists. But, most observers think that cybercrime is the most significant challenge facing us in cyberspace. Certainly, in terms of real-world effects on a day-to-day basis, far more users of the Internet are affected by cybercrime than have ever yet been injured in a cyber war or had their website hacked by an insurgent. The reason has, naturally, to do with the nature of cyberspace—and in particular the problems of anonymity, asymmetry, and action at a distance.

CYBERCRIMES AND THE SUBSTANTIVE LAW

The application of criminal law to cybercrimes raises issues of substantive law, procedure, and forensics. While in the real world distinguishing a crime from an accident is relatively straightforward, the exercise is much less easy in cyberspace. In the end, this unique characteristic makes prosecuting cybercrime particularly difficult.

Substantively, though the law is still evolving, we have, for the most part, developed an adequate set of laws for offenses involving unauthorized intrusions into cyber systems. These intrusions diverge from traditional crime but can be readily analogized to more old-fashioned common law concepts like trespass. Steadily, laws have adapted to make clear that hacking intrusions are crimes in and of themselves, as is trespass, and we are now building an adequate legal system to deal with situations similar to the concerted denial of service attack on Estonian systems. If that event had occurred in the United States, it likely would have been criminal under the Computer Fraud and Abuse Act (CFAA).[2] As we shall see, there are some reasons to think that the CFAA is overbroad and criminalizes innocent behavior, but we cannot say that we lack criminal laws to deal with illegal activity.

Criminal law has also adapted fairly readily to situations in which computer systems are not the object of the crime but are used as tools to commit crimes of a more traditional nature. Using computers to commit fraud or access child pornography does not involve any legally relevant distinctions from the use of note paper or the mails to commit the same offenses. In general, criminal law focuses on the illegal conduct itself and is suitably neutral as to the means by which the crime is committed. Some legislatures have perhaps gone too far beyond this construct and made it a crime to commit a particular offense (e.g., theft) using a computer, but in general that response seems unnecessary (in contrast, for example, to offenses that are rendered more serious through the use of a weapon). Still, this expansion, while unnecessary, is little more than a distraction from the generally appropriate structure of criminal law.

To these substantive challenges of criminal law, one must add another piece—the significant forensic challenges of actually solving the crime. In the real world, proximity is frequently a necessity for a successful crime. Much traditional crime requires the physical presence of the criminal and is done face-to-face and one-on-one. Not so with cybercrime, which can be done at a distance and (as anyone who has received a Nigerian fraud solicitation knows) in bulk on a one-to-many scale. And, because the physical presence requirement helps to delimit physical criminality, it also makes capture easier—a factor whose absence makes identifying and prosecuting cybercrime a significant challenge.

Thus, today we face a vexing situation, where high-profit criminality can occur with low risk of capture. This turns our deterrence model of law enforcement on its head. Deterrence only works when there is a credible threat of response and punishment (the degree of punishment mattering less than the degree of certainty of being caught). But, deterrence cannot work without attribution and the nature of cyberspace makes attribution viciously difficult.

Finally, there is a cultural dissonance between the public's view of traditional crime and the dynamics of cyberspace. Law enforcement professionals generally focus on solving crimes. Despite changes occasioned by the response to September 11, they continue to do less work on prevention. Likewise, the public tends to leave prevention to the professionals. What little prevention we do is generally defensive in nature (e.g., putting locks on doors) and leaves offensive investigative function to others. Thus, the dynamic is for the public to take relatively little responsibility for its own protection—again, an understandable policy when the neighborhood police patrol can be effective, but not the best posture when the criminal neighborhood is global. In effect, every computer is a border point—between countries or for entering a home. We have yet to fully come to grips with that reality.

NIGERIAN SCAMS

For most people, the most significant criminal threat in cyberspace is the prospect of fraud or identity theft. Here, the law has developed in ways that make sense, but the actors who commit the crimes are so far removed from American jurisdiction (or for that matter, the jurisdiction of any Western nation) that the prospects for using the criminal law effectively are minimal.

Consider, for example, the by now too-familiar case of Nigerian scam artists—known as 419 fraudsters after the section of the Nigerian criminal code that prohibits fraud. This is just the modern day computer version of an old time fraud known as "an advance fee scheme." Under the advanced fee scheme, the dupe is offered an opportunity to share in a percentage of millions of dollars that are available, if only the recipient will help the criminal—who often poses as a corrupt government official—transfer the money illegally out of Nigeria. The intended victim is scammed—either by sending information to the criminal that allows the crook to steal his identity (e.g., blank letterhead stationery, bank name and account numbers, and other identifying information) or by having the victim provide some advance fee money to the official to be used for transaction costs and bribes.

In the later variation, the victim is asked to send money to the criminal in Nigeria in several installments of increasing amounts for a variety of reasons. Of course, the millions of dollars do not exist, and the victim eventually ends up with nothing but loss. For obvious reasons, the Nigerian government is not sympathetic to the victims of these schemes. After all, they are theoretically complicit in a scheme to remove funds from Nigeria in a manner that is contrary to Nigerian law.

What makes this scam so effective is two-fold: First, the anonymity of the Internet makes the scammer practically invulnerable to effective identification and, even if identified, to extradition. Second, the borderless and near-costless nature of the Internet makes it possible for the scammer to send out tens of thousands, if not hundreds of thousands or millions, of fake solicitation e-mails. Even if the massive majority of recipients properly recognize the scam, a few trusting innocent souls (or, less sympathetically, a few corrupt souls seeking illegal gain) will always respond.

Which actually raises an interesting question that is worth pausing to briefly consider—why are the Nigerian scams so blatant? After all, they come with so many clues that they are scams (misspelled words and transparent come-ons) that we tend to think that only a really naïve person would respond. It turns out that's exactly the point. A recent sociology study suggested that the Nigerian scams (and other blatant scams like it) are bad on purpose. The scammers are actually trolling for the naïve and the uninformed. The idea is that sending a spam load costs the scammers nothing, but what costs them a lot is spending time cultivating a mark for the con.

So they want to identify easy marks early on, and the best way to do that is to be so silly and blatant and overt that only an easy mark will respond. That way they invest their time in fish they are likely to reel in and not in ones that will be hard to catch. The best part is that they actually make the victims do the work. By deleting their e-mails and not responding, we are self-selecting out of the pool; those who answer are advertising their gullibility.

THE RUSSIAN BUSINESS NETWORK

Unlike the Nigerian scammers, who are traditional fraudsters using new tools that give them greater range and scope, the Russian Business Network (known as the RBN) is truly a child of the Internet; it couldn't really exist without it.[3]

The RBN was an Internet service provider, run by criminals for criminals. Its founding date is unclear, but it may go back as far as 2004. The RBN was allegedly created by Flyman, a 20-something programmer who is said to be the nephew of a well-connected Russian politician. Though its initial activity appears to have been legal, it quickly morphed into something more. It provided domain names, dedicated servers, and software for criminals—a one-stop shopping center for those who want to be active on the Internet. The RBN is sometimes called a bullet proof network because, in effect, users are capable of hiding their criminal activity and are bullet proof against prosecution or discovery in their country of origin.

To a large degree, the RBN was just another business: it offered access to bulletproof servers for $600/month and highly effective malware (price $380 per 1,000 targets) and rented out botnets at the bargain basement price of $200 per bot. All this came with free technical support, patches, updates, and fixes.[4] In its heyday, the RBN was responsible for some of the largest criminal hacks to date. One example would be the infamous Rockfish incident, in which users were tricked into entering personal banking information on the web, resulting in losses in excess of $150 million.[5] In another incident, a keystroke logger program (one that records keystrokes input on a keyboard—like a password entry) was introduced on the computers of most of the customers of the Bank of India. The RBN is also said to have provided some support for Russia during the Georgian and Estonian conflicts.

Under severe pressure from the Russian government, which was deeply embarrassed by some of the RBN's activities, the RBN officially closed its doors in 2008—though many suspect that rather than closing, they simply moved offices to another location. Still, it is encouraging to see that some forms of international cybercrime cooperation are possible.

KILLING THE BOTNETS

It is even possible, though very difficult, to actually take steps to cut off a criminal network at the knees and kill it. The effort requires a great deal of time and the investment of significant resources, but it can be done.

The United States has begun a program of using *in rem* actions to prevent servers from continuing to host botnets used for distributed network attacks. *In rem* is a legal Latin term that means "against the thing." Most lawsuits are against a person. This less frequent legal action is against a thing, like the servers controlling a botnet. The virtue of an *in rem* action is that one does not need to know who owns, or controls the thing. You just need to know where the thing itself is.

This new program was first deployed in April 2011 against the Coreflood botnet. The Coreflood botnet infected more than two million computers around the world. Its operators used the system to steal more than 500 gigabytes of sensitive banking information, resulting in untold financial losses to corporations and individuals.[6] To combat this threat, the federal government used a unique legal tool, filing a civil complaint, authorizing it to have identified Coreflood control servers redirected to networks run by the nonprofit Internet Systems Consortium (ISC). When bots reported to the control servers for instructions—as they were programmed to do periodically—the ISC servers would reply with commands telling the bot program to quit.

No American law enforcement agency had ever before sought such authority. It required the application of several novel theories of law, both relating to the jurisdiction of the court and to the court's authority to order equitable relief of the sort needed to destroy the botnet. Most notably, the government sought (and received) authority to send software commands to computers owned by private individuals that had, unknowingly, been infected. As support for this action, the government relied on two statutes that broadly spoke to its authority to enjoin fraudulent activity but did not specifically speak to the applicability of the law to computer networks.[7] Though nothing is ever certain in cyberspace, reports suggest that the government's efforts to disrupt Coreflood have been successful.[8]

A reasonable review of the Coreflood effort suggests that the legal foundations of the action are, at a minimum, debatable. Certainly, some service providers who might seek to resist the types of orders entered in the Coreflood case will have an argument that the *in rem* seizure is beyond existing authority; the procedure has never been used before and has not been tested in an adversarial proceeding in court. For those who think that *in rem* proceedings are worthy of replication, the ambiguity in the law does counsel consideration of confirmatory legislative action.

ONLINE PIRACY

The government has also used *in rem* proceedings to fight online piracy (that is, the illegal download of movies or music in violation of the rights of the copyright holder). For example, in *Operation In Our Sites v. 2.0,* coordinated seizure orders were executed against 82 domain names of commercial websites allegedly engaged in the illegal sale and distribution of counterfeit goods and copyrighted works. This is controversial.

Even more controversial are recent legislative proposals to combat piracy by requiring ISPs to divert internet traffic away from domain names that are identified as trafficking in pirated content. Critics say that the effort won't work (it is a web after all) and that it is inconsistent with projects to secure the web, like DNSSEC. (These are the bills that generated the Internet protest we noted earlier—the ones with an air of insurgency about them.) Proponents say (accurately) that piracy is rampant on the web and that something needs to be done.

THE LIMITS OF INTERNATIONALISM

Despite the success with using international pressure to disrupt the RBN (if it is, indeed, a success), severe procedural difficulties limit the effectiveness of criminal law in addressing transnational cybercrime. Most American procedural criminal law requirements are premised on the assumption that the crimes to be investigated and prosecuted have occurred within the geographic boundaries of the United States. In the rare cases where cybercrimes are geographically limited in this way, these procedural requirements are suitable. But, the reality is that cybercrime is predominantly (and almost exclusively) transnational in character.

In many ways, the situation is much like the challenge facing state law enforcement officials prosecuting Depression-era bank robberies. The perpetrators could escape investigation and prosecution simply by changing jurisdictions and hiding behind differing laws. The problem is best exemplified by

Clyde Barrow's famous fan letter to the Ford automobile company, thanking it for providing the means by which he and Bonnie escaped justice.[9]

The solution, of course, was to federalize the crime of bank robbery and, effectively, eliminate the boundary problem. But, what the U.S. government could do with the stroke of a federal legislative pen takes, in the international context, years and years of work. Today, we are just at the beginning of constructing a transnational set of procedural rules for cybercrime. For the most part, information sharing across national boundaries is slow and limited—far slower and more limited than the nimbleness with which criminals can change their tactics. Substantive convergence of the law is even further in the future and may well prove impossible.

To date, the only effort to develop a unitary procedural approach to cybercrime is the Convention on Cybercrime developed by the Council of Europe.[10] It aspires to create a single set of cyber laws and procedures internationally in order to insure that there is no safe harbor for cybercriminals. But, the process is slow—only 36 countries have ratified the Treaty in 11 years. Significant cultural and legal hurdles (e.g., differing American and European approaches to "hate" speech) have further slowed convergence. Thus, in the criminal domain, the single most significant question is one of extraterritoriality and engendering cooperation from international partners.

The signatories to the treaty (notably, they do *not* include Russia and China) have agreed to pass common laws criminalizing cybercrime and to cooperate in the transborder investigation of cyber incidents. The transborder efforts have, however, been hampered by adherence to outdated modes of cooperation. Countries sharing cyber information must still proceed through Mutual Legal Assistance Treaties (MLATs) and Letters Rogatory—processes first developed in the 1800s.

The growing consensus, therefore, is that the Convention on Cybercrime doesn't work on at least two levels—operationally and strategically. Operationally, the Convention's procedures are widely regarded as ineffective, slow, and cumbersome. What is necessary, in the first instance, is an effort through the Council of Europe to adopt more rapid response mechanisms that work in real-time. The technology for such an effort is readily available in the current interconnected environment.

Reopening the treaty for modifications of this sort is likely to be a challenge—but one with a potentially significant long-term benefit. If that course was deemed inexpedient, perhaps a better option would be to act on a bilateral basis. Failing an effort to revise the Convention, the United States can, and should, negotiate bilaterally to achieve the same effect with a coalition of the willing.

Strategically, the absence of China and Russia from the Convention makes it a bit of a paper tiger. If they refuse to bind themselves to assist in the prosecution of cybercriminals, they become, in effect, a safe haven. The international community needs to move beyond the current structure to a naming and shaming campaign modeled on that developed to combat money laundering by the Financial Action Task Force (FATF).

The FATF was created based on the recommendation of the G-7 back in 1989 and brought together a task force of experts in banking and law enforcement to create a set of recommendations for best practices in defending against illegal financial activity. The FATF has moved beyond recommendations to a routine system of self-inspection. More importantly, the FATF uses the same standards to publicly identify high-risk and noncooperative jurisdictions that do not implement adequate safeguard. Creating a similar Cybercrime Action Task Force should be a top priority for identifying and combating countries that serve as havens for bad actors.

THE OVERBROAD CFAA

Despite our overall success domestically with updating American criminal law to account for cybercrime, we still have a few substantial issues to deal with. One problem facing the criminal law is the difficulty in actually defining some of the terms—especially with regard to a second form of criminal activity—intrusion into a computer system without the authorization of the owner of the computer. Conceptually, this makes great sense. It is an unobjectionable premise that it ought to be a crime to hack into someone else's computer without their permission.

The problem is that the CFAA's definition of this type of crime is overbroad. The problem begins with the language of the CFAA (18 U.S.C. § 1030), which makes it a crime to access a computer "without" or "in excess" of "authorization." In some ways, both of these make sense, especially if you substitute the word "permission" for the legal term "authorization." If an intruder hasn't been given permission to use a computer at all or if he has only been given it by you for a limited purpose, and violates that limitation by rooting around in other cyberfiles, that's an act that clearly ought to be punished.

But, how do we determine what the limits of your authorization are? Since the term is not defined in the law, the courts have looked to contractual agreements that govern the use of a computer or Internet system. These agreements are known as the Terms of Service or ToS. They are those long, detailed legal terms that everyone clicks on to "accept" before they sign up for, say, a Facebook account. But, this means that private corporations can in effect establish what conduct violates federal criminal law when they draft such policies.

This is potentially quite broad a definition—indeed, an overbroad one. Consider this: Three federal circuit courts have agreed that an employee who exceeds an employer's network acceptable use policies can be prosecuted under the CFAA. This means that, for example, an employer's limitation on personal use of the Internet could, in theory, be the ground for a prosecution of an employee who accessed a Fantasy Football league webpage. As of the writing of this chapter, only one federal court has disagreed with this interpretation and the Supreme Court has yet to resolve the issue.

The effect is to create computer crimes for activities that are not crimes in the physical world. If an employee photocopies an employer's document to give to a friend without that employer's permission, there is no federal crime (though there may be, for example, a contractual violation). However, if an employee e-mails that document, there may be a CFAA violation.[11] If a person assumes a fictitious identity at a party, there is no federal crime. Yet, if they assume that same identity on a social network that prohibits pseudonyms, there may again be a CFAA violation. At least one federal prosecutor has brought criminal charges against a user of a social network who signed up under a pseudonym in violation of terms of service—the infamous Lori Drew case, involving a mother whose Internet abuse caused a teenager to commit suicide.[12]

Revisions to the CFAA are being considered as this book goes to press, for precisely these reasons. As part of the ongoing process of legislative development, the law may be modified to focus on malicious hacking and identity theft and include an exclusion that avoids criminalizing behavior that happens to take place online, in violation of terms of service or an acceptable use policy. Only time, however, will tell.

LIMITS ON SELF-HELP

The CFAA (and other laws) also poses a problem for private sector actors who want to engage in self-help. The failure to develop structures that effectively protect the private sector from cyber intrusion creates a challenge for private sector actors who are obliged to defend their own networks: consider the cyber problem from the perspective of the private sector actor whose systems are subject to an attack. The vulnerability is particularly acute as we come to realize that our adversaries *may* be planning acts that are designed to target private infrastructure.[13] Private sector actors who are contemplating a response to such attacks may well find themselves on the horns of a dilemma—neither able to rely on the government to defend them nor legally authorized to respond themselves.

As with other actors in the cyber domain, those defending private sector networks will frequently be unaware of the identity of their attackers, and they may often be equally unable to distinguish a true attack from a probe or an unlawful intrusion. In such an ill-defined situation, those who act in response to an attack may do so in violation of the law.

First, and foremost, many of the most reasonable actions that a private sector actor would take in defense of their internal network are likely to violate the CFAA. As we have discussed, under the CFAA, it is a crime to intentionally access any protected computer (i.e., one used in or effecting interstate or foreign commerce) without authorization, or in excess of authorized access, and thereby obtain information from the computer.[14] But, the most successful defensive measures often involve using beacons or other forms of surveillance inside the malicious actor's computer to identify the source of the attack. Once identified, an effective countermeasure might be to flatline the offending IP address, that is, arrange for it to be taken down. This type of defensive countermeasure (sometimes going by the name "hackback") is almost certainly a crime in and of itself. Almost invariably, any protective action by a private sector actor will involve accessing a protected computer without the authorization of its owner (who may sometimes even be an innocent intermediary) and obtaining information from it. As a result, virtually every aspect of private sector self-help is, at least theoretically, a violation of the CFAA and therefore a crime. The specter of criminal prosecution may disable or deter private sector self-help and may also have the effect of causing the private sector to outsource protective activities overseas.[15]

ECONOMIC ESPIONAGE

Finally, in closing our discussion of cybercrime, it is useful to think of the rather ambiguous case of economic espionage, that is, spying directed at economic secrets, not national security ones. In such cases, there is no direct threat to America, but the effects are just as real.

And, it isn't just the large corporations who suffer. The story is told (based on a classified source) of an American furniture company that had its furniture designs stolen through a malicious hack from China. Within months, they were seeing their own designs being offered, at lower prices, from a Chinese manufacturer.[16]

That is just but one example of many. According to the Office of the National Counterintelligence Executive (NCIX), the threat is pervasive. In the recent report, *Foreign Spies Stealing US Economic Secrets in Cyberspace*,[17] the NCIX detailed some of its conclusions: "Foreign economic collection and industrial espionage against the United States represent significant and growing threats to the nation's prosperity and security. Cyberspace—where most business activity and development of new ideas now takes place—amplifies these threats by making it possible for malicious actors, whether they are corrupted insiders or foreign intelligence services (FIS), to quickly steal and transfer massive quantities of data while remaining anonymous and hard to detect."

The NCIX noted, in particular, that

Chinese actors are the world's most active and persistent perpetrators of economic espionage. US private sector firms and cybersecurity specialists have reported an onslaught of computer network intrusions that have originated in China, but the IC [Intelligence Community] cannot confirm who was responsible[;] Russia's intelligence services are conducting a range of activities to collect economic information and technology from US targets. Some US allies and partners use their broad access to US institutions to acquire sensitive US economic and technology information, primarily through aggressive elicitation and other human intelligence (HUMINT) tactics. Some of these states have advanced cyber capabilities.[18]

Plainly, all of this activity is both a cybercrime and, at the extremes, a significant cyber threat to national security. At some point, economic espionage (especially of companies in the Defense Industrial Base) blends into national security espionage, and criminality becomes spying. The line between the two is fuzzy indeed, making cybercrime yet another avenue for the broader cyber conflict.

8
Chapter

Cyber Conflict and
the Constitution

Einstein 2.0 is an intrusion detection cybersecurity system deployed by the federal government to protect the federal cyber networks. Its successor program, Einstein 3.0, not only detects cyber intrusions of the federal network but also seeks to actively prevent them. In the next iteration, these programs will increasingly be deployed on private networks to protect critical infrastructure. And, therein hangs a tale—and a Constitutional issue worthy of consideration.[1]

A SHORT INTRODUCTION TO INTRUSION DETECTION AND PREVENTION SYSTEMS

An intrusion detection system, like Einstein 2.0, operates through two principal systems. The first is what one might call a look-up system. Every piece of malicious code is unique; it has what is known as a signature (essentially, an identifying code component that serves as a marker for the program). When we spoke about the problem of distinction, we were speaking of the difficulty of identifying malicious code. Eventually, however, with effort, the code can be identified and its unique characteristics can be mapped.

The detection program has a database of known malicious code signatures on file and constantly compares incoming messages with the malicious signatures. When it finds a match, it sends an alert to the recipient. For the federal system, Einstein 2.0 gets its database of malicious signatures from a variety of sources, including both commercial sources like Symantec (a private Internet security company) and classified sources at the NSA.

The second system, less definitive and more probabilistic, is what is known as anomaly detection. In essence, the Einstein 2.0 program knows what normal

Internet traffic looks like and can produce an alert when the incoming traffic differs from normal by some set tolerance level. Notably, the Einstein 2.0 system is a gateway system that screens traffic as it arrives at federal portals and does not stop any traffic.

Einstein 3.0, the next generation of program, is based on a classified NSA program known as Tutelage and is different in several respects. Its goal is to go beyond detection of malware (and an alert) to actual intrusion prevention. After all, simple detection is a bit like telling someone "you're being robbed," after the bank robber is already inside the vault. It is, naturally, far more valuable to prevent the robber from getting into the bank in the first instance. To do this, Einstein 3.0 must intercept all Internet traffic bound for federal computers before it is delivered, delay it temporarily for screening, and then pass it along if it is nonthreatening, or quarantine the malware, as appropriate. And, for that system to be effective, the Einstein 3.0 screening protocols must reside *outside* the federal government firewalls, on the servers of trusted Internet connections.

THE LEGAL DEBATE

There is little real legal debate over the operation of Einstein 3.0 as applied to government networks. Almost all scholars who have examined the question agree with the conclusion reached by the Department of Justice's Office of Legal Counsel: it is appropriate and necessary for the government to monitor traffic to and from its own computers.[2] Disagreement is much more likely to be over how deeply a government-owned and -operated system, such as Einstein (call it Einstein 4.0, if you want), may be inserted into private networks, either to protect the government or to protect private sector users.

The question is whether such a system would pass Constitutional muster, though its full operation would require amendment of several existing statutory restrictions—amendments whose political viability is highly questionable. Thus, while we begin with a discussion of the legality of the system, we should not lose sight of the related question of its advisability as a matter of policy.

Content versus Noncontent

To begin with, current doctrine makes it clear that the noncontent portions of the intercepted traffic are not protected by the Fourth Amendment (the Constitutional amendment that protects against unreasonable searches and seizures).[3] The Supreme Court addressed these questions in a related context in two 1970-era cases: *United States v. Miller*[4] and *Smith v. Maryland*.[5] In both cases, the question was, in effect, to what degree did an individual have a constitutional protection against the wholesale disclosure of information about him that had been collected by third parties? And, in particular, could an individual use the Fourth Amendment to prevent the government from using data it had received from a third party collector without a warrant?

In both cases, the Court answered with a resounding "no." Along the way, it developed an interpretation of the Fourth Amendment that has come, unsurprisingly, to be known as the third party doctrine—one has no Constitutional rights to protect information voluntarily disclosed to others. The reasoning is that, by disclosing it, the data owner has given up any reasonable expectation of privacy that he might have had.

Applying this doctrine, in *Miller,* the Court held that financial information voluntarily disclosed by an individual to a bank was not protected by the Fourth Amendment against subsequent disclosure to the government. Likewise, in *Smith,* the Court held that an individual's telephone toll records—that is, records of the phone numbers called by the individual—were not protected against disclosure. In effect, the Court adopted a gestational theory of Fourth Amendment privacy—just as you can't be a "little bit pregnant," you cannot, according to the Court, be a "little bit public and a little bit private." What you disclose to anyone else is fair game for everyone else. Though many have decried this doctrinal result,[6] there is only modest prospect of a change in the Court's view of the Fourth Amendment.

In the context of cyber conflict and intrusion detection systems, the same result follows almost *a fortiori.* Noncontent header information in Internet traffic (IP addresses, "to" and "from" lines, and such) are likewise not protected as a matter of constitutional law. Because the information has been provided to the information service provider, it loses any privacy protection it might have and a government-operated Einstein 4.0 is free to scan the noncontent portions of a message for malware.

Consent and Banners

This legal analysis gets us only part of the way to an answer, however. The *Miller/Smith* rule does not, of course, permit the use of an intrusion prevention system to routinely scan the content portions of an Internet exchange. Those portions—the actual messages themselves—remain private, just as telephone conversations are private. As a result, a government program typically may not review that content without probable cause and a warrant. (To think of this clearly, just think of the difference between the address on the outside of the envelope—which anyone can read—and the letter inside—which is protected by law from disclosure.)

One problem with this is that in the cyber realm the line between content and noncontent is not so clear. Is the web address you type in "content" or not? In many ways, it looks like a noncontent address on the outside of the envelope. But, domain names on the Internet often reveal the website's content in ways a regular address does not. If you go to aa.org, then we know you are visiting Alcoholics Anonymous, with all of the resulting inferences.

Even more saliently, the content portions of an Internet transmission may also be the portions of a message that contain malware. Indeed, it would be an extremely poor rule that permitted screening of only noncontent information for malware, as that would simply draw a map for malfeasant actors as to how to avoid the intrusion detection systems. As a consequence, any intrusion detection or prevention system that we want to deploy *must* inherently have the ability to look at the content of communications if it is to be effective. Bridging that gap—finding a Constitutionally-permissible way of looking at content—is the difficult question.

Protecting Federal Cyberspace

For Internet traffic directed to federal computers, the content/noncontent distinction is comparatively easy to solve. As the Department of Justice assessed it, Fourth Amendment concerns (and also most statutory concerns) can be addressed by using a robust form of consent.

Interestingly, the consent concerns are more for the recipient (some federal employee or agency) than for the sender. Not unreasonably, the Office of Legal Counsel concluded that the sender loses his privacy interest in the content of an Internet communication when it is delivered.[7] After all, he intended the recipient to get the message and lawfully the recipient may do with it what he likes (including putting it in the spam folder). There is little, or no, interest (once the mail is delivered to its intended recipient) in fooling the recipient into doing the wrong thing.

So, in Einstein 2.0 and 3.0, the main consent concern is actually for the recipient employee, who might have a privacy interest in the contents of the e-mail, as against his federal employer who would be screening the content of his incoming mail.[8] As to those employees, however, the government can (and typically does) make consent to e-mail monitoring a condition of employment, reinforced by login click through banners that warn the employee that his e-mail will be monitored. In the past, it has done this, lawfully, to prevent government resources from being used for illegal or inappropriate purposes (say, downloading pornography) and that legal meme has simply been translated to the cybersecurity realm.

Federal Assistance to the Private Sector

This analysis paints a good roadmap for how the government can (and has begun to) expand its presence into the private sector (where neither the sender nor the recipient is a federal employee or agency). The extension has begun through voluntary agreements with closely aligned government contractors in the Defense Industrial Base (DIB), known as the DIB Pilot.[9] To foster their ability to do business with the federal government, those companies agree to monitor incoming Internet traffic using government-provided threat signature information. Here, again, as in the case of communications bound for the federal government, the noncontent addressing information is not protected by the Fourth Amendment; the senders have no expectation of privacy as against the recipient, and the recipient employees consent to scrutiny of the communications as a condition of employment.

This voluntary consent model is readily expandable to almost any industry that is dependent on federal financing. Already, there is talk of extending this model to the financial and nuclear industries.[10] A more problematic extension might be to the healthcare industry or the education community, but those problems are likely more ones of policy than of law. However broad the expanse of this voluntary consent model, it seems likely to occupy a significant fraction of the field.

Even if the legal gap is bridged, that still leaves a large policy question: Do we really want the NSA (or any portion of the government, for that matter) to be inspecting the private communications of American citizens? Legal does not, after all, mean wise.

BUT IS IT GOOD POLICY?

As a result, even though it is likely lawful to expand the federal government's protection of critical infrastructure, we are doing so in a cautious way. Most notably, instead of the NSA actually running an Einstein 4.0 program on the private sector networks, the DIB Pilot program involves two limitations that are not legally necessary: First, the Einstein program is actually run by ISPs who transmit Internet traffic to the private sector companies who are to be protected by it, using both software and threat signatures provided by the NSA. Second, because of fears that NSA's direct involvement in the program might raise the specter of Big Brother and the government collection of private communications, the private sector DIB Pilot members are not required to provide any feedback to the NSA on the effectiveness of the program (though they may voluntarily provide some data on network intrusions).[11] Thus, NSA is generally cut off from any private-to-government communications and cannot possibly gain access to private sector content.

From this pilot, we have already learned two things. First, some critics of the government say that there is really no need for any federal intervention at all. They argue that the private sector has made large investments in cybersecurity and that it is generally more nimble and more knowledgeable in key respects about its systems than the federal government could ever be. There is some support for this proposition: A recent internal DoD study suggested that the DIB Pilot's effectiveness has been mixed with some success and some failures to meet expectations. Notably, in this test phase, only two of 52 discovered incidents relied on classified NSA signatures.[12]

But, neither the private sector nor the government thinks that the DIB Pilot is unnecessary. And, there is at least some evidence that the government (and more particularly, the NSA) is a value added contributor to cybersecurity in the private sector. We can all agree that the private sector is more agile than the government and that, in our free-market society, the private sector ought to be the cybersecurity provider of first choice. Certainly, nobody would ever claim that the federal government is always better at providing cybersecurity. Even with its modest success, the DIB Pilot suggests that, in some cases, it can be a superior provider of information or technology. After all, when Google was hacked by the Chinese in Operation Aurora, it turned to the NSA for assistance in analyzing the intrusion. At least to some degree, cyber market leaders, like Google, recognize the value of federal cyber-assistance.

More fundamentally, however, the DIB Pilot shows how a fear of government intervention can have a tendency to hamstring the effectiveness of our collective approach to cybersecurity. This may not necessarily be a bad thing; there are sometimes societal values that are greater than efficiency and effectiveness. But, we should be clear about the choices we are making.

As noted earlier, in order to overcome lingering privacy-protective suspicions of its motives, NSA agreed to forgo any mandatory feedback from the DIB Pilot partners on the effectiveness of the NSA-provided threat signatures. This was a pragmatic decision. NSA made the judgment that since the enhanced security provided to the DIB was important enough, it was willing to avoid the political controversy that might arise if it was suspected of performing secret wire taps and threatening civil liberties. Even if the suspicion was false, its common acceptance would have paralyzed the Pilot program and killed it before it even began.

But, we should make no mistake. This form of self-limitation is not intended to enhance effectiveness or efficiency. On the contrary, there can be little doubt that NSA's response and its ability to provide signature threat information to all of the members of the DIB Pilot would be enhanced by incorporating information on effectiveness derived from the members' experience. Nobody who wants to foster product improvement purposefully constructs an OODA loop with a limited feedback component.

In short, though it is likely that the government could lawfully have expanded NSA's role through a strong consent model, to include its active participation in the DIB Pilot, we have, instead, deliberately chosen not to include the feedback loop for political reasons.[13]

This course will inevitably make us less effective. As a pragmatic judgment of the politically possible in America today, it is probably a wise decision. As a policy for effective cybersecurity, it is the second best option.

OODA LOOPS
> OODA stands for "Observe, Orient, Decide and Act." It is a conceptual means of examining commercial operations or learning processes (originally designed by the military).
> OODA loops always have a feedback component, so one can learn by doing.

THE REST OF THE NET

And what, then, of the remaining Internet traffic—private-to-private traffic that is not directed to or from a critical infrastructure industry? Here, the legal limitations on the scrutiny of private content network traffic are at their highest and are likely to prevail. This is not to say that the private sector Internet is without protection. On the contrary, as we shall see, the protections are quite robust. But, what it does mean is that the American government is likely to have little, if any, active role in the protection of the general Internet.

For many in the cyber community, that is the right result. Others, however, look at this dichotomy and see a trend toward a bifurcated Internet—one portion a closed, walled garden protected by high-security and the other, a virtual free-fire zone reminiscent of the Wild West in the mid-1800s. Neither model seems optimal. The walled garden loses the vibrancy, transparency, and ease of borderless access that are the main characteristics of the Internet; it is, if you will, Internet-lite; all the features without the pizzazz. The Wild West, however, is a lawless domain, where nobody is safe.

There must be a better way. One reasonably safe prediction is that governments will come under increasing pressure to provide security services on the Internet. This will come to pass, notwithstanding the fears of a threat to civil liberties, but only with significant oversight. If that is the case, then the Constitutional issues will come back to the fore. To that end, let us consider two theoretical grounds on which the government might proceed to protect the entire Internet (at least in the United States), while hastening to note again, that a lawful plan is not necessarily a wise one as a policy matter:

First, one might argue that wholesale scrutiny of network traffic is reasonable, based on the prevalence of malware in Internet traffic. If the government were to minimize nonmalware traffic intercepts (by deleting any nonmalicious traffic from its own servers after screening) and forgo criminal prosecution, it could argue that broad-based scrutiny is akin to a sobriety checkpoint on the highway—a necessary special needs administrative inspection that is acceptable precisely because of the harm it averts.[14]

Somewhat more ambitiously, the government could adopt a law, making consent to malware intrusion detection systems an implied condition of access to the Internet. Here, the analogy would be to the implied consent laws that have been adopted by many states with respect to sobriety tests. In these states, acceptance of a driver's license and the right to travel on the public roads brings with it mandatory consent to a sobriety test—refusal itself is a crime.[15] One can imagine the adoption of such a regulatory system for the Internet.

All of which is to say, by way of introduction to the topic, that there is probably a wide scope of constitutionally permissible activity for the government, even on the private networks of the Internet. Exactly how far the government is permitted to go, in the end, is more likely a question of wise policy than it is of constitutional law.

9

Chapter

Dataveillance and Cyber Conflict

We generally conceive of cyber conflict as one involving the use of cyber weapons of some form—malware intrusions, surreptitious decryption techniques, espionage and theft of data, or hardware attacks. But, there is another way to think of the cyber conflict—as the natural battleground for enhanced analytical tools that are enabled by cyber technology. If our goal is to combat terrorists or insurgents (or even other nations), then the cyber domain offers us the capacity not just to steal secret information through espionage, but to take observable public behavior and information and use cyber tools to develop a more nuanced and robust understanding of their tactics and intentions. Likewise, it can be used by our opponents to uncover our own secrets—a topic to which we will return in a later chapter.

Traditionally, the concept of surveillance has been taken to mean an act of physical surveillance—for example, following someone around or planting a secret camera in an apartment.[1] As technology improved, our spy agencies and law enforcement institutions increasingly came to rely on even more sophisticated technical means of surveillance,[2] and so we came to develop the capacity to electronically intercept telecommunications and examine e-mail while in transit.[3]

To these more traditional forms of surveillance, we must now add another: the collection and analysis of personal data and information about an individual or organization. Call the phenomenon "dataveillance," if you wish, but it is an inevitable product of our increasing reliance on the Internet and global communications systems. You leave an electronic trail almost everywhere you go.

Increasingly, in a networked world, technological changes have made personal information pervasively available. As the available storehouse of data has grown, so have governmental and commercial efforts to use this personal data for their own purposes. Commercial enterprises target ads and solicit new customers. Governments use the data to, for example, identify and target previously unknown terror suspects—to find so-called clean skins who are not in any intelligence database. This capability for enhanced data analysis has already proven its utility and holds great promise for the future of commercial activity and counter-terrorism efforts.

Yet, this analytical capacity also comes at a price—the peril of creating an ineradicable trove of information about innocent individuals. That peril is typically supposed to stem from problems of misuse; in the government sphere one imagines data mining to identify political opponents, and in the private sector we fear targeted spam. To be sure, that is a danger to be guarded against.

But, the dangers of pervasively available data also arise from other factors. Often, for example, there is an absence of context to the data that permits or requires inaccurate inferences. Knowing that an individual has a criminal conviction is a bare data point; knowing what the conviction was for and in what context allows for a more granular and refined judgment.

The challenges arising from these new forms of analysis have already become the subject of significant political debate. One need only think of the controversy surrounding the most ambitious of these—the Total Information Awareness (TIA) program. TIA was a research program initiated by the Defense Advanced Research Projects Agency (DARPA) in the immediate aftermath of September 11. Its conception was to use advanced data analytical techniques to search the information space of commercial and public sector data, looking for threat signatures that were indicative of a terrorist threat. Because it would have given the government access to vast quantities of data about individuals, it was condemned as a return of Big Brother.[4]

Compare that condemnation with the universal criticism of the government for its failure to connect the dots during the Christmas 2009 bomb plot attempted by Umar Farouk Abdulmutallab.[5] This gives you some idea of the cross-currents at play. The conundrum arises because the analytical techniques are fundamentally similar to those used by traditional law enforcement agencies, but they operate on so much vaster a set of data, and that data is so much more readily capable of analysis and manipulation, that the differences in degree tend to become differences in kind. To put the issue in perspective, just consider a partial listing of relevant databases that might be targeted: credit card, telephone calls, criminal records, real estate purchases, travel itineraries, and so on.

One thing is certain. These analytical tools are of such great utility that governments will expand their use, as will the private sector. Old rules about collection and use limitations are no longer technologically relevant. If we value privacy at all, these ineffective protections must be replaced with new constructs. The goal then is the identification of a suitable legal and policy regime to regulate and manage the use of mass quantities of personal data.

THE COMPUTING AND STORAGE REVOLUTION

The growth of dataveillance is inevitable. It reflects a fundamental change caused by technological advances that, like King Canute's fabled tide, cannot be stopped or slowed. Increasingly, the cyber conflict will be fought, and won, by those who use data to their best advantage. The opportunity—or problem, depending on one's perspective—derives from two related, yet distinct trends: increases in computing power and decreases in data storage costs.

Many are familiar with the long-term increase in the power of computers. It is most familiarly characterized as Moore's Law—named after Intel computer scientist Gordon Moore, who first posited the law in 1965. Moore's Law predicts that computer chip capacities will double every 18 to 24 months.[6] Moore's law has been remarkably constant for nearly 30 years. Processor capacity today is roughly more than one million times faster than processor speed in 1970.

The power of this processing capacity—which translates almost directly into processing speed—is immense. It is what drives the information technology tools that power Google and Amazon and make Walmart's purchasing system a reality. It also, more problematically, makes financial fraud and DDoS attacks a reality as well. But, all the same, the trend is clear. Though no one predicts that processing speed will double indefinitely—surely a physical impossibility—there is no current expectation that the limits of chip capacity have been reached.

To this trend, one must also add the remarkable reduction in the costs of data storage. Data storage costs have also been decreasing at a logarithmic rate, almost identical to the increases we have experienced in chip capacity, but with an inverse slope. What this means in practical terms is that in 1984—less than 30 years ago—it cost roughly $200 to store a megabyte of data. By 1999, that cost had sunk to 75 cents. Today, you can buy 100 megabytes of data storage capacity for a penny. On E-Bay, you can frequently purchase a terabyte storage device for your desktop for under $100. A terabyte is roughly 1 trillion bytes of data—a huge volume for storing simple alphanumeric information. Here, too, the prospects are for ever-cheaper data storage. One can readily imagine peta-, exa-, or even yottabyte sized personal storage devices.[7] If that is for the individual, imagine what a large corporation or a government can purchase and maintain.

Therefore, the story of technology today requires us to answer the question: "What happens when ever-quicker processing power meets ever-cheaper storage capacity?" Anyone who uses Gmail knows the answer to that question. No longer do you have to laboriously label, file, and tag your e-mail. One may now simply store all the e-mails he or she wants to retain and use a simple natural language search algorithm to pull up relevant e-mails from storage when needed. The storage cost of Gmail to the user is zero—Google offers it for free—and the processing time for any search request for the average individual is measured in, at the most, seconds, not minutes.

Here is how IBM Chairman Samuel J. Palmisano put it in a speech he gave in September 2011:

> We're all aware of the approximately two billion people now on the Internet—in every part of the planet, thanks to the explosion of mobile technology.
>
> But there are also upwards of a trillion interconnected and intelligent objects and organisms—what some call the Internet of Things.
>
> All of this is generating vast stores of information. It is estimated that there will be 44 times as much data and content coming over the next decade . . . reaching 35 zettabytes in 2020. A zettabyte is a 1 followed by 21 zeros. And thanks to advanced computation and analytics, we can now make sense of that data in something like real time. This enables very different kinds of insight, foresight and decision-making.[8]

In other words, we live in the world of Big Data. Data is now pervasively available and pervasively searchable. For large-scale databases of the size maintained by governments or companies, the practical limitations lie in the actual search algorithms used and how they are designed to process the data, not in the chips or the storage units. The changes that will come from this new cyber reality are profound.

OUTDATED LAW AND POLICY

Ten years ago, surveying the technology of the time—which, by and large, was 100 times *less* powerful than today's data processing capacity—Scott McNealy, then CEO of Sun Microsystems, said, "Privacy is dead. Get over it."[9] He was, it seems, slightly wrong. Pure privacy—that is, the privacy of activities in your own home—remains reasonably well-protected.[10] What has been lost, and will become even more so increasingly, is the anonymity of being able to act in public (whether physically or in cyberspace) without anyone having the technological capacity to permanently record and retain data about your activity for later analysis.

American law has a phrase to describe this phenomenon; it is "practical obscurity." Derived from a Supreme Court case, *Department of Justice v. Reporter's Committee*,[11] the origin of the phrase is instructive in illuminating the effects of the change in technology.

Back in the late 1980s—the veritable dawn of time for computers—the Department of Justice went to a great deal of trouble to create a database with information about the criminal records of known offenders.[12] At the time, such records were kept in disparate databases that were not connected to each other; arrest records might be held by a local police station, charging records by a district attorney, and disposition and sentencing records by a state court. Federal records were, of course, held by still other law enforcement, attorney, and court institutions.

All these records were generally public and, in theory, available for inspection by the press or private citizens. But in practice the records were so widely scattered among so many data-holders that no newspaper or individual could incur the expense of finding all the information and creating a comprehensive dossier on any individual. They were, in a phrase, "practically obscure." Only the federal government had the degree of need and adequacy of resources to undertake the task of creating, at great expense, the precursor of what is today the National Crime Information Center. At very great cost, the Department of Justice began the collection of criminal records on a small number of criminals who were of national interest.

The *Reporter's Committee* case was a powerful expression of the strength of the paradigm of practical obscurity. A CBS news correspondent and a press organization filed a Freedom of Information Act request with the Department of Justice asking for the collated dossier, or rap sheet, on alleged Mafia figures. Their reasoning was, it seems, quite persuasive; since the information was all public when found in disparate databases, it did not lose that public character when collected by the federal government. And, if it was public information, then it was clearly subject to disclosure under the Freedom of Information Act (FOIA).

The Department denied the FOIA request, and a unanimous Supreme Court—whose membership at the time included jurists ranging from liberal Justice William Brennan to conservative Justice William Rehnquist—upheld the denial. According to the Court, "Plainly there is a vast difference between the public records that might be found after a diligent search of courthouse files, county archives, and local police stations throughout the country and a computerized summary located in a single clearinghouse of information." Because of that difference, the Court concluded that the "privacy interest in maintaining the practical obscurity of rap-sheet information will always be high."[13]

Today, the Court's confident assertion that obscurity will always be high has proven to have a half-life of less than 20 years. Large data collection and aggregation companies, such as Experian and ChoicePoint, hire retirees to harvest, by hand, public records from government databases.[14] Paper records are digitized and electronic records are downloaded. These data aggregation companies typically hold birth records, credit and conviction records, real estate transactions and liens, bridal registries, and even kennel club records. One company, Acxiom, estimates that it holds on average approximately 1,500 pieces of data on each adult American.[15]

Since most, though not all, of these records are governmental in origin, the government has equivalent access to the data, and what they cannot create themselves they can likely buy or demand from the private sector. The day is now here when anyone with enough data and sufficient computing power can develop a detailed picture of any identifiable individual. That picture might tell your food preferences or your underwear size. It might tell something about your terrorist activity. Or your politics.

Back in 1993, *New Yorker* cartoonist Peter Steiner[16] famously lampooned that "[o]n the Internet, nobody knows you're a dog." Today, as one observer has said, they not only know you are a dog, but they know your favorite leash color and whether or not you have been neutered.[17] It is all in some pervasive database somewhere.

THE POWER OF DATA ANALYSIS

This analytical capacity can have a powerful influence in cyber conflict—and in particular in revealing links between the cyber persona and the real world activities of individuals. When we speak of the new form of dataveillance, we are not speaking of the comparatively simple matching algorithms that cross check when a person's name is submitted for review—when, for example, they apply for a job. Even that exercise is a challenge for any government, as the failure to list Abdulmutallab in advance of the 2009 Christmas bombing attempt demonstrates.[18] The process contains uncertainties of data accuracy and fidelity, analysis and registration, transmission and propagation, and review, correction, and revision. Yet, even with those complexities, the process is relatively simple technologically. The implementation is what poses a challenge.

By contrast, other systems of data analysis are far more technologically sophisticated. They are, in the end, an attempt to sift through large quantities of personal information to identify subjects when their identities are not already known. In the commercial context, these individuals are called potential customers. In the cyber conflict context, they might be called Anonymous or Russian patriotic hackers. In the terrorism context, they are often called clean skins because there is no known derogatory information connected to their names or identities. In this latter context, the individuals are dangerous because nothing is known of their predilections. For precisely this reason, this form of data analysis is sometimes called knowledge discovery, as the intention is to discover something previously unknown about an individual. There can be little doubt that data analysis of this sort can prove to be of great value. A few examples will illustrate the point.

Consider first Non-Obvious Relationship Analysis (NORA), a system developed for the purpose of identifying potential threats to Las Vegas casinos.[19]
NORA collects data about casino players, hotel guests, employees, and vendors.[20] It cross-references that information with data about subjects of interest
(e.g., Vegas cheats, card counters, in-house casino incidents and arrests, and
even problem gamblers who have self-reported). The intention is not only to
immediately identify subjects of interest, but also to identify the seemingly
good guys (e.g., customers, employees) who are connected to these subjects
of interest in nonobvious ways. Does employee X, for example, share a former
address (say, while in college) with known cheater Y? Is accounts payable employee A buying equipment from someone he knows?

The results of such a wide ranging analysis can be stunning. In a typical year, NORA will identify employees who are also playing at the casino (a
policy violation at some casinos), cheaters playing with false identities, and
employees who have undisclosed connections to known cheaters or vendors.

The story of Ra'ed al-Banna, a Jordanian who attempted to enter the U.S.
at O'Hare Airport on June 14, 2003, also illustrates the value of computer dataveillance.[21] Ra'ed al-Banna was carrying a valid business visa in his Jordanian
passport and, on the surface, appeared to be an unremarkable business traveler from the Middle East.

The Department of Homeland Security operates a sophisticated data
analysis program called the Automated Targeting System (ATS) to assess the
comparative risks of arriving passengers. Based on those assessments, the inspection resources of Customs and Border Protection (CBP) are allocated.[22]
The system is essential, given the sheer volume of travelers to America. In a
typical year, approximately 350 million people sought entry across our borders, and more than 85 million of those arrived by air.[23] Since more than
350 million individuals cannot, obviously, be subject to intense scrutiny, some
form of assessment and analysis must be used to make choices about how and
when to conduct inspections. ATS is that system.

ATS flagged al-Banna for heightened scrutiny.[24] His pattern of travel and
his prior record of entry to the United States combined to suggest that he
should be subjected to secondary screening—a form of enhanced, individual-
ized review where a passenger is pulled from the main line of entrants and individually questioned. During the secondary interview, al-Banna's answers were
inconsistent and evasive—so much so that the CBP officer who conducted the
interview decided to deny his application for entry and ordered him returned
to his point of origin.[25] As a matter of routine, al-Banna's photograph and
fingerprints were collected before he was sent on his way.

There the story might have ended since CBP officers reject entry applications daily for a host of reasons, but al-Banna proved an unusual case. More
than a year later, in February 2005, a car filled with explosives drove into a

crowd of military and police recruits in the town of Hillah, Iraq.[26] More than 125 people died—the largest death toll for a single incident in Iraq until that time. The suicide bomber's hand and forearm were found chained to the steering wheel of the exploded car (why they were chained is a fascinating question of psychology). When the fingerprints were taken by U.S. military forces, a match was found to the fingerprints taken from al-Banna 20 months earlier in Chicago.

Now, of course, nobody knows what al-Banna intended to do that day when he arrived at O'Hare. It is impossible to prove a counter factual. Perhaps he was only headed to visit friends, but the CBP officer who interviewed al-Banna later said, "I was shocked. That it was so close to home, that I actually interviewed someone who not only was capable of doing but actually did something like that. You never know who you are interviewing or what they are capable of doing."[27] Without the data analysis provided by ATS, it is nearly certain that al-Banna would have entered the United States—who knows for what purpose.

Most similar successes are not made public. Often, the factors that form part of the analysis cannot be revealed, and successes in identifying terrorist suspects—or, in other contexts, members of a criminal organization—would be negated by disclosure of the success. Only al-Banna's death made his case fit for public disclosure.

That does not mean that a careful observer cannot discern the outlines of other cyber intelligence successes based on data analysis in recent events. When David Headley was arrested for allegedly seeking to commit terrorist acts in Denmark, news reports suggested that one of the key factors in his identification was his pattern of travel to the Middle East and his efforts to conceal those trips from the government.[28] Dataveillance of his travel both provided the trigger to ask questions and the factual cross-check on the veracity of his answers. Likewise, when Najibullah al-Zasi (who tried to explode a bomb in Times Square) was arrested, one factor that was publicly disclosed as a ground for suspicion was his travel to Pakistan.[29]

Both of these incidents, which involved serious threats of violence, would appear to have been thwarted, at least in part, through some form of successful dataveillance, that is, using knowledge discovery techniques to target investigative resources based on a careful risk assessment of seemingly innocent individuated facts.

Our failures also seem to arise when these sorts of cyber analytic techniques are used ineffectively. In the case of the 2009 Christmas bomb plot, not only was Abdulmutallab's name provided by his father, but the evidence suggests that other, less specific NSA intercepts existed that might have generated a suspicion of Nigerian travelers.[30] Add in his reported purchase of a cash ticket and the alleged rejection of his visa application by the United Kingdom[31] and the case seems to be the precise sort of concatenation of facts which, individually, amount to little but, collectively, paint a more cautionary picture. In the wake of the failed bombing attempt, there are already calls for even greater efforts to connect the dots of terrorist threats and that will mean more dataveillance, not less.[32]

* * *

In short, given its utility, cyber dataveillance is here to stay whether we like it or not. The only question is when and how we monitor and control the government's use of the techniques so that we get the benefits of the growth in data surveillance without the potential harms to civil liberties. We turn to that question in the next chapter.

10

Privacy for the Cyber Age

Given the utility of the sort of data analysis we have just seen and the likely persistence of the terrorist threat, it is, as a matter of practical reality, unlikely that governments will eschew these analytical tools anytime soon, if ever. Though some for whom privacy is paramount yearn for a return to the days when practical obscurity was a reality,[1] a realistic appraisal suggests that these dataveillance tools are likely a permanent part of the national and international landscape for the foreseeable future. That is not necessarily a bad thing since these tools play a strong and useful role in our counter-terrorism efforts.

Yet, as should be evident by now, the use of such analytical tools is not without risks. The same systems that sift layers of data to identify concealed terrorist links are just as capable, if set to the task, of stripping anonymity from many other forms of conduct—personal purchases, politics, and peccadilloes. The question then remains how do we empower data analysis for good purposes while providing oversight mechanisms for deterring malfeasant uses?

ANTIQUE PRIVACY

Our current privacy-protective architecture, or, if one prefers, our anonymity-protective architecture, is simply not up to the task. It is, to a very real degree, an antique relic of the last century. The relevant Supreme Court precedents date from the 1970s, as does the 1974 Privacy Act.[2] Is it any wonder that the current structure of law does not match the technological reality?

As we saw in Chapter 8, the third party doctrine developed by the Supreme Court in *Miller* and *Smith* back in the 1970s at the dawn of the computer era, means that information you disclose to a third party is not protected by the Fourth Amendment. In the context of intrusion-protection systems, that meant that the government was free to screen noncontent information for malware since that sort of addressing information was disclosed to your service provider to allow the delivery of your Internet message or command. In the context of data privacy, it also means that there is no Constitutional protection against the collection and aggregation of your cyber data (credit card purchase and the like) for purposes of data analysis and piercing the veil of anonymity.

Therefore, all that is left to protect anonymity are the statutory protections created at the federal level by Congress.[3] Some laws, like the Right to Financial Privacy Act (RFPA),[4] create sector-specific privacy protections. Reacting to *Miller*, the RFPA prevents banks from willy-nilly providing financial data to the government, instead, requiring the issuance of a subpoena and notice to a customer who has the right to object to the inquiry. Likewise, the Health Insurance Portability and Accountability Act[5] has stringent rules regarding medical privacy and limiting the types of disclosures that doctors, hospitals, and insurers can make.

By and large, however, in the national security dataveillance sphere, there is no sector or activity-specific set of protections.[6] Rather, privacy advocates seek to protect privacy (or anonymity) by requiring the government to adhere to broad principles of privacy protection. These principles, known as the Fair Information Principles,[7] were first developed in the United States and have now become the touchstone of most privacy protective regimes. They are embedded in the Privacy Act of 1974 and lie at the core of the European Union's 1995 Privacy Directive.[8] In brief summary—which does not do them justice for want of detail—the principles are:

- *Collection limitation:* The collection of personal information should be lawful and limited to that which is necessary. Where feasible, the collection should be consensual.
- *Data quality:* Those collecting information should strive to ensure that it is accurate, relevant, and complete.
- *Purpose specification:* Data should be collected for a specific purpose. Data should not be repurposed to other uses without disclosure and consent, if at all.
- *Use limitation:* Data should be used only for a specific purpose and should be disclosed only for the purpose collected.
- *Security safeguards:* Information collected should be protected against loss or theft.
- *Openness:* The collection, use, and security of data collected should be fully disclosed and transparent to the public.
- *Individual participation:* Individuals should be allowed to access data collected about themselves and should be afforded a chance to correct any errors they perceive.

- *Accountability:* Those who collect and hold data should be accountable for their adherence to these norms.[9]

In the United States, these principles are procedurally implemented through Privacy Impact Assessments (PIAs) and through the publication of System of Record Notices (SORNs).[10] The PIA, conducted by the government, is a detailed analysis of how a particular set of personal information is collected, stored, protected, shared, and managed. The SORN is the public notification of the existence of systems that collect and hold data. Taken together, the two requirements are intended to provide for the openness and accountability that will allow the public to remain assured that those collecting data are adhering to these principles.[11]

The problem is that a conscientious and fair application of these principles is, in many ways, fundamentally inconsistent with the way in which personal information can be used in the context of counter-terrorism or cyber insurgency dataveillance. Recognizing this fact is not, at this juncture, to make a normative judgment, but merely to make the descriptive point that the way in which dataveillance programs, like the Automated Targeting System that discovered al-Banna, function is at odds with these principles.

Consider that the collection limitation principle calls for the collection of the least amount of information and, where feasible, acquiring the consent of those about whom the data is being collected. Effective terrorism dataveillance, however, relies on the breadth of the collection for its success since the unknown connection will often come from an unexpected data field and the collection often occurs without the knowledge of, much less the consent of, the data subject.

Likewise, the purpose specification principle, if fully applied, would significantly degrade the analytical utility of many knowledge discovery systems. Often, the data of interest that gives rise to a previously unknown connection is one that was collected for a different purpose and intended for a different use. To take the most prosaic example, imagine that a phone number is collected from an air traveler so that the airline may contact him, and his frequent flyer number is collected so that his loyalty account may be credited. When those data fields are used for another purpose—for example, to identify potential connections between known terrorists and those who are otherwise unknown—these purpose and use limitation principles are violated. Yet, that is precisely how systems like ATS operate and, in retrospect, it is a method that might have identified the 9/11 terrorists before their attack, if it had been available at the time.[12]

Perhaps, even more pointedly, the principles of openness and individual participation are challenging to implement in the counter-terror context. Full disclosure of the methods of operation of a dataveillance system would often make it easier, for those wishing to do so, to evade it. The notion of allowing potential terrorists to see exactly what data is and is not held about them simply seems impossible to contemplate.

The problem, of course, is that in this modern world of widely distributed networks with massive data storage capacity and computational capacity, so much analysis becomes possible that the old principles no longer fit. We could, of course, apply them but only at the cost of completely disabling the new analytic capacity. In the current time of cyber threat that seems unlikely. Alternatively, we can abandon privacy altogether, allowing technology to run rampant with no control. That, too, seems unlikely and unwise.

What is needed, then, is a modernized conception of privacy—one with the flexibility to allow effective government action but with the surety necessary to protect against government abuse.

MODERNIZING PRIVACY

Our privacy laws and our conceptions of privacy cannot withstand the technological change that is ongoing and the cyber conflict that is developing. We must put theories of data availability and anonymity on a sounder footing—a footing that will withstand the rigors of ever-increasing computational capacity. To do so, we need to define what values underlie our instinctive privacy-protective reaction to the new technology, assess how realistic threats of abuse and misuse are, and create legal and policy incentives to foster positive applications, while restraining adverse ones.

Though a comprehensive new anonymity-protective legal structure has yet to be developed, the outline of one can already be discerned. Old ideas of collection and purpose limitations will be forced by technological change to yield a greater emphasis on use limitations. Even those limitations will need to be modified so that our concern is not with uses that are mere analyses but rather with uses that constitute the imposition of adverse consequences. The new system will be based on the new answers to three broad questions:

- What is privacy?
- What new structural systems do we need?
- What old rules need to be rethought?

What Is Privacy?

Privacy is really a misnomer in many ways.[13] What it reflects is a desire for the independence of personal activity, a form of autonomy. We protect that privacy in many ways. Sometimes, we do so through secrecy, which effectively obscures both the observation of conduct and the identity of those engaging in the conduct. In other instances, we protect the autonomy directly. Even though conduct is observed and the actor identified, we provide direct rules to limit action—as, for example, in the criminal context where we have an exclusionary rule to limit the use of illegally collected evidence.

The concept of privacy that most applies to the new information technology regime and the use of data in a cyber conflict is the idea of anonymity or practical obscurity, a middle ground where observation is permitted—that is, we expose our actions in public—but we are not subject to identification or scrutiny. The information data-space is suffused with information of this middle-ground sort, for example, bank account transactions, phone records, airplane reservations, and Smartcard travel logs, to name but a few. They constitute the core of transactions and electronic signature or verification information available in cyberspace. The anonymity that one has in respect of these transactions is not terribly different from real-world anonymity. Consider, as an example, the act of driving a car. It is done in public, but one is generally not subject to routine identification and scrutiny.

Protecting the anonymity we value requires, in the first instance, defining it accurately. One might posit that anonymity is, in effect, the ability to walk through the world unexamined. That is, however, not strictly accurate, for our conduct is examined numerous times every day. Sometimes, the examination is by a private individual, for example, one may notice that the individual sitting next to them on the train is wearing a wedding ring. Other routine examinations are by governmental authorities—the policeman in the car who watches the street or the security camera at the bank or airport, for example. As we drive down the road, any number of people might observe us.

So, what we really must mean by anonymity is not a pure form of privacy akin to secrecy. Rather, what we mean is that even though one's conduct is examined, routinely and regularly, both with and without one's knowledge, *nothing adverse should happen to you without good cause*. In other words, the veil of anonymity—previously protected by our practical obscurity—that is now so readily pierced by technology must be protected by rules that limit when the piercing may happen as a means of protecting privacy and preventing governmental abuse. To put it more precisely, the key to this conception of privacy is that privacy's principal virtue is as a *limitation on consequence*. If there are no unjustified consequences—that is, consequences that are the product of abuse, or error, or the application of an unwise policy—then, under this vision, there is no effect on a cognizable liberty/privacy interest. In other words, if nobody is there to hear the tree, or identify the actor, it really does not make a sound.

The appeal of this model is that it is, by and large, the model we already have for government/personal interactions in the physical world. The rule is not that the police cannot observe you; it is that they require authorization of some form from some authority in order to be permitted to engage in certain types of interactions, which are identified here as consequences. The police normally cannot stop you to question you without reasonable suspicion, cannot arrest you without probable cause, cannot search your house without probable cause, and cannot examine a corporation's business records about you without a showing of relevance to an ongoing investigation. We can and should build structures that map the same rules-based model of authorization linked to consequence as the appropriate model for the world of dataveillance.

Thus, the questions to be asked of any dataveillance program are: What is the consequence of identification? What is the trigger for that consequence? Who decides when the trigger is met? These questions are the ones that really matter, and questions of collection limitation or purpose limitation, for example, are rightly seen as distractions from the main point. The right answers to these questions will vary, of course, depending on the context of the inquiry, but the critical first step is making sure that we are asking the right questions.

What New Structural Systems Do We Need?

Once defined, how do we protect anonymity?[14] The traditional way is with a system of rules and a system of oversight for compliance with those rules. Here, too, modifications need to be made in light of technological change.

Rules, for example, tend to be static and unchanging and do not account readily for changes in technology. Indeed, the Privacy Act—the central statute intended to protect individual privacy against government intrusion—is emblematic of this problem; the principles of the Privacy Act are ill-suited to most of the new technological methodologies, such as distributed databases. Thus, we have begun to develop new systems and structures.

First, we are changing from a top-down process of command and control rule to one in which the principal means of privacy protection is through institutional oversight. To that end, the Department of Homeland Security was created with a statutorily-required Privacy Officer (and another Officer for Civil Rights and Civil Liberties).[15] The more recent Intelligence Reform and Terrorism Prevention Act,[16] and the Implementing Recommendations of the 9/11 Commission Act of 2007[17] go further. For the first time, they created a Civil Liberties Protection Officer within the intelligence community. More generally, intelligence activities are to be overseen by an independent Privacy and Civil Liberties Oversight Board.[18]

Indeed, these institutions serve a novel dual function. They are, in effect, internal watchdogs for privacy concerns. In addition, they naturally serve as a focus for external complaints, requiring them to exercise some of the functions of ombudsmen. In either capacity, they are a new structural invention on the American scene—at least, with respect to privacy concerns.

The second significant change concerning how we address privacy concerns lies in the new focus on results rather than on legal rules. We are using that new focus to drive and force technological change and encourage technologies that allow us to manage the connections between observation and identification according to new rules. The paradigmatic example of this shift is the mandate in the Intelligence Reform and Terrorism Prevention Act of 2004[19] for the creation of an information sharing environment. That recommendation grew out of work done by the Markle Foundation and the 9/11 Commission, and recognizes the need for enhanced interconnectivity among federal databases.[20] We must, as they say, connect the dots more effectively.

Recognizing the reality of technological change, Congress took a different track in the IRTPA. It simply defined the results it expected and tasked the Office of the Director of National Intelligence to issue the guidelines and develop a system that protects privacy and civil liberties in the development and use of the information-sharing environment.[21] To enhance transparency and oversight, it also required that these guidelines be made public, unless nondisclosure is clearly necessary to protect national security.[22]

Instead of a static set of rules adopted once and for all, we now anticipate an iterative process. The oversight institutions put in place will evaluate the efficacy of the tools deployed. Based on that evaluation—and, likely, in light of further technological changes—the information-sharing environment will be dynamically modified as necessary.

Finally, and perhaps most significantly, the very same dataveillance systems that are used to advance our counter-terrorism interests are equally well suited to assure that government officials comply with the limitations imposed on them in respect of individual privacy. Put another way, the dataveillance systems are uniquely well equipped to watch the watchers, and the first people who should lose their privacy are the officials who might wrongfully invade the privacy of others.

Indeed, there are already indications that these strong audit mechanisms are effective. Recall the incident in the 2008 presidential campaign in which contractors hacked into Barack Obama's passport file.[23] In this instance, there was no lawful reason for the disclosure of the file; it was disclosed purely for prurient, political reasons. As a result, candidate Obama suffered an adverse consequence of disclosure, which had not met any legal trigger that would have permitted the disclosure. A strong audit function quickly identified the wrongdoers and allowed punitive action to be taken.[24]

We can, therefore, be reasonably confident that as we move forward in establishing a consequence-based system of privacy protection we are also moving toward a point where the legal structures and technological capabilities to support that system are being put into place.

What Old Rules Need to Be Rethought?

Perhaps, the greatest dangers, however, lie in questions that we have yet to ask—at least those that have not yet been heard.[25] These are questions about the nature of wrongs and the nature of punishment. While these new dataveillance technologies mean greater success in identifying, solving, and punishing wrongful conduct, such as terrorism, they are equally capable of identifying, solving, and punishing wrongful conduct of a more morally ambiguous nature.

Consider, as an almost trivial example, the use of red light cameras in several major American cities. Before the development of this technology, drivers running red lights were identified only infrequently when they had the bad luck to run the light in the presence of a police officer. Now, with automated cameras, the rate of capturing wrongful red light runs is higher.[26] The same is increasingly true of a host of other offenses. Given the rate and scope of technological development, the trend will only continue.

This change—the use of technology to make it more likely (if not certain) that violations of law will be observed—will work powerful effects on the deterrence component of law enforcement and, if properly applied, on criminal and espionage type activities in cyberspace. We now calculate the optimal level of punishment by discounting the real punishment to account for the likelihood of getting caught. A 10-year sentence with a 1-in-10 chance of capture arguably has an effective deterrent value of one year in prison. When the chance of capture increases, the effective deterrent does as well.

An interesting corollary to the development of new technologies is that they will, inevitably, require either a reduction in punishments across the board or a much better, and narrower, definition of wrongful conduct. As technology trends towards near perfect enforcement, society will need to re-examine its definition of what constitutes a wrong. To put it prosaically, in a world where we could identify every Senator who has illegally smoked a Cuban cigar or every individual who has exceeded the speed limit by the least amount, we might well need to change our definition of those acts as wrongful. Increasingly, we will need to consider how we can best enhance individual autonomy, and that may necessitate decreasing the sphere of governmental authority.

Thus, one of the unseen perils to dataveillance is not, as most privacy advocates suppose, the increased likelihood that the state will abuse its power by targeting for adverse consequence those who have committed no crime, for example, a person whose only act is to engage in political protest. The new structures and systems we are putting in place are likely to be capable of protecting against abuse. The real peril is that our conception of the state's ambit has grown so broad that the state may soon lawfully use its powers to target wrongful conduct that ought not, truly, to be deemed wrongful.

THE COMING INTERNATIONAL PRIVACY WAR

There is one looming cloud on the privacy horizon that ought to be highlighted—a coming conflict between the privacy values of the United States and those of the European Union. According to the European Union, cloud-based companies who collect personal data are violating fundamental human rights. As E.U. Commissioner Vivian Redding has said: "We . . . believe that companies who direct their services to European consumers should be subject to E.U. data protection laws. Otherwise, they should not be able to do business on our internal market."[27] Indeed, the EU plans to back up new data privacy requirements with rules that fine businesses five percent of their global turnover if they breach the requirements.[28]

This is going to be a challenge for the rule of law in cyberspace. Nobody will know what law applies: Imagine you are a company, seeking to do business in Europe. What if some other country (say the one(s) where your server(s) are maintained) contends that its law also controls the business and that law is inconsistent with Europe's? What about the law of the home country (say, the United States), where the data storage provider is headquartered? The conflict of applicable laws will create great uncertainty and uncertainty breeds hesitancy and the loss of entrepreneurial vibrancy. Conflicting legal and technical requirements have the potential to crush innovation.

The globalized nature of the Internet and the distributed nature of cloud architecture suggest the need for a universal set of rules to protect privacy—rules of general applicability for cloud services everywhere on the network. But, there is little reason to be sanguine about the prospects for a satisfactory global privacy regime.

The alternative, however, is equally problematic. If the development of privacy rules and regulations is left to individual countries, we are likely to see one of three results: One (presaged by the EU's actions) will be unilateralism as countries try to impose their own privacy views on an unruly network. They will hold providers who use cloud services hostage as a condition of access to a market; in effect trying to balkanize the Internet. Another possibility is a rush to the bottom as countries compete to attract commercial cloud services by minimizing privacy protections. The most likely, however, is a privacy war as the United States and the European Union contest to impose their will. This is the worst possible result, pitting natural allies against each other.

* * *

It will be a significant challenge to determine the right answers to many of the substantive questions posed in this chapter. There will be substantial policy issues to resolve, for example, in determining what, if any, triggers might be created for denying an individual employment in a nuclear facility or refusing to let him board a plane. Yet, these are the questions that must be answered.

The improvements in computational power and data storage costs will not slow down, and we cannot expect to stop the deployment of new anonymity-invasive technology. Indeed, any effort to do so is doomed to failure before it has begun.

Therefore, rather than vainly trying to stop progress, or trying to fit the new technologies into old principles of privacy that no longer apply, we will need to go about the business of answering the hard policy questions. Instead of reflexively opposing technological change, a wiser strategy is to accept the change and work within it to channel change in beneficial ways.

This will require a rethinking of privacy—both a re-conception of what we think it means and a reconfiguration of how we think it is to be protected. It may be true that privacy is dead, but for those who truly want to protect privacy, the motto should be: "Privacy is dead. Long live the new privacy."

11
Chapter

No More Secrets

We live in a world in which there are no more secrets. In Chapter 9, we saw how that applied to individuals who coveted their privacy. In this chapter, we look briefly at how the end of secrecy is transforming governments.

Actually, to be fair, it is an overstatement to say that there are no more secrets—some secrets still exist. But, what is fairer to say, and is exceedingly accurate, is that the half-life of secrets (i.e., the length of time that they can be maintained) is diminishing rapidly. Where in the past a government could hope to obscure its actions from view for an almost indefinite period of time, today the power of cyberspace and the information conflict it engenders make that expectation entirely unreasonable.

WIKILEAKS

The transparency aspect of the WikiLeaks story is well known and widely remarked on. Using a series of servers and an anonymization protocol, WikiLeaks accepts and publishes documents provided to it by sources within governments.[1] Though the site has published documents with provenance as wide ranging as Zambia and Abu Dhabi, its most notable (or perhaps notorious) publications have involved a number of American documents, including the video of a wartime friendly fire incident, raw tactical intelligence from the battlefields of Iraq and Afghanistan, and a trove of classified State Department cables.[2]

Opinions vary as to the efficacy of WikiLeaks transparency efforts. To be sure, some of the most apocalyptic predictions (that nobody would talk to American diplomats ever again) have proven to be overblown. On the other hand, reliable reports suggest that the WikiLeaks disclosures have had significant public repercussions, ranging from increased tensions in U.S.–Mexican relations,[3] to threats to the leader of the Zimbabwean opposition leader,[4] to reports that the Taliban have collated a list of people who helped the United States and have targeted them for killing.[5] Indeed, some analysts have even said that the public disclosure of America's opinion of the Tunisian leader played a role in catalyzing the Tunisian rebellion that sparked the surge in Middle East unrest and led to the Arab Spring.[6] It would be easy to overstate the case, but it seems clear that we increasingly live in a world where secrecy is losing ground to transparency, with significant effects.[7]

To be sure, this problem is not unique to cyberspace. But, the availability of transparency enhancing technology in the cyber domain will increase the frequency and salience of transparency in our public discourse. Put simply, there is a significant difference in degree between the leak of the *Pentagon Papers*[8] to the *New York Times* and the massive data dumps practiced by WikiLeaks. This difference in degree borders on a difference in kind, and it will require a sea-change in how our national security system operates—one for which it is not well-prepared.

As a recent American Bar Association report put it: "The national security community traditionally relies upon information monopoly providing it with strategic advantage. This assumes that the government has information that its competitors or adversaries do not. Given the ubiquity of information in open sources, the irresistible benefits that come from networking information and the vulnerability of cyberspace, this assumption should be seriously challenged inside and outside of government. It is increasingly likely that others will have the same information, either because they have stolen it from you or because they have been able to develop it independently."[9] Policy makers (especially in the national security domain) have long been accustomed to consultation behind closed doors and our structures for policy making presume that capacity. Though we have long had to accommodate the process to occasional leaks of information (some of great significance), the transparency of cyberspace reflects a quantum change in those expectations for which our policy making institutions are not ready.

EVEN THE MOSSAD CAN'T KEEP SECRETS

In the world of Big Data, even the most experienced and competent intelligence agencies are having a hard time keeping secrets. They fail to learn the lessons of data analytic transparency at their own peril.

A perfect case in point (albeit a very macabre one) involved the death of a Hamas operative in Dubai. On January 19, 2010, Hamas commander Mahmoud al-Mabhouh, one of the founders of the group's military wing, was murdered in his hotel. Suspicion naturally fell immediately on Israel since the government would be one of the few in the world with both a motive to kill al-Mabhouh and the means to do so.[10]

Suspicion soon became proof. The law enforcement authorizes in Dubai were able to identify a hit squad with more than 20 members who were responsible for the killing, many of whom had traveled to Dubai on fraudulent passports. How they did it shows just how hard it is to keep secrets these days.

To begin with, some of the team members were spotted on security camera footage in the hotel acting suspiciously—two were seen putting on disguises in the bathroom and two others hung out in the lobby in tennis clothes for hours on end. But, the hotel surveillance footage was just the beginning of the story. According to an Israeli investigative reporter, Ronen Bergman,[11] the hit team apparently did not anticipate the ability of the Dubai authorities to piece together bits of data from across disparate databases.

For starters, the hit team's activities were tracked through a series of transactions using prepaid debit cards. The operatives used all the same type of card issued through MetaBank in Iowa. They were also connected through phone call records. The team used phones in Austria as a relay station to route calls between each of them. As Bergman put it: "since dozens of calls were made to and from this short list of Austrian numbers over a period of less than two days the moment that the cover of a single operative was blown and his cell phone records became available to the authorities, all others who called or received calls from the same numbers were at risk of being identified."

Another piece of the puzzle was a trick that America had taught the Dubai authorities—the analysis of travel records. Dubai authorities searched their customs and immigration databases to identify anyone who had entered and left Dubai shortly before and after the killing. They then cross-referenced this result against the lists of visitors who were in Dubai during al-Mabhouh's previous visits to the United Arab Emirates. This created a target list of possible suspects, which could be match against hotel registries. Video footage of check-in then matched faces to names.

As a consequence, the Dubai authorities were able to compile a meticulous video record of the Mossad hit team, both on the day of the murder and on their earlier visits to Dubai.[12] Finally, the Dubai authorities published the passport photos of the suspects—leading, in the end, to a near-certain identification.

And, of course, it isn't just Mossad who has problems—all spy agencies do. The development of technology has made it very difficult, for example, for an undercover spy to move around with a covert false identity. Too many trails in cyberspace can provide evidence that a false identity is a recent creation. The credit card was issued recently; the biometric data on the passport links to the person's true identity in a database somewhere; the claimed employment record can't be verified. All of these basic background facts are now subject to ready research on the network, making revelation of the falsity an increasingly easier task. We may well be reaching the point where human spying with a fictitious identity is a thing of the past thanks to the Internet.[13]

DEANONYMIZATION

The Internet also makes it possible to pierce the veil of anonymity through technical means. If data starts with an identification tag, that tag is, in the end, nearly impossible to remove.

For example, according to two computer science researchers at the University of Texas, while Twitter and Flickr only have a 15 percent overlap in users, both networks can be de-anonymized with only a 12 percent error rate. Likewise, two MIT students built a program that analyzed Facebook friends and were able to predict the sexual orientation of people with a high degree of accuracy. And, according to Carnegie Mellon researchers, gender, birthdate, and zip code information are enough to uniquely identify 90 percent of the people in America. In short, if you really exist, your anonymous data isn't so anonymous. And if you don't—that's clear too.

OFFICIAL SECRETS AND THE ESPIONAGE ACT

So, what's a government to do?[14] If you accept provisionally the need for secrets of some form (how to build an atomic bomb, say), what steps can a government legitimately take to keep secrets?

One possibility, of course, is prohibition. We can make it a crime to disclose government secrets. The application of such a law is, however, problematic for any number of reasons.

First, as a substantive matter, the main American law addressing the disclosure of national security secrets is the World War I–era Espionage Act provision,[15] whose text is, as one scholar has put it, "marred by profound and frustrating ambiguities."[16] As currently interpreted, the law is vague and of uncertain application in part because the text might facially apply to situations that many would consider legitimate activities (such as whistleblowers or reports in the press).

Worse yet, the law dates from a time when acts of espionage were acts of personal disclosure and when the most sophisticated means of communication were the telegraph and the radio. Little in the current law has any real application to the modern challenges of the Internet, where espionage may occur at a distance and its perpetrators can readily hide behind the cloak of anonymity.

These ambiguities are problematic for two interrelated reasons. First, vague laws do not give citizens notice of what it is that is prohibited. Second, vague laws may cause uncertainty in lawful prosecutions of those, like

WikiLeaks, who appear to have a malevolent intent but whose actions may be immunized from prosecution by a lack of clarity in the law.

Indeed, the Espionage Act's language is capacious and could be read to criminalize all sorts of lawful activity protected by the First Amendment to the U.S. Constitution. Accordingly, it has been interpreted narrowly to save it from First Amendment attack, but that has made it less effective. To fit current needs, a more targeted law would need to be drafted that both respects important press freedoms and still punishes more direct breaches of classified national security information.

Second, as a practical matter (and as we have seen already) the realities of the Internet are likely to frustrate any prohibitory rule. Often (though not always as the case of Bradley Manning, the alleged WikiLeaks source of American documents, illustrates) the source of the secret materials will be obscured by anonymity. Frequently, as the Mossad case shows, the piercing of secrets will come not from a leak but from the patient piecing together of open-source materials to develop a clear picture of otherwise cloaked activity. And, even more often, those who might be the objects of any prohibition are often effectively outside of any one country's jurisdiction. It makes little difference if American law makes the publication of classified information a crime if those who publish the information have gotten it through the Internet and released it in, say, Malaysia.

Finally, as with so many issues of this sort, it is not clear where America's equities truly lie. Though the government feels aggrieved by the publication of State Department classified cables on the WikiLeaks website, the extraterritorial application of our own secrecy laws to non-Americans (like WikiLeaks founder, Julian Assange) could create a precedent that, in the long run, we may not like. Consider, as a hypothetical, the *Washington Post* reporter who receives an anonymous leak (say, through a Tor onion router) and publishes the

---

TOR

Tor (a freeware program operated by The Tor Project—torproject.org) is an anonymizing tool used worldwide by journalists, human rights activists, hackers, law enforcement officers, and anyone else who wants to. Tor uses cryptography to encrypt messages and builds a volunteer network of servers around the globe to bounce encrypted traffic in a way that evades detection.

It is called an onion router because trying to get to the original source is like trying to peel back the layers of an onion—it's almost impossible. Those using Tor software are able to conceal their originating IP address from discovery. Activists say that Tor protects personal freedom and privacy. Governments say it protects secrecy. WikiLeaks says it promotes transparency. And, criminals don't say much, but are glad to use it to conceal their actions.

confidential minutes of the Chinese Politburo. How would America react to a prosecution of that reporter for violating the Chinese equivalent of the Espionage Act? Not well, one suspects, and with some justification.

EMBRACING TRANSPARENCY

We will never do away with government secrets. So long as they hold value, secrets will be worth keeping. Some, like the timing of the raid on Osama bin Laden, will be significantly time limited in value; others, like the names of individuals who are American intelligence sources in China, will be nearly timeless. But, so long as there is an incentive to maintain them, there will be secrets. The challenge will be to keep them secret for long enough to make them useful. The threat of untimely disclosure may well force governments to act more quickly while the information they hold can still provide them with an advantage. More importantly, for those timeless secrets that remain, governments will be obliged to spend increasing amounts of scarce resources to protect the information they hope to keep.

Given this reality, governments will need to adapt to a world where transparency is the norm, rather than the exception. Indeed, in many cases transparency can actually increase security. If we learned only one thing from the 9/11 attacks, it is the need to connect the dots. But, connection requires sharing; there are increasingly strong incentives to share information (both within the U.S. government and with allies) rather than keep it close-hold. We have come to think that the value of integrating data and sharing it more widely outweighs the costs from the risk of exposure of that information as it becomes more widely available. But, the hard reality is that those risks are real and need to be managed: Data analytics—so powerful in the analysis of private individual data—is of equal utility in probing government data. The citizens' loss of privacy is the governments' loss of secrecy.

But, equally important, we need to give serious thought to our definitions of what is secret and why we keep it. Joel Brenner, the former head of the National Counterintelligence Executive (a bureau in the intelligence community that tries to identify efforts by foreign governments to gain intelligence from the United States) gives a good example of how we overclassify information and have too many secrets. In 2007, he did a review of the official confidential U.S. government analysis of the then-forthcoming French Presidential election (the one eventually won by Nicolas Sarkozy) and compared it to the open source information that could be gleaned from the *New York Times,* the *Washington Post,* and *LeMonde.* His conclusion: "no information in the official reports" could not have been found in the open source literature.[17] The only ground for classification was to obscure what it was that the American government was reading—as if the fact that we were reading the newspapers was a secret in and of itself.

In the end, the only answer will be for governments to more clearly and consciously identify their crown jewels of truly secret information—things that protect the lives of its agents, protect the secrecy of its methods, or give it a decisive information advantage that can actually be used—and devote all their resources to their protection. Secrecy for secrecy's sake, or to prevent embarrassment, or to avoid public disclosure of differences of opinion or uncomfortable truths is, in the end, inevitably going to come to an end. Old business models premised on long-term secrecy cannot survive the cyber revolution.

12
Chapter

Encryption and Wiretapping

In 2010 the government of India approached Research In Motion (RIM), the manufacturer of Blackberry devices, with a demand. India wanted to monitor the encrypted e-mails and Blackberry messages (a form of Internet chat) that passed across RIM's servers between corporate clients. And, it wanted help in decrypting the encrypted messages. This was, the Indian government argued, essential to allow it to combat terrorism. And, they added, if you don't give us this access, we'll pull your wireless license and close down Blackberry in India. Faced with the loss of more than one million Indian corporate customers, RIM compromised—it found a way to share with the Indian government details on where to find the encrypted messages the government wanted—in effect identifying the servers where the information originated—without actually decrypting the messages itself.[1]

In making this arrangement (and, by all reports, placating the Indian government), RIM nicely illustrated two distinct, yet linked, issues that relate to the security of cyber communications, and are deeply imbedded in all aspects of the conflict in cyberspace. One is the issue of encryption—when and how communications and information can be encoded and decoded so that only the people you want to read the information can have access to it. The other is wiretapping—that is, whether and under what rules someone can intercept messages in transit and divert or copy them to their own purposes. The linkage between the two seems apparent. Wiretapping a message you cannot decrypt still leaves the content of the message concealed and even unencrypted information is safe if the transmission channels are absolutely secure. Those engaged in a conflict in cyberspace want both capabilities—to intercept/divert information and to decode it so that they can read its contents.

And, therein hangs a tale. India is not alone in its interest in being able to read people's encrypted mail. Other governments from Dubai and China to the United States have the same interests—for good or for ill. Indeed, late in 2010 and, again, in 2012 the U.S. government disclosed tentative plans to expand its wiretapping laws to apply to encrypted email transmitters like BlackBerry, social networking websites like Facebook, and software that allows direct peer-to-peer messaging like Skype.[2] How well (or poorly) a nation achieves this objective bears directly on its ability to successfully win conflicts of espionage, crime, and war in cyberspace—and also on how great or little intrusion the government makes into the communications of its private citizens.

* * *

The Internet is a means, essentially, of transmitting information across large distances at a ridiculously rapid pace. All of the various types of attacks we have seen described in the preceding chapters are, fundamentally, based on the ability to corrupt the flow of accurate information—whether by stealing a portion of it for misuse, disrupting the flow so that accurate information doesn't arrive in a timely manner, or inserting false information into an otherwise secure stream of data. If the confidentiality and integrity of the information being transmitted cannot be relied on, then the system or network that acts based on that data is vulnerable. That, in a nutshell, is the core of much of cyber warfare—the ability to destroy or corrupt the flow of information from your enemies through espionage or attack—and the collateral real-world effects of that destruction.

What if your data could not be deciphered or altered (or, slightly less useful, but almost as good, if you could make your data tamper-evident, so that any corruption or interception was known to you)? If your goal is to protect your own information from attack, there are a number of ways by which you might achieve that objective. One of the earliest defensive measures taken in cyberspace was a method as old as human history—data and information were protected by encryption.

The idea behind encryption as a defensive mechanism is not, as we shall see, a perfect solution. But, what it can do, if done properly, is ensure that your information is confidential and can't be read by anyone else. It also, in contemporary usage, can provide you with a means of confirming that the information has not been tampered with in any way (since it uses modern algorithms, any alteration of the data would result in a gibberish product). Encoding information can keep it secret and sealed. Properly used, it can also allow you to share information with a trusted partner while excluding others.

But, this expansion of cryptographic capabilities to protect cyber networks comes with an uncertain cost to order and governance. Advances in cryptographic technology have made it increasingly difficult for individuals to crack a code. Code breaking is as old as code making, naturally. But, as the run of technology has played out, encryption increasingly has an advantage over decryption, and recent advances have brought us to the point where decryption can, in some cases, be effectively impossible. This has the positive benefit of allowing legitimate users to protect their lawful secrets, but it also has the inevitable effect of distributing a technology that can protect malevolent uses of the Internet. If the U.S. government can encrypt its data, so can China, or the Russian mob, or a Mexican drug cartel.

An alternative strategy that works in concert with encryption is to make your information transmission immune to interception. Here, too, the changes wrought by Internet technology have made interception more difficult and enhanced the security of communications. In the world of telephone communications, for example, intercepting a communication was as simple as attaching two alligator clips to the right wire—hence the word wiretapping. Communications through the Internet are wholly different; the information being transmitted is broken up into small packets that are separately transmitted along different routes and then reassembled when they arrive at their destination. This disassembly of the data makes effective interception appreciably more difficult.

These two technological developments have led to controversy over critical policy issues that bear on cyber conflicts today: Can a government require the manufacturers of encryption technology to limit their distribution to prevent strong cryptography from falling into malevolent hands? And, can they require communications transmission companies to assure the government access to communications? Can they, in effect, require that code makers build in a back door by which they can access and decrypt encrypted messages? And, can they require ISPs to provide them access to the data as it transits the net?

And, if they can, under what rules would these back doors be accessed? At the whim of a government? Or, only with an appropriate court order? Under what sorts of standards?

THE BASICS OF ENCRYPTION

Encryption, or secret writing, is one of the oldest forms of human activity. Secret coding has been around almost as long as there have been secrets worth keeping. One of the earliest instances is recorded in *The Histories* by Herodotus, who described how secret writing techniques saved the Greeks from being conquered by Xerxes, the King of Persia. A Greek, witnessing the buildup of the Persian fleet sent a message to Sparta, warning of Xerxes' plans. To keep the message from being intercepted, he concealed the writing beneath the wax covering of a wood tablet. Forewarned and prepared, the

Greeks were able to assemble their navy and defeat the Persian fleet at the battle of Salamis.[3]

But, simply hiding a message (beneath wax on a tablet or in a hollowed out pen, or the heel of a shoe) isn't strictly speaking encoding the message. It merely provides a means of preventing the message from being intercepted and detected while en route. Encryption, or encoding, is intended to keep the message secret even if it is physically intercepted.

Conceptually, encryption involves three separate components that come together—the plaintext, the algorithm, and the key. The plaintext is the substance of the message that the sender wants to convey. Of course, this information doesn't have to be a text at all; it can be the firing code for a nuclear missile or the formula for Coca Cola products; or, quite literally, any data of any form that is more valuable to the sender if not known to anyone.

The algorithm is a general system of encryption; in other words a general set of rules for transforming a plaintext. An example of an algorithm is a cipher where, say, each letter of the plaintext (assuming it is actually a written text) is replaced with another letter. The algorithm here is "replace each letter with another." The third, and most vital, component of an encryption system is the key, that is, the specific set of instructions that will be used to apply the algorithm to a particular message. A cipher key might therefore be "replace the letter with the letter which is five letters after it in the English alphabet." Using this simple algorithm and key, the plaintext "cat" would then be converted to the word "hfy" and that result would now be known as the ciphertext. The critical feature, of course, is that as an initial premise, only someone who has the algorithm and the key can decrypt the ciphertext, so even if it is physically intercepted, the contents remain confidential.

We've been creating cyphertexts for quite a long time. Earliest mentions of coded writing can be found in the *Kama Sutra* (which counseled women to record their liaisons in secret writing). Julius Caesar's use of codes was so common that the type of algorithm he used (the letter shift system mentioned previously) is actually sometimes called the Caesar shift cipher.[4]

Of course, where some seek to keep secrets, others seek to reveal them. It is one of the truisms of encryption that the key to keeping a secret is the key—not the algorithm. The algorithm—the general method—is often too widely known to be a usefully kept secret. So, the strength of the key—how hard it is to guess—defines how good the encryption product is.

To return to the Caesar shift cipher, if we restrict ourselves to just shifting the alphabet, there are only 25 possible keys to use, depending on how far down the alphabet we shift the letters. That's a pretty weak key—if someone knows the general algorithm the key can be cracked with brute force in a short time period. If we loosen the algorithm a bit however, and instead of a shift rule apply a rule that allows any rearrangement of the 26 letters of the English alphabet, then the number of keys increases astronomically to well over 400 septillion (!) different possible arrangements, making a brute force effort to discover the key difficult indeed.

OF CODES AND CIPHERS

Technically, a cipher replaces plaintext at the level of a letter, while codes replace higher level items (e.g., a word or phrases). Thus, a code might be "apple = President."

Codes have the advantage of being much less subject to frequency analysis of the sort developed in the ninth century. On the other hand, codes are much less flexible than ciphers (since they are limited to the predefined code substitutions) and the loss of a codebook can be catastrophic for the secrecy of the messages it has been used to encode.

By contrast, cipher keys are more flexible in encrypting content and more readily created, distributed, and, if need be, changed. As a general rule, one can say that ciphers are of greater utility than codes.

Of course, brute force is not the only method of breaking a cipher. Since at least the ninth century (when the method of frequency analysis was first reported by Arab scholars),[5] it has been well established that a cipher can be broken by analysis rather than by brute force. Frequency analysis is relatively simple to describe. It rests on the knowledge that, for example, in English the letter "e" is the most common vowel. Other common letters in regular usage include "a," "i," "n," "o," and "t." With this knowledge derived from analysis external to the code, the deciphering of a ciphertext is made much easier. It is far more likely than not that the most frequently used cipher letter, whatever it may be, represents one of these common English letters. In a ciphertext of any reasonable length, there is virtually no chance, for example, that the most common cipher letter is being used to signify a "q" or a "z."

This sort of knowledge makes decryption easier and reduces the need for a brute force approach. Indeed, it is a fair assessment of the art of cryptography that, until the dawn of the computer era, those decrypting ciphers had the upper hand. Either the keys themselves could be stolen or they could be decrypted using sophisticated techniques, like frequency analysis. Even the notoriously difficult German Enigma code from World War II eventually yielded to analysis.

THE PRIME NUMBER, PUBLIC KEY REVOLUTION

There things stood for a number of years. Those who wanted to keep secrets were at a fundamental disadvantage—in order to transmit a secret message they first had to exchange a (secret) key to the message. Besides the possibilities of backward analysis to determine what the key was, there were all sorts of problems with the exchange of keys in the first instance. They could be lost, stolen, revealed, or compromised in any number of ways. By their very nature, private keys were only good for as long as they were private.

In the late 1970s, however, enterprising cryptographers developed a way to encrypt information using the multiplication of two impossibly large prime numbers and certain one-way mathematical functions (a one-way function is one that only works in one direction; most mathematical functions, like addition and subtraction, work in both directions—you can get the results from the precursors or the precursors from the results, so to speak). With one way functions, a recipient can publish the result of his impossibly large multiplication as a public key. People who want to send the recipient a message can use the public key to encrypt their message. And, since only the recipient knows how to break down this impossibly large number to its original primes, only he can decrypt the message.[6] Today, you can embed this type of encryption into your e-mail system using a program that can be purchased over the Internet for less than $100. If the users at both ends of a message use this form of public key encryption, the secret message they exchange between themselves becomes, effectively, undecryptable by anyone other than the key's creator,[7] unless, of course, a hacker attacks the creation of the key at its source, by breaking into the key generation algorithm, in some way.

This last scenario was thought to be entirely theoretical and outside the box. Nobody could break into the key generation process—until someone did. In March 2011, the leading manufacturer of public encryption security key devices (those little key fobs that people carry around and which generate random six-digit numbers every 60 seconds), the company RSA—named after its founders Rivest, Shamir and Adelman, who discovered and invented public key mathematics—was hacked.[8] The product, known as SecureID token, was a way of granting remote access to a set of servers for people who are working offsite. Later, in May 2011, someone who had access to the stolen RSA data, used that knowledge to attack the systems of Lockheed Martin (a major defense contractor) and attempted to gain access.[9] Given the sophistication of the breach at RSA and the focus of the attack on a defense contractor, espionage rather than theft was suspected, and inferences have been drawn that another state-actor (probably the Chinese) was behind the attack. Whatever the source, this experience demonstrates that for even the strongest of encryption keys, key security is vital.

THE KEY ESCROW CONTROVERSY

But, the U.S. government is not going to hack RSA or any other key generator. And so, the government's solution: if we can't decrypt information by analysis or brute force, we should force those who manufacture encryption software to build into the system a back door decryption key that would allow the government to read any encrypted messages. These decryption keys would be stored (or escrowed) with a trusted third party (say, a judge at a federal court) who would only release the key under specified, limited circumstances. Hence, this cluster of issues often goes by the name of key escrow—a system where the makers of technology would be required by law to include decryption keys that governments can get access to. Needless to say, many privacy advocates opposed this effort—and their opposition was successful.

In the 1990s, the FBI sought to require encryption technology manufacturers to include such a back door that went by the name of Clipper Chip.[10] In part, opposition to Clipper was based on civil liberties objections, but it was also based on a practical realization that the government, itself, was a beneficiary of strong encryption to protect its own secrets and on the recognition that the United States had no monopoly on the development of encryption algorithms. If the United States required back doors in American products, the market would naturally tend to favor non-American products and our own national security system would have a back door into our own secrets.[11]

Indeed, at this juncture, encryption technology is widely available, with exceedingly strong encryption keys. Free software (for example, that provided by TrueCrypt.Org) with a 256 bit key size, is readily available and easy to install, as are open source public key encryption programs. In effect, with the death of the Clipper Chip back door movement, it is now possible to encrypt data in a way that cannot be decrypted after even a year of effort.[12]

WIRETAPPING—YESTERDAY AND TODAY

Pre-Internet, wiretapping was an easy physical task. Early telephony worked by connecting two people who wished to communicate through a single, continuous wire (typically made of copper). The image that captures this concept most readily is of a telephone operator moving plugs around on a board and, by that effort, physically establishing an end-to-end wire connection between the two speakers.

That made wiretapping easy. All that was required was attaching a wire to a terminal post and then hooking the connection up to a tape recorder. The interception didn't even need to be made at the central Publicly Switched Telephone Network (PSTN) switching station. Any place on the line would do. And, there was (with limited exceptions) only one American telephone company, AT&T, and only one system, so coordination with the PSTN was easy if it was authorized.

Things became a little more complicated when AT&T broke up into the Baby Bells, but the real challenge came with the development of new communications technologies. As microwave, FM, and fiber optic technologies were introduced, the technical challenges of intercepting communications increased as well.[13] The technological difficulty in intercepting communications grew exponentially in a relatively short period of time.

Today, the problem is even more complex. In addition to cellular telephones, we now have instant messaging and e-mail and text messaging for written communications. If you want to communicate by voice, you can use Skype (a web-based video conferencing system), or Google Chat (an embedded browser-based chat program).[14] Businesses use web-teleconference tools for teleconferences and many people (particularly in the younger generation) communicate while present in virtual worlds through their avatars. Twitter and Facebook allow instant communication between large groups of people.

In short, we have created an almost infinite number of ways in which one can communicate.[15] When combined with the packet-switching nature of Internet web transmissions, and the development of peer-to-peer networks (that completely do away with centralized servers), the centralized PSTN network has become a dodo. Indeed, the Internet Engineering Task Force (the organization that sets standards for operation of the Internet) has rejected requests to mandate an interception capability within the architecture of the Internet communications protocols, making interception of Internet-based transmissions even more difficult.[16] With these changes, the laws and policies for authorized wiretapping have, effectively, become obsolete.

CONTEMPORARY COMMUNICATIONS SYSTEMS
Skype
X-fire
Google Chat
Google Apps
Go-To-Meeting
Quick Connect
Reddit
Tumblr
Facebook
My Space
Second Life
EVE Online
Chat Anywhere
Napster
Grokster
LimeWire

WIRETAPPING AND CHANGING TECHNOLOGY

The law enforcement and intelligence communities face two challenges in administering wiretap laws in the age of the Internet—one of law and one of technology. The legal issue is relatively benign and, in some ways, unencumbered by technical complexity. We need a series of laws that define when and under what circumstances the government may lawfully intercept a communication. For the most part, the authorization issues are ones involving the updating of existing authorities to apply explicitly to new technologies. The technical issue is far harder to solve—precisely how can the desired wiretap be achieved?

Legal Authorization

In *Katz v. United States,*[17] the Supreme Court held that the Fourth Amendment applied to electronic communications, and that a warrant was required for law enforcement-related electronic surveillance conducted in the United States. *Katz* was codified in the Omnibus Crime Control and Safe Streets Act of 1968, with particular requirements for such interceptions laid down in Title III.[18] In general, Title III prohibits the interception of "wire, oral, or electronic communications" by government agencies without a warrant and regulates the disclosure and use of authorized intercepted communications by investigative and law enforcement officers.

Reflecting its pre-Internet origins, Title III originally covered only wire and oral communication. It has since been modified to take account of technological changes and now covers all forms of electronic communication (including, for example, e-mails).[19] The law also regulates the use of pen register and trap and trace devices (i.e., devices designed to capture the addressing information of a call, such as the dialing information of incoming and outgoing phone calls). In general, this noncontent information may be collected without a warrant or showing of probable cause, unlike the content portions of a message.[20]

As a core part of its structure, Title III also incorporates certain privacy and civil liberties protections. It permits issuance of an interception warrant only on a judicial finding of probable cause to believe that the interception will reveal evidence that "an individual is committing, has committed, or is about to commit" certain particular criminal offenses.[21] Title III has minimization requirements, that is, it requires the adoption of procedures to minimize the acquisition and retention of nonpublicly available information concerning nonconsenting U.S. persons who are not the targets of surveillance, unless such a person's identity is necessary to understand the law enforcement information or assess its importance. In other words, if while investigating a terrorist case, the wiretap intercepts a conversation with a doctor, or a lover, or a pizza salesman that is not relevant to the investigation, that conversation must be minimized and information not meeting that standard may not be disseminated. Most significantly, electronic evidence collected in violation of Title III may not be used as evidence in a criminal case.

As Title III applies in the law enforcement context, the Foreign Intelligence Surveillance Act (FISA) authorizes the collection of communications for certain intelligence purposes. Passed in 1978, the Act creates the mechanism by which such orders permitting the conduct of electronic surveillance could be obtained from a specialized court—the Foreign Intelligence Surveillance Court (FISC). This court was, initially, authorized to issue orders for targeting electronic communications in the United States of both U.S. and non-U.S. persons based on a showing of probable cause of clandestine intelligence activities, sabotage, or terrorist activities, on behalf of a foreign power. The law was subsequently expanded to authorize the court to issue warrants for physical searches (1994), the use of pen registers/trap and traces (1999), and the collection of business records (1999).

To obtain a FISC order authorizing surveillance, the government must meet the same probable cause standard as in a criminal case; it must make a showing of probable cause to believe that the target of the electronic surveillance is a foreign power or an agent of a foreign power. As with Title III, the law imposes minimization obligations on the agency intercepting the communications.[22]

Technical Capacity

While amending the laws authorizing wiretaps to accommodate changes in technology has been, for the most part, a ministerial exercise of amending legislation, the same cannot be said of maintaining the technical capacity to tap into the ever-changing stream of communications.

In 1994 Congress attempted to address this problem through the Communications Assistance for Law Enforcement Act, known as CALEA.[23] CALEA's purpose was to insure that law enforcement and the intelligence agencies would not be left behind the technology curve, by requiring telecommunications providers to build the ability to intercept communications into their evolving communications systems.

CALEA, in effect, imposed a new technical requirement on communications providers. Initially, many digital telephone systems did not have interception capabilities built in.[24] CALEA required providers to change how they built their telecommunications systems so that they had that capacity—an effort that could be achieved, generally, without interfering with subscriber services. (As an aside, CALEA also provided for a federal monetary subsidy to the telecommunications providers to pay for the changeover.)

As originally adopted, CALEA's requirements were applicable only to facilities-based telecommunications providers, that is, companies who actually owned the lines and equipment used for the PSTN and Internet. Information services providers (in other words, those who provide e-mail, instant messaging, chat, and other communications platforms that are not dependent on traditional telecommunications) were excluded, at least in part because those forms of communication were still in their infancy and of relatively little importance.[25]

Finally, and perhaps most importantly, CALEA didn't say that telecommunications providers had to give the government a way of decrypting encrypted messages that were put on its network for transmission. A telecommunications provider only had to decrypt messages if it provided the encryption services itself. So, if an individual independently used encryption at the origin of the message, all that CALEA required was that the telecommunications provider should have a means of intercepting the encrypted message available when authorized to do so.

THE WIRETAPPING PROBLEM TODAY

Hence the problem, which is two-fold: Cybercriminals, cyber spies and cyber warriors are increasingly migrating to alternative communications systems—ones like Skype and virtual worlds that are completed disconnected from the traditional PTSN networks covered by CALEA. And, along the way, they are increasingly using encryption technology that prevents law enforcement, counter-espionage, and counter-terrorism experts from having the ability to listen in on communications.[26] On the wiretapping front, the problems are both technical and legal.

Technologically, the distributed nature makes true interception capabilities extremely difficult. In a peer-to-peer network, there is no centralized switching point. In a packet switching system, where the message is broken in many parts, there is no place on the network where the whole message is complied, save at the two end points. While peer-to-peer systems can be used for illegal activity (e.g., illegal file sharing[27]), they are also an integral part of legitimate file-sharing activities.[28]

Instead, the government must use sampling techniques to intercept portions of a message and then, when a problematic message is encountered, use sophisticated techniques to reassemble the entire message (often by arranging for the whole message to be redirected to a government endpoint). The FBI developed such a system in the late 1990s, called Carnivore.[29] It was designed to sniff packets of information for targeted messages. When the Carnivore program became public, the uproar over this sort of interception technique forced the FBI to end the program.

It is said that the NSA uses a packet sniffing system, called Echelon, for intercepting foreign communications traffic that is significantly more effective than Carnivore ever was.[30] Indeed, according to the *New York Times,* the Echelon system was at the core of the NSA's post-9/11 domestic surveillance system.[31] While little is publicly known about the capacity of the Echelon system, one observer (an EU Parliamentary investigation) has estimated that the system could intercept three million faxes, telephone calls, or e-mails per minute.[32]

In order for a system like Carnivore, or Echelon, to work, however, the routing system must insure either that traffic is routed to the sniffer along the way or that the sniffer is physically located between the two endpoints. But, therein lies the problem: many of the peer-to-peer systems are not configured to permit routing traffic to law enforcement sniffers.

CHANGING LAW—ADDRESSING NEW CHALLENGES

To address these problems, the U.S. government has spoken publicly of its intent to seek an amendment to CALEA. According to public reports, the government would seek to extend CALEA's wiretapping requirements for traditional telecommunications providers to digital communications technologies. Doing so would, according to the government, close a growing gap in existing surveillance capabilities that increasingly places criminal or espionage activity behind a veil that the government cannot pierce—a phenomenon the government calls Going Dark.

The proposed changes would have three components: (1) an expansion of CALEA's decryption requirement to all communications service providers who give their users an ability to encrypt their messages; (2) a requirement that foreign-based service providers doing business in the United States have a domestic office to which the government may go where interceptions can take place; and (3) a requirement that providers of peer-to-peer communications systems (like Skype) alter their software to allow interception. The government, speaking through Valerie Caproni, the General Counsel for the FBI, has argued that these proposed changes (which are expected to be the subject of legislative consideration in the coming years) would not give additional wiretapping authority to law enforcement officials, but simply extend existing authority "in order to protect the public safety and national security."[33]

The principal legal issues in this proposal will, as before, involve authorization rules and standards for operation. Presumably, if the government is to be taken at its word, they will be seeking no greater interception authority than exists today for wire communications, that is, routinized access to non-content header information joined with a probable cause standard for access to content.

In some conceptions, the CALEA expansion might also implicate the Fifth Amendment protection against self-incrimination. In general, the Constitution says that an individual cannot be compelled to give evidence against himself through testimony. When questioned he is, by law, entitled to stand mute and say nothing.

Imagine an individual who encrypts messages he sends across the Internet. The courts have yet to determine whether or not an effort to compel that individual to disclose the decryption key constitutes a violation of his Fifth Amendment privilege. In general, the answer to the question will turn on whether disclosing the decryption key is thought of more like the production of a physical object (such as the physical key to a lock box), which may be compelled, or like the production of a person's mental conceptions (such as the memorized combination to a safe), which may not be.[34]

These Fifth Amendment considerations are likely to be of limited applicability. Even in many peer-to-peer applications (like Skype), the encryption keys are held by a centralized provider who uses the user-generated keys to enable encrypted communications from a variety of different platforms where the user might log in. In effect, to make the system more convenient, the user allows a third party coordinator (here, Skype) to have access to the key. In doing so, Fifth Amendment protections are likely waived.

Moreover, despite the widespread availability of encryption tools that provide solid security, it seems that nobody uses them—not even the bad guys. Every year, the U.S. court system publishes a report on the wiretapping activities of the federal government. In the 2010 report,[35] of the more than 3,100 wiretaps authorized, only 6 had any encryption in use. Even those six cases didn't stop the government's efforts; it was able to get the evidence it was seeking every time.

At the bottom, however, the issues raised by the nascent proposal are more policy questions than legal questions. Consider a short list of these sorts of questions:

Is implementation of an expanded CALEA even technically feasible in all cases? How will software developers who are providing peer-to-peer services provide access to communications when there is no centralized point in the network through which the data will have to pass? Presumably, this will require developers to reconfigure their software products in ways that permit the interception and decryption.

Think, for example, of an open-platform encryption program like TrueCrypt (that is, one that is developed by a public consortium and where the underlying code is open to all for inspection), where users retain sole possession of their own generated keys. Here, the users might retain Fifth Amendment rights against self-incrimination that would protect them against the compelled disclosure of their keys, but could CALEA be amended to require that software commercial vendors who manufacture such programs include decryption back-doors? The answer is unclear.

And, even if they could, what then? Depending on how broad the modified CALEA requirements are, the economic costs of modifying the existing platforms could run into the millions, if not billions, of dollars. When CALEA was first implemented, the federal government made funds available to offset the costs of the upgrades.[36] Would it do so again, and to what degree?

More significantly, what would be the security implications of requiring interception capabilities in new technologies? Building in these capabilities would necessarily introduce potential vulnerabilities that could be exploited, not by those who would have authorized access, but rather by hackers who found a way to crack the capabilities of the protection itself.[37]

And, finally, there are issues to be considered in connection with international perceptions of American conduct. In recent years, efforts have been made by various foreign governments to secure access to Internet communications.[38] It is difficult, if not impossible, for the United States to oppose such efforts in international forums when its own policy favors expansions of interception capabilities domestically. Indeed, our stated public policy favors Internet freedom, in large part as a way of energizing democracy movements around the world[39]—a policy that is difficult to square with a domestic move toward greater governmental interception capabilities.

THE FUTURE OF ENCRYPTION

Jay Wack has the air of an evangelical preacher. He looks the part too, with black wrap-around glasses that shade his eyes. But, Wack isn't preaching religion in the classical sense. Instead, he is preaching a new conception of encryption. Wack works with Ed Scheidt, who is one of the grand old men of cryptography. When the CIA commissioned a new sculpture for its offices in Langley, Virginia, they wanted one that stood out—so they asked a sculptor, Jim Sanborn, to construct a sculpture with a puzzle in it. Sanborn, in turn, collaborated with Scheidt, to put 4 separate code sections on the Kryptos sculpture. Today, more than 20 years after the sculpture was first unveiled, only 3 of the code sections have been decrypted. The fourth remains unsolved, and Ed Scheidt has moved on to new encryption challenges.

The problem with encryptions systems, as Wack and Scheidt will tell you, is that they are based on static encryption keys, that is, keys that apply only at either end of the communication chain. In other words, the sender uses a particular key to encrypt the information on the front end, and then the recipient uses the same key (or a related one) to decrypt it on the other. The key is independent of the message and can travel separately from the message.

The direction Wack and Scheidt are headed in is a novel one. They are creating dynamic keys that actually travel with the information being transmitted. What this means, in practice, is that an encryption header can travel with any digital object—and so authorize access to the content contained in a data set. In the end, instead of the encryption protecting the transmission of information from point to point, the encryption will be directly attached to the content and protect the information itself. Even when the data is at rest in a computer system, the dynamic encryption will limit who can see it (and even allow people with different permissions to see different parts of the data set). One beauty of this approach is that it will solve a persistent problem in communications security—how to deal with different levels of secrecy and access. Using dynamic keys, each bit of data is associated with a level of permission access.

This new approach also provides a way of getting around the problem of trust. As encryption is commonly practiced today, you have to trust the entity that is issuing the encryption keys. But, in the real world, as Wack will tell you, "trust is not a transitive event."[40] Just because Jim trusts Steve and Steve trusts Bob, doesn't mean that Jim should necessarily trust Bob. They may well have different reasons to trust people and apply those reasons in different ways. But, the modern system of key issuance is based on transitive trust; everyone accepts encryption standards that are accompanied by a certificate of issuance. Right now, more than 600 different companies and institutions issue those sorts of certificates that are used to verify the authenticity of messages and websites.

What happens when someone hacks one of the certificate issuing authorities? Sadly, we know the answer now. As we discussed in chapter 6, an Iranian hacker (who some suspect of working for the Iranian government), hacked DigiNotar, one of the certificate issuers. He used his access to DigiNotar's certificate systems to create certificates for various websites. Among those subject to attack were sites operated by major Internet players like Google, Microsoft, and Mozilla. The certificates would let the hacker spoof users of the sites and redirect traffic to places they thought were legitimate—and then allow him to collect, for example, their e-mail traffic.[41]

The use of dynamic keys offers the promise of breaking this cycle of the abuse of trust. When encryption follows the data, permission to access the information will be allowed locally, without the need for reference to a centralized certificate authority. From a user's perspective, that looks like a great improvement.

From the perspective of governments worldwide, however, it may be a problem. Dynamic encryption may make wiretapping irrelevant. If data or information can be encrypted at both ends, and also while in transit, intercepting the data may not really advance your interests since it will be undecipherable. In the never-ending tug-of-war between those who want the ability to destroy or corrupt the flow of information from your enemies through espionage or attack, and those who want to protect that information from destruction or corruption, the protectors seem to be gaining the upper hand. Whether that's a good thing or a bad thing depends on where you sit. It's great for democracy advocates in the Middle East but problematic for signals intelligence experts at the NSA.

13

Chapter

The Devil in the System: Hardware Failures

Some cyber threats arise, not from direct software attack on the system, but from threats that originate from within the system itself. Some of those threats might arise from insider activity—as when an enemy agent successfully poses as an insider to gain access to the cybersystem. Conceptually, however, this insider threat (whether to a U.S. government target or a private commercial target) poses no problems distinct from those posed by any other instance of insider espionage—the only difference is the means by which the insider theft occurred. Put another way, when Private Bradley Manning allegedly downloaded files onto a CD-ROM to give to WikiLeaks, what he did wasn't in practice that much different than if he had copied the files on a photocopier—quicker and easier to be sure, but not categorically distinct.

Likewise, the systems we have developed and put in place to protect against more traditional insider threats of espionage—security clearances and background checks—are likely also appropriate to counter the insider cyber threat. Thus, there is little reason to suspect that any organizational or process issues exist that are unique to cyber insiders.

The same cannot be said of the insider threat posed to cyber systems by the workings of the hardware within the various routers, switches, operating systems, and peripherals that comprise the real-world manifestations of cyberspace or in the code in the software purchased from foreign sources. History records several examples where a state actor has taken advantage of its position as a system supplier to surreptitiously introduce hardware changes into systems and subject those systems to its own control or influence.

In the past, hardware intrusion of the sort we are discussing involved production equipment instead of computer hardware. For example, according to the Farewell Dossier (a collection of documents released by former Soviet

KGB Colonel Vladimir Vetrov, codenamed Farewell), the United States sup-
plied flawed gas generators and turbines for use by the Soviet Union in its gas
pipelines.[1] At least one former government official has said that our hardware
and software operation against the pipelines caused a massive explosion.[2]

But, there is no reason to think that only manufacturing equipment is
subject to manipulation. Just a while ago, for example, AT&T was considering
subcontracting some of its production work to a large Chinese telecom company, Huawei. As it was preparing to do so, AT&T got a phone call from the
NSA, warning the company that if it wanted to continue providing equipment
to the American government, it had better reconsider any contractual agreements with Huawei. "The NSA called AT&T because of fears that China's intelligence agencies could insert digital trapdoors into Huawei's technology that
would serve as secret listening posts in the U.S. communications network."[3]
Huawei says that suspicions about its relationship with the Chinese government are false, and has even formally asked the U.S. government to investigate
the issue.[4]

For these reasons, it is a matter of significant concern that over the past
decades the U.S. government has become increasingly reliant on commercial off-the-shelf technology (sometimes known by the acronym COTS) for
much of its cyber supply needs. Indeed, counterterrorism experts have sometimes opined that American reliance on COTS computer technology, which
is often manufactured and/or maintained overseas, poses a greater vulnerability to U.S. cyber systems than traditional cyber attacks. In testimony before the House of Representatives in July 2011, the Department of Homeland
Security confirmed publicly that it was aware of situations where electronic
equipment had come pre-loaded with malware, spyware, or other forms of
hardware intrusion.[5]

The Cyberspace Policy Review conducted by President Obama early in his
administration put the problem this way: "Counterfeit products have created
the most visible supply problems, but few documented examples exist of un-
ambiguous, deliberate subversions. . . . The challenge with supply chain attacks
is that a sophisticated adversary might narrowly focus on particular systems
and make manipulation virtually impossible to discover."[6] Or, as the Defense
Science Board (a science review team reporting to the Secretary of Defense)
opined in 2007: "The current systems designs, assurance methodologies, acquisition procedures, and knowledge of adversarial capabilities and intentions
are inadequate to the magnitude of the threat."[7]

The situation has changed little since these reports were issued. For this
reason, the Comprehensive National Cybersecurity Initiative (CNCI) (first
issued in 2008 and released in declassified form in 2010) identified "global
supply chain risk management" as one of the initiatives critical to enhanced
cybersecurity.[8] Yet, the United States has a very limited set of systems and

processes in place to respond to this challenge. Indeed, there is a disconnect between our counter-intelligence, which is often aware of risks to our cyber supply chain, and our procurement processes, which cannot have access to classified information regarding supply chain threats. Setting aside intelligence concerns, the prospect of creating a black list of unacceptable products for purchase is fraught with problematic issues regarding liability and fidelity. And, even if we could devise a means of giving the procurement process access to sufficient information and if liability issues could be overcome, it might well be the case that no significant alternative sources of supply exist.

Nor, of course, is the problem limited to the government (though that will be our focus in this chapter)—it applies to private-sector systems too. Consider the following: in April 2012 it was announced that a Canadian company that makes equipment and software for critical industrial control systems had planted a backdoor login account in its flagship operating system, potentially allowing attackers to access the devices online. The backdoor, which cannot be disabled, is found in all versions of the Rugged Operating System made by RuggedCom. The login credentials for the backdoor include a static username, "factory," that was assigned by the vendor and can not be changed by customers. Using the backdoor, Rugged can access their customers' systems for maintenance, but a malicious actor can, likewise, access the system if it knows the access information.[9] In short, the problems relating to hardware intrusions in the chips of our systems are some of the most wickedly difficult to address; we have no solutions, only approximations of slightly better practices. It's a dim prospect, but that is the reality.

WHERE WE ARE TODAY

At present, there are only two notable structures in operation within the U.S. government that provide a means of addressing supply chain security issues—and neither is particularly adept or well suited to the task.

One is the Committee on Foreign Investment in the United States (CFIUS). CFIUS is an inter-agency committee authorized to review transactions that could result in control of a U.S. business by a foreign person (known as covered transactions), in order to determine the effect of such transactions on the national security of the United States.[10] If CFIUS determines that the proposed transaction poses a risk of some sort, it may prohibit the transaction altogether or, far more frequently, it may enter into a mitigation agreement that puts in place mechanisms and requirements that it deems necessary to ameliorate the risk. Though CFIUS was initially created to focus on the sale of companies that would result in foreign control of defense-critical industries, in the post-9/11 world it has come, as well, to focus on sales that will effect critical infrastructure (such as the now-infamous sale of port facilities to Dubai

Ports World). This focus has, on at least one publicly acknowledged occasion, involved the review of a purchase that implicated cybersecurity concerns.[11]

Likewise, an interagency working group known as Team Telecom reviews questions relating to the acquisition of an ownership interest in American telecommunications companies by foreign interests. The Federal Communications Commission has statutory authority to review transactions where a foreign entity seeks to purchase more than a 25 percent indirect ownership stake in U.S. common carriers licensed by the FCC. When such a transaction is proposed, the FCC will, as a matter of policy, defer to the Executive Branch and coordinate the application with the Executive Branch for national security, law enforcement, foreign policy, or trade concerns. The applications are referred to Team Telecom, which is co-chaired by staff from the Department of Homeland Security and the Department of Justice, including the FBI, and which also includes representatives from the Departments of Commerce, Defense, State, and Treasury, and the Office of the United States Trade Representative. Based on its review, Team Telecom may have no comment on an application or may request that the FCC condition the grant of the application on compliance with assurances made by the applicant in either an exchange of letters or a formal security agreement. In this way, as well, the U.S. government will on occasion have a process in place for addressing cyber assurance concerns that result from the foreign purchase (note that both processes are limited to the acquisition of ownership interests) of an interest in a cyber-related industry.[12]

In recent years, a number of *ad hoc* working groups have sprung up to consider the COTS challenge. Many of them operate in a classified environment. A recent survey by the co-chair of the ABA Information Security Committee identified no fewer than five separate industry and federal initiatives.[13] The most notable are two recent data-collection initiatives documenting the extent to which counterfeits infiltrate our supply chain: a recently completed study by the Department of Commerce, which documented the prevalence of counterfeit parts in the Navy's IT supply chain,[14] and ongoing pilots within the CNCI, Task 11, collecting detailed data on vendors, components, product integration, and deployment of cyber products within DoD and DHS.[15]

THE REALITY OF THE THREAT

If you ask counter-intelligence experts which they fear more, American vulnerability to an external cyber attack or the potential compromise of the operation of the hardware innards of our computers and Internet switches, they almost certainly will say that the hardware threat is more challenging. The globalization of production for both hardware and software makes it virtually impossible to provide either supply chain or product assurance.[16]

The vulnerability is made acute by the fact that the U.S. government (and the private sector) have come to rely on COTS technology. These COTS technologies have many obvious advantages. They are generally cheaper than custom-built proprietary solutions and, because they are produced in the private sector, they are modified and upgraded more rapidly in a manner that is far more consistent with the current technology life cycle. Particularly in the cyber realm, where upgrades occur with increasing frequency, reliance on COTS allows government and the private sector to field the most modern equipment possible.

One example of the COTS phenomenon, as recounted by an International Telecommunications Union workshop, will serve as an example: "In the mid-1980's, the DoD mandated the use of the ADA programming language. ADA never gained popularity in the commercial sector, which used programming language evolved from [more common commercial] programs such as Cobal and Fortran to C and C++. While ADA was optimized for real time and rapid conversion of analog to digital information, much faster microprocessors and digital sensors circumvented most of these advantages."[17] As a consequence, ADA fell into disuse and the DoD systems moved away from their specially designed, noncommercial programming language to a commonly available commercial one. But, in doing so, the United States adopted a structure that was vulnerable to the same types of attacks and hacking as commercial systems. The vulnerabilities that come from running commercial operating systems on most government computers would not exist in the same way if our computers operated on a noncommercial system.[18]

This is equally true for our hardware purchases. Because COTS systems have an open architecture design (that is, broadly speaking, a structure that is readily open to plug and play hardware additions, and modifications), few of them have integrated security architecture. Increasingly, knowledge of the design of the systems and their manufacture is outsourced to overseas production. We therefore live in a world where a significant fraction of the innards of our computers are manufactured overseas, often in plants located in peer-competitor nation-states.[19] Likewise, much of the service of existing systems is conducted overseas.

THE CHALLENGE AHEAD

A process for dealing with these vulnerabilities is by no means clear. It is unlikely that the U.S. government and private sector will return to a time when all of its systems were "made in the USA." Doing so would be prohibitively expensive and would forego a substantial fraction of the economic benefits to be derived from the globalization of the world's economy.

A "made in the USA" response would not eliminate the COTS problem, as even hardware constructed in the United States could be built with malicious intent. However, the origin of hardware components may create a significant difference in the nature of the problem. For U.S.-built components, the threat is in the nature of an insider threat, and we can have reasonable confidence that the quality control and security processes of the U.S.-domiciled manufacturer are intended to negate that threat, rather than foster it. For non-U.S. companies, the same will often be true, at least for components manufactured in countries that take an equivalent approach to hardware assurance.

But, we may sometimes have less confidence in the efficacy of those processes in countries where quality control and security are less well-developed. Even more troubling, we may sometimes reasonably doubt whether the company's processes are truly designed to achieve those goals or whether the intent works at cross-purposes with America's interests. It is significantly more difficult for the inspection processes of the purchaser to provide for hardware or software assurance than it is for those of the manufacturer.[20]

And so, though the continued purchase of COTS from a globalized supply chain is inevitable, it would be inappropriate to disregard the threat posed by the foreign origin of much of our hardware. And, notably, the risk is not posed simply by the hardware purchases we make. Many of the service functions that our cyber domain requires are also procured from foreign providers. The commonplace chestnut is the complaint that all of the helplines are answered in India, but the far more significant fact is that many of the repair and maintenance services used for our cybersystems are also provided by foreign suppliers—and so the risk is not just that we purchase hardware from overseas sources but that we rely on those same sources for much of our operational repair and maintenance capacity.

The CNCI recognized this vulnerability with its initiative to "develop a multi-pronged approach for global supply chain risk management." But, "multi-pronged approach" is often code for "this is a very big problem that we don't have a handle on." Thus, it is somewhat distressing (though utterly unsurprising) that the CNCI initiative to address this problem consists of little more than anodyne platitudes: "This initiative will enhance Federal Government skills, policies, and processes to provide departments and agencies with a robust toolset to better manage and mitigate supply chain risk at levels commensurate with the criticality of, and risks to, their systems and networks."[21] Far more concrete action is necessary, perhaps, even action that is moderately intrusive on the free flow of globalized commerce.

INTELLIGENCE AND COTS

One possible answer to the COTS problem might be better intelligence collection. After all, if NSA or the CIA were able to glean, from their sources, information about potential hardware intrusions, that would be a good thing—or so it would seem. Unfortunately, the complexity of how to get that information (some of which may already exist) to government consumers has, so far, prevented us from taking effective action.

The problem is both a legal one and a practical one. For one thing, there are always issues that arise when we consider disclosing of the results of the government's intelligence analysis—we risk revealing our own sources and methods. This will have practical saliency when we examine questions of supply chain security (or, more accurately, insecurity). Disclosing concerns in such a public way ("don't buy that computer") will plainly paint a picture of what the government knows.

In addition, while the government may be in a position to say that the risk from a purchase is high, there are no guarantees—and that creates ambiguity for the private sector and procurement officers. How then to respond to an inquiry from a domestic company that is also considering a systems purchase—especially, say, an inquiry from a company that provides support to the U.S. defense or intelligence communities through its own manufacturing? Under current law, if such a company inquires as to the government's knowledge about a supplier, the unfortunate answer they must receive is "we can't tell you."

The intelligence community has no authority to create, in effect, a blacklist of suspect suppliers in the supply chain. In any event, the effort would create all sorts of potential liability questions: How certain are you? How often must you update or modify your assessment (and what would be the resource commitment to do so)? In short, the intelligence community can, and does, share such concerns within the U.S. government but is presently legally disabled from disseminating the same information to critical private-sector stakeholders. This is one legal area that clearly requires work.

SOME THOUGHTS ON A WAY FORWARD

We need to give more concerted attention to the problems posed by the insecurity of our supply chain. Our current system (which, in a very limited way, reviews threats to our supply chain in some situations where a foreign entity takes corporate control of a critical systems manufacturer) plainly does not serve (and was not intended to serve) so broad a purpose. It is safe to say that under the current CNCI initiatives the U.S. government is still in the information gathering stage as it seeks to assess the scope of the problem and devise a workable set of solutions.

Recent recommendations for addressing the COTS problem reflect the difficulties that face us in devising a comprehensive solution. As the Defense Science Board recognized (and, indeed, recommended), the U.S. government will continue to purchase commercial goods for use.[22] It simply is untenable to suppose that the United States will ever forgo the economic benefits of a globalized purchasing system. Yet, such a system inherently carries with it the risks associated with the offshore production of goods and services critical to an infrastructure.

But, strategies to eliminate the risk are nonexistent and those required to mitigate it seem to be mostly nibbling around the edges. The Defense Science Board, for example, recommends:

- increased intelligence efforts to understand adversarial intentions;
- allocation of assurance resources on a prioritized basis to missions whose failure would have the greatest impact;
- better quality DoD software (to make malicious attacks more readily observable);
- development of better assurance tools and programs;
- better knowledge of suppliers' processes and trustworthiness; and
- a robust research agenda.[23]

Likewise, the Department of Commerce, Office of Technology Evaluation, recommends relatively modest steps:

- creation of a centralized counterfeit reporting database;
- clarification of the Federal Acquisition Regulations to allow a best value purchase of IT components;
- federal guidance to industry on the scope of criminal and civil liability for dealing with counterfeits and responsibility for reporting to the federal government;
- broader law enforcement investigations of counterfeit activities;
- federal leadership in disseminating best practices to industry;
- international agreements to limit the flow of counterfeit technology; and
- better lifecycle planning to reduce the need to rely on problematic and unreliable vendors.[24]

The reality, however, is that these steps will not eliminate the risk to cyber assurance posed by the use of commercial systems. The dispersed nature of the cyber domain only serves to exacerbate the international character of the problem and render it seemingly insoluble. To supplement the ongoing CNCI Task 11 initiatives, America needs to charter a broad-based study program (perhaps through the National Academies of Science) focused exclusively on the problem of COTS and supply chain security. Developing a comprehensive risk mitigation plan is both essential and, likely, the best that can be achieved.[25] As the Cyberspace Policy Review put it, "[a] broad, holistic approach to risk management is required rather than a wholesale condemnation of foreign products and services."

Here are a few suggestions for additional steps that do not, thus far, appear to have been actively considered:[26]

- We should consider expanding governmental review authorities to include situations where foreign entities take control of service activities that affect the cyber domain, or where foreign influence is achieved without purchasing full control (as in, say, a lease arrangement). Neither of these situations falls within the current domain of CFIUS or Team Telecom—yet the threat is no different whether Cisco's router production system is purchased by a foreign entity or all service for the routers is provided by that same foreign entity.
- We should also consider actions that would diversify the types of hardware and software systems that are used within the cyber domain. Such a diversification would, in effect, create a herd immunity against attack by malicious actors through both software and hardware intrusions.[27] For federal actors (and other governmental actors), creating herd immunity might be as simple as changing the Federal Acquisition Regulations to require product purchasing diversity.
- If we, in fact, believe that a monoculture of having a single major supplier is a problem for the federal government, it would, a fortiori, be a problem for the private sector. One can conceive of a more stringent enforcement of the antitrust laws to compel a diversification of operating systems in the private sector.
- Perhaps most saliently, major federal hardware purchases need to change their procurement rules so that they systematically evaluate the security of the products provided by their suppliers. These evaluations ought to encompass a wide range of factors: Who owns the company? Who manages it? What is its physical security like? How often does it audit its own products for defects and/or tampering? These are detailed questions of minutiae to be sure, but asking these sorts of questions is the only way to reduce the risk of hardware intrusions across the board. And, if well conceived, federal procurement standards would drive private sector standardization as well.

To be sure, these suggestions are moderately controversial. Yet, it seems self-evident that in the absence of concerted action the potential vulnerability posed by the reliance on COTS will not be alleviated. But, the hard truth is equally discomfiting. For as long as the purchase of hardware products occurs on the global market (which is to say, for the foreseeable future and beyond), there will be a significant risk of hardware intrusion. That risk can never be eliminated. It can only be managed and reduced.

Part III

Enduring Questions

Sometimes the best way to approach a problem is to step back and ask bigger, more fundamental questions. Up until now, this book has looked at the question of cyber conflict from a relatively narrow perspective of "what is?" What is our encryption policy? What is the problem with COTS purchase? And, what is our best response to those problems?

In Part III, we will try and reverse the lens and ask "what ought?" What ought to be the role of the government in the cyber domain? What do first principles tell us about how the government should be organized? Or, about the role of international institutions?

This approach is avowedly more theoretical and normative (though we still do a lot of describing). Because, when you come right down to it, the cyber domain is an artificial construct. Unlike the land, sea, or air around us, it is not naturally occurring. Humans built it—initially in the image of a gee-whiz technological marvel to help with scientific research and today, increasingly, in the image of a critical (dare we say, indispensable) part of our society and culture. On the Internet today, you can rally a political protest or consult a doctor. You can order shoes or divorce your spouse. You can chat with friends about your common interest in Civil War minutiae or read the front page of a newspaper published half-way around the world.

In this human-constructed domain, we are capable of ordering our responses in ways that aren't driven by the mandates of nature. We know what a ship looks like because it can only look like one broadly defined thing if it is to function. In cyberspace, on the other hand, we can build what we will—and so it is worth asking what we want.

The first two chapters of Part III look at this question from the perspective of economic theory—what do fundamental economic principles tell us about the optimal role of the government and its relationship to the private sector? In the third chapter, chapter 16, we flip that around and ask about the idealized vision of how the private sector can, and should, protect itself.

The next two chapters (17 and 18) look at the government itself and those organizations that have grown up in America over the past 30 years to deal with the cyber domain. Having asked the broad question about the government's best function, we puzzle out how and why the government is the way it actually is—and whether or not that's the right structure to have.

In the last chapter of Part III, we return to a fundamental theme—that the Internet knows no borders—and look at the implications this has for international approaches to Internet governance and cyber conflict between nations. Sadly, this view is a bit of a dim one, as the prospects for effective international approaches to the problems of cyber conflict are not, to put it delicately, very robust.

14
Chapter

The Economics of Cybersecurity

As we have already seen, in January 2010 Google released disturbing news: It had been the subject of a "highly sophisticated and targeted attack" that had originated in China, resulting in the "theft of intellectual property" from Google. The attacks seemed to be targeted at Chinese human rights activists. And, Google was not alone. At least 20 other major companies, spanning sectors including the Internet, finance, and the chemical industry were also targeted.[1] At its core, the attack apparently attempted to corrupt some of Google's source code.

Though the attribution of responsibility for cyber intrusions is notoriously difficult to accomplish, there seems to be little doubt that official Chinese authorities were behind the attack. Indeed, one of the classified State Department cables released by WikiLeaks reports that the operation was authorized by the Politburo Standing Committee,[2] the rough equivalent in authority of America's National Security Council. The intrusion seems, therefore, to be of a piece with China's notorious efforts to maintain control over Internet access by its citizens and is, in many ways, unsurprising.

Far more surprising, however, was the next disclosure about Google: that it had turned to the National Security Agency (NSA) for help.[3] Google sought to take advantage of the NSA's expertise in information assurance. In other words, it wanted the NSA to help it evaluate the vulnerabilities in its hardware and software and assess how advanced the intruders were. Using NSA expertise, Google would have a better understanding of how its systems were penetrated. Google, in turn, would share with the NSA any information it had about the precise nature of the malware code that was used to corrupt its system.

This cooperation agreement between Google and NSA is notable for a number of reasons. First, note the fact that Google turned to the NSA for assistance and not to the Department of Homeland Security (DHS), which has the nominal responsibility for assisting in the protection of private sector infrastructure. Second, the more fundamentally transformative aspect of the agreement is that Google looked to anyone in government at all for assistance.

Google's business model is controversial in Silicon Valley. But, whatever one thinks of their commercial approach, nobody doubts their technical expertise. Google, along with other major cyber actors such as Facebook and PayPal, service providers like Verizon, and software manufacturers like Microsoft, is at the cutting edge of cyber innovations. Yet, even with that deep and sophisticated base of knowledge, Google was compelled to seek governmental assistance.

Informally, private sector leaders in the IT/Telecoms space often say they don't need anything from the government.[4] Indeed, their repeated refrain is that government involvement will simply stifle innovation rather than foster security. That argument has (as we shall see) great appeal. Yet, one of the most sophisticated players in the entire domain, Google, turned to the government for help. What does that say about the desirability of public/private cooperation in cybersecurity?

From the government's perspective, the need for robust and effective cooperation seems self-evident. It is a commonplace to note that 85–90 percent of the cyber infrastructure is owned and operated by private entities. (Though, notably, no authoritative source for this figure can be found.[5]) Most government cyber traffic travels on nongovernmental cybersystems. Those systems, in turn, are used to control or communicate with a host of other critical infrastructures—the transportation system, the electric grid, the financial markets, and the like. Thus, core national security functions of command, control, communications, and continuity are all dependent, to greater or lesser degrees, on the resilience of the private sector networks. With that context, the federal government must, it seems, be deeply concerned with private sector cybersecurity.

And yet, public and private actors often do not coordinate well together. The challenge for the federal government is how to integrate its efforts with those of the private sector. To date, the results have been less than stellar, at least in part because of private sector resistance to the concept.

What is the nature of public/private cooperation in cyberspace? Why does it work the way it does? To understand the nature of public sector/private sector cooperation, we must understand the fundamental economics that drive cybersecurity. Only then can we understand the nature of the government's role in providing for a common defense, and the government's ability to regulate the cyber domain and control externalities.

AN INTRODUCTION TO THE ECONOMIC THEORY OF CYBERSECURITY

In considering the appropriate scope for government intervention, it is useful to examine basic principles and consider a theoretical model of when governmental activity is warranted. This is not to say, of course, that the theoretical model governs our decision making; but it often serves as a useful guidepost for examining the question. And, to be sure, what this chapter has to say on the topic is not novel—but a brief review is in order.[6]

As a matter of theory and of ideological commitment (born of the independence inherent in the foundations of the Internet), most private sector leaders will tell you that there is no need for much, if any, government assistance in the cybersecurity market. All they require, they will tell you, is for the government to enable the sharing of more information by clarifying legal uncertainties (described more fully in the next chapter) and then get out of the way. A closer examination of the theoretical argument suggests, however, that there is some significant room for governmental engagement and, indeed, it explains, partially, why Google went to the NSA. The theory runs something like this:

A public good is a good that is both nonrivalrous and nonexclusive.[7] These are technical terms in economics, but their meaning is actually relatively easy to understand: To be nonrivalrous means that use of the good by one person does not affect its use by others. An example of a nonrivalrous good would be a movie theater showing—the fact that I am watching the movie doesn't affect whether or not you can watch it (though, if I don't turn off my cell phone, perhaps that is untrue!). Similarly, to be nonexclusive means that the availability of the good to one person means that it is also available to every other person. An example here might be a fishing ground in international waters—anyone who has a boat can go and fish. Note that these two examples show how the concepts of rivalry and exclusivity are different. A movie theater is exclusive (since you can limit who gets in) and a fishing ground is rivalrous (since if I over-fish the ground then there are no fish for anyone else).

Public goods are relatively rare things. Everyone can use them and use by one person doesn't affect how others use them. The classic example of a public good is national defense. The enjoyment of defense services provided to protect one citizen does not affect the protection enjoyed by another citizen (we all benefit equally), and defense services provided to one citizen are enjoyed by all other citizens (everyone is defended if one is). The opposite of public goods is, of course, private goods (like, say, a shoe). These cannot be used by more than one person (at least, at the same time!) and their use by one person affects potential uses by others (see Table 14.1).

Public goods are, typically, beset by two problems—free riders and assurance. Free rider problems arise when an individual hopes to reap the benefits

Table 14.1 Public Goods, Private Goods, and Cybersecurity Products

	Nonrivalrous (Use by A does not affect use by B)	Rivalrous (use by A affects use by B)
Nonexclusive (Use by A does not prevent use by B)	*Public Goods* National Defense Clean Air Cybersecurity Threat Information	*Common Pool Goods* Fishing Grounds Parks Early Internet (?)
Exclusive (Use by A prevents use by B)	*Club Goods* Private Club Movie Theater Secure Network	*Private Goods* Shoes Automobiles Cybersecurity Firewalls and Intrusion Detection Systems

of a public good but refuses to contribute to its creation because he thinks others will do so even absent his participation. For example, if I thought that the government would provide for a police service no matter what I did, it would be in my own best interests to try and get the police services without paying any taxes. The assurance problem is the opposite side of the coin and exists when people refuse to invest in the production of a public good because they believe there will never be enough cooperative investment to produce the good and, thus, that the investment would be futile. If we are thinking about setting up a police service, I won't put money into it unless and until I'm convinced that enough of my fellow citizens will also put money into it to make it worth my while.

The classic solution to this conundrum is governmental intervention. When a public good is viewed as necessary but cooperation is unavailing, the government coerces its citizens to cooperate through taxation or some other mandate and provides the public good. Paying taxes for national defense (or police) isn't optional. We've formed a government to make it mandatory.

So, what is cybersecurity? Is it a public good that the government should provide? Or, is it a private good—something that we can count on the private sector to create? The answer helps to define what a good public/private partnership would look like. Unfortunately, the answer is not a simple yes or no conclusion. It turns out that some parts of cybersecurity are better provided by the government, while others are better provided by private companies.

Security Information as a Public Good

Security in cyberspace, like physical security in the kinetic world, is a market good. People will pay for it and pay quite a bit. But, as in the real world, security in cyberspace isn't just one product. Instead, it is a bundle of products and services, some of which operate independently and others of which act only in combination. These goods are purchased in an effort to protect networks, hardware, data in transit, and stored data from theft, destruction, disruption, or delay.[8]

Since many products are involved, it isn't surprising to realize that you can buy them from many different sources. Just as some security in the physical world can be purchased directly in the private market, so too in cyberspace, many security systems (e.g., anti-virus software and intrusion detection systems from Symantec) are private goods, bought and sold by private companies. These products actually meet the formal definition of a private good since Symantec can control who uses them and sell them exclusively to clients. Indeed, evidence from the financial sector suggests that cybersecurity is to a very large degree a private good, adequately provided by the private sector.[9]

There is, however, one aspect of the bundle of cybersecurity products that appears to be a public good—threat and vulnerability information about new and evolving cyber intrusions.[10] That sort of information is a classic public good. It can be given to one person to use without affecting how another might use it and everyone can use the information when it is made available. This public good–like nature of information about cyber threats and vulnerabilities helps to explain the substantial focus of many on the laws and regulations regarding information sharing; our legal mechanisms haven't adequately captured the nature of the information being shared and are thought to be an impediment to the wide distribution of this public good, rather than enhancing that activity. It also explains, at least partially, why Google might look to the NSA for assistance. They seek a public good, namely, information about threats to their systems.

This way of thinking about cybersecurity information is also consistent with our understanding of the incentives that are likely to drive the decision by any individual or company considering whether or not to disclose the information about threats and vulnerabilities in its system. There are a host of reasons why private sector actors are very reluctant to make such disclosures (especially of vulnerabilities). These include risk of loss of reputation and trust, risk of liability and indemnification claims, negative effects on financial markets, signals of weakness to adversaries, and risks to job security and individual career goals.[11] Treating information as a public good tends to overcome these factors and to recognize that, at an individual actor level, the private market for information may not work as well as we would like it to.

Private Good, with Externalities

But, what about the private sector's claim that it doesn't need any government assistance at all (except, perhaps, for better threat and warning information)? Even here, economic theory suggests there might be a role for government, though in this case we might be a bit cautious about getting too enthusiastic. It turns out that government intervention may do more harm than good—even if it might be theoretically warranted.

Even if cybersecurity is a private good, often the sale of private goods causes public harms—what economists call an externality. The technical definition of an externality is when the activity between two economic actors may directly and unintentionally modify a third-party's cost–benefit analysis.[12] The practical definition is that something I do privately, affects you. A classic example might be if I keep a dog in my house—his barking disrupts your sleep and that's an externality. These external effects can be either negative (if my dog keeps you from sleeping) or positive (if he protects the entire neighborhood from burglars).[13]

ZERO-DAY EXPLOITS

Should anyone doubt that there is a true private market in cybersecurity (albeit one with significant externalities), consider the market in zero-day exploits (that is, previously unknown vulnerabilities). Cyber hacker entrepreneurs expend great intellectual capital in discovering these exploits and marketing them on the black market. Truly unique and unusual zero-day exploits can sell for as much as $50,000. There is even a royalty provision in some sales where the discoverer gets a continuing payment for as long as the vulnerability remains unpatched.

But perhaps the oddest aspect of the market is this: the market isn't limited to malicious actors. It has been reported that the U.S. government (through the NSA) often buys zero-day exploits from discoverers and may pay over six-figure amounts for the product.

Many cybersecurity activities have positive external effects. By securing my own server or laptop against intrusion, for example, I benefit others on the network since my computer cannot be hijacked, say, into a botnet and used to attack other people. Indeed, almost every security measure performed on any part of cyberspace improves the overall level of cybersecurity by raising the costs of attack.[14]

But, cybersecurity also has negative external effects, in two ways. The first is a diversion effect: Methods of protection, such as firewalls, have the effect of diverting attacks from one target to another; making improvements in one actor's security equivalent to a decrease in security for systems that are not as well-protected (even though that owner has not sought to increase his or her own vulnerability).[15] If I have a really good intrusion detection system and you don't, guess who the hackers go after.

The second negative effect is a pricing problem that reflects the failure of the private market. Sometimes, the price of a product doesn't have all of the costs of the product built in. A typical example is air pollution, where the long-term costs from adding carbon to the atmosphere (whatever they may be—I'm taking no side in the global warming debate here) aren't part of the cost of the car or of the gasoline used to drive it. When costs like that aren't included in the price of a product, the product is too cheap and somebody else ends up paying the costs in the end.

The costs of cybersecurity failures are like that. When software fails to prevent an intrusion or a service provider fails to interdict a malware attack, Microsoft and Verizon don't bear the expense of fixing the problem. Instead, the end user who owns the computer pays the costs (to clean his machine, or recover his stolen identity). In general (there are a few exceptions), no mechanism exists by which the software manufacturer or ISP can be made responsible for the costs of those failures. In this way, security for the broader system of the entire Internet is a classic market externality whose true costs are not adequately recognized in the prices charged and costs experienced by individual actors.

Recognizing that cybersecurity can have both positive and negative external effects can be confusing and poses a significant policy challenge. Either circumstance suggests a role for government. But, identifying which factor predominates is essential, since the characterization will point to differing policy directions. Private goods that cause positive externalities are typically subsidized. Not enough of the good exists and we want to encourage investment. By contrast, private goods that cause negative externalities are taxed, regulated, or subjected to a liability regime. We want less of the good or we want the producers to internalize the external costs and reduce the level of production to one commensurate with its true costs.

That doesn't end the problem, because the government is itself an economic actor—and sometimes it makes mistakes too. There are two reasons to be skeptical of the government's engagement in the private sector's provision of cybersecurity. First, as with any governmental interference in the marketplace, there are good reasons to doubt the ability of the government to systematically make the right choices. In a perfect world, experts could tell us the right answer, but in the real world sometimes the answer we get to is defined more by lobbyists and influence than by analysis. We call this sort of problem rent-seeking behavior, and it often adversely affects decision making.[16] We have good reason to be concerned that the subsidies, taxes, and regulations enacted will not foster the right result, but rather the result that concerted lobbying efforts favor (think, for example, of the ethanol subsidies that have been around for years even though everyone knows they are not a good investment). This concern is not unique to the cyber arena. It happens whenever government regulates and those who are affected seek economic advantage. But, the problem is no less real just because it is common.

Second, and more uniquely an aspect of cybersecurity, the pace at which transformations happen has increased exponentially. This has the impact of hastening technological changes. But, the government makes policy through slow-moving hierarchical decision-making structures. It takes too long for laws and regulations to be passed, and by the time they are passed they are out of date. As one expert, put it: "The attackers are two years ahead of the defenders, security vendors, who are two years ahead of market, which is two years ahead of compliance, and legislation is five years behind that. . . . [Legislatively mandated cyber security] practices may be even more stale once enacted. It's unlikely the law could ever keep pace, given the glacial pace of legislation."[17] In short, our policy making apparatus can't turn inside the cyberspace innovation radius. Or, as one colleague has put it, the government is using a Ford sedan policy making system to manage the cyberspace Porsche system.[18]

So, even though we recognize that some government regulation of cybersecurity may be necessary as a result of the externalities that exist, we should have a deep skepticism of the capacity of the government to exercise that authority in a timely manner that successfully deals with the problems. Put bluntly, by the time a notice and comment rulemaking has taken place, the technology at issue will likely have been made obsolete. Indeed, in the time it typically takes to write a federal rule, under Moore's law the average speed of computer processors doubles; the law is chasing technology and can never catch up.

Self-Governing Structures

So the government might be able to help, but it has structural reasons for being a poor choice. How about the private sector? Can it police itself and set up rules without government intervention to take care of the external effects?

Probably not. Some scholars have suggested that it is possible. They've argued that cyberspace is what we call a common pool resource.[19] Common pool resources are ones, like a fishing ground or an unfenced field, where the exclusion of users is difficult and use of the good or resource effects other users. You can't keep ships out of a fishing ground and fishing by one person diminishes the availability of the fish to someone else. It is reasonable to argue that the physical bandwidth and servers that make up the Internet may well be, precisely, such a common resource.[20]

In some limited circumstances, the users of common pool resources can self-organize and act collectively to govern their use.[21] One well-known example of this involves the collective regulation of lobster catches by the lobstermen of Maine, where all of the lobstermen got together and shared the lobster catch equitably.[22] But, this type of self-governance only works when everyone using the resource knows all the other users. In that case, where the number of users is relatively small, there are high social and reputational costs for violating social norms. If a lobsterman cheats on his catch limit, his friends will know and he will become a social outcast. While that may have described the Internet at the dawn of the computer age (the first network had only four nodes on it!), it hardly describes the cyber domain today. At this point, cyberspace is so diffuse that a truly successful self-governing structure is hard to imagine. The resource is too large, there are too many users, and the dynamics of its governance are highly unpredictable.

There are some who suggest that the Internet's capacity for collaborative work (sometimes known as crowdsourcing) makes it different. They point to the success of Wikipedia as an example of successful self-organization enabled by the interconnectedness of the Internet. This is intriguing, in theory, but has yet to produce many practical cybersecurity successes.[23]

Finally, economic theory also points to one other possible answer to the problem of cybersecurity—a solution sometimes known as club goods. These are resources (like a club room or a movie theater) from which some users may be excluded but where access is controlled such that the resources are nonrivalrous (that is, not effected by other users). In the cyberspace context, this would be the equivalent of creating a walled garden domain with a limited number of users, the way AOL once did. Unfortunately, while this result may work for limited special purpose domains (like the U.S. government's classified networks), it is almost self-contradictory as a general matter. A limited Internet not connected to the World Wide Web is no Internet at all.

* * *

In sum, there are certain aspects of the security problem (most notably, security information) that can, probably, be fairly characterized as public goods—and for these a governmental role is pretty clear. But, the remaining security goods are either private goods with recognized externalities (and grave challenges of government regulation) or common pool resources (with equally grave challenges of private sector coordination). For these later categories of goods, devising an appropriate public policy is truly a "wicked problem."[24]

15
Chapter

The Role of Government Regulating the Private Sector

Now that we have a good understanding of the economics of cybersecurity, we are better positioned to ask questions about the role of the government in providing cybersecurity. The theoretical model helps to explain, for example, why a significant fraction of the policy debate about cybersecurity and public/private partnerships revolves around the challenge of effective security information sharing. Because threat and vulnerability information may have the characteristics of a public good, it is in society's interests to foster their creation and distribution.

The information in question will relate, broadly speaking, either to specific threats from external actors (for example, knowledge from an insider that an intrusion is planned) or to specific vulnerabilities (as, for example, the identification of a particular security gap in a particular piece of software). In both situations, the evidence of the threat or vulnerability can come in one of two forms: either nonpersonalized information related to changes in types of activity on the network, or personalized information about the actions of a specific individual or group of individuals.[1] Needless to say, the use by the government of Personally Identifiable Information (PII) in the second category is of greater concern to civil libertarians than the sharing of network traffic information.[2]

It is often said that existing legal restrictions prevent the private sector from effectively creating cybersecurity. Some of these restrictions are said to relate to the inability of the government to adequately share threat information with the private sector. Other restrictions are said to limit how the private sector shares information with the government or amongst itself. If this were true—if existing laws restrained and restricted either of these—that would be a policy dissonance. On closer examination, however, the truth is more nuanced. Many of these legal limitations appear to be less constricting than they are perceived to be. In the end, what really restricts cooperation are the inherent caution of lawyers who do not want to push the envelope of legal authority and/or policy and economic factors that limit the desire to cooperate.

But even caution has a cost, which is why in August 2012 Congress considered (but rejected) a bill to clarify the law and incentivize information sharing. Having failed to change the law, however, we are left to reflect on the ambiguities in the current legal structure.

INFORMATION SHARING FROM THE GOVERNMENT TO THE PRIVATE SECTOR

Some suggest that the principal barriers to an effective public/private partnership in combating cyber threats are limitations on the ability of the government to share threat and vulnerability information with the private sector. Sometimes (perhaps often) the government has collected this information using sources and methods that are classified, and disclosure of the information risks a compromise of those sources and methods. Less frequently, the existence of the threat or vulnerability is itself classified information since disclosure of its existence or scope might adversely affect security. If this were true—if the government really knew something that could protect the private sector networks, but laws prevented that information from being shared—that would be a serious disconnect between law and reality.

Thankfully, it isn't likely that this is what is happening. For the most part, these problems are ones of policy, rather than law. No legal barrier exists preventing the government from giving members of the private sector the required security clearances; it is simply a matter of inadequate resources. Likewise, though the private sector complains that the alert information it gets from the government is late and slow in coming, the untimeliness in the process is more the product of the need for internal review and the government's insistence on accuracy over timeliness than it is of any legal barrier to sharing. And, indeed, this policy choice may be the right one, since inaccuracy will erode governmental credibility, but that cannot gainsay its adverse collateral effect of inefficacy.

As Google's request for assistance to the NSA demonstrates, there are plainly situations in which company-specific assistance can be rendered by the government. Indeed, the Google experience is in the midst of being generalized. Recently, the Department of Defense announced the continuation of the pilot project described earlier for sharing threat signature information with ISPs who, in turn, use that information to protect the systems of private corporations that are part of the Defense Industrial Base (DIB).[3] This pilot program is voluntary and involves only the one-way transfer of information from the government to the private sector—a structure that alleviates most, if not all, of the legal concerns about government surveillance activities.[4] More broadly, the Obama Administration's draft cybersecurity legislation would codify authority for DHS to provide assistance to the private sector on request.[5] At the bottom, then, these problems are not likely to be ones of law, but rather, ones of commitment.

PRIVATE-TO-PRIVATE AND PRIVATE-TO-GOVERNMENT SHARING

Consider next, the privacy laws that are often said to limit the ability of the private sector to cooperate with the government or amongst itself. Here, again, if the law prohibited the private sector from giving threat information to the government or if it prohibited Verizon from sharing threat and vulnerability information with Sprint, that would be a significant problem. But, again, the problems are less about the law than about caution.

Two portions of the Electronic Communications Privacy Act (ECPA),[6] Title I relating to wiretapping (sometimes spoken of as an amendment to the Wiretap Act)[7] and Title II relating to the privacy of electronic communications (often called the Stored Communications Act [SCA]),[8] are applicable. These laws were created to protect privacy and to impose checks and balances on law enforcement access to private citizens' communications. As such, they serve important public policy goals.

But, it is equally true that the laws are of old vintage. Passed initially in 1986, they were largely drafted to address issues relating to the telephone network, and, it is fair to say, have yet to be fully modernized to come to grips with today's Internet-based communications technologies. Some ISPs argue that the ambiguous nature of the laws and their applicability prevent them from acting to protect their customers and networks by making it legally uncertain whether or not they can use certain communications information to protect consumers and/or share certain information voluntarily with the government for the purposes of cybersecurity.

The arguments for ambiguity are, however, somewhat overstated. Both laws have exceptions reasonably related to the protection of service provider networks.[9] Thus, the seeming uncertainty attending the law is rather overblown. There is, however, a residual question, and the source of the ambiguity lies in the scope and frequency of the information sharing at issue.

The law permits a tailored approach, that is, one of limited scope, reasonably related to the cybersecurity threat. It may not necessarily be read to authorize ongoing or routine disclosure of traffic information by the private sector to any governmental entity. To interpret them so broadly might be inconsistent with the promise of privacy that undergirds the Wiretap Act and SCA. Yet, routine sharing may be precisely what is necessary to effectively protect the networks; it may be that the right way to protect against malware is to passively monitor *all* the traffic on the net. But, it is likely that such a dragnet approach would run afoul of the law, and the line between a tailored approach and a dragnet approach is often hard to draw. Hence, though the statutory limitations are not as stringent as might be imagined, they do have some effect, and pity the service provider who is trying to determine when his permissibly tailored sharing becomes impermissibly routine.

SO WHY THE HESITATION?

All of this leaves us with another puzzle: If the law does not prohibit the sorts of information sharing that both the public and private sector say they want, why is there so much hesitancy and resistance to doing it effectively? On the government side, we have already seen some reasons: there are resource constraints, a desire for accuracy over efficacy, and, in the end, no doubt, a cultural resistance to sharing classified information outside the government.

On the private sector side, the reasons are similar. Service providers (or more accurately the lawyers for service providers) are inherently cautious and want to avoid litigation and controversy at all costs. Likewise, there may be good business reasons why a service provider might prefer not to impose new terms of service on its clients in an overt way (by, say, requiring them to consent to sharing of private information as a condition of service) that engenders controversy. Moreover the private sector, not unreasonably, fears revealing information and vulnerabilities that may give competitors an advantage. Seen in this light, then, complaints about the law's ambiguity are merely expressions of a desire to have the federal government, by law, provide liability protection and relieve the service providers of the ill will that might attend such an amendment. Trying to avoid litigation and a difficult public relations battle are less persuasive reasons for failing to act than real ambiguity, but they are nonetheless rational business judgments that may provide a good ground for legislation.

In August 2012 Congress considered legislation that would have clarified this issue. Provisions to clearly authorize routine sharing of cyber-threat information were prominent throughout the debate on Capitol Hill, both in the House-passed Cyber Intelligence Sharing and Protection Act and in the Senate-considered Cybersecurity Act of 2012. Both failed to pass at least in part because of privacy and civil liberties concerns.

TRUE PUBLIC GOODS—GOVERNMENT AS PROTECTOR

There is another way to think about the government's role and the interaction with the private sector—a way that, effectively, removes the private sector from the equation. Just as the private sector is not responsible for national defense in the kinetic world, we might conceive of cybersecurity as an analog to police services or national defense, that is, as a public good that can be readily provided directly by the government. In truth, the analogy to police services may be quite apt—for security of that sort is provided at a baseline level by the government, but private sector actors are free to supplement the public sector's actions with their own private methods.

But, if we were to adopt this model—to, in effect, make the government the protector of the network—we would need to authorize the government to engage in an active defense (which is to say, an offensive capability of some form). This certainly is the theory of action that the Pentagon is contemplating.[10] So far, the government's efforts have been limited to voluntary information sharing.[11] But, one could readily imagine the government concluding that protecting critical infrastructure is too important to be left to the private sector.

Those sorts of efforts—in effect allowing DHS or NSA to deploy active defenses on the private networks—would raise a host of constitutional and policy problems. On the level of legal limitations, the government's inspection of private-to-private Internet traffic would raise significant Fourth Amendment concerns.[12] While much of the network traffic information (i.e., noncontent information, like the To and From lines and related IP addresses) is unlikely to be protected by the Constitution, network traffic inspection is not sufficient to fully protect the network.[13] Any operational system intended to prevent malicious intrusions must, of necessity, also inspect the packets of information containing highly personalized information including the content of the information conveyed—for malware may reside anywhere in the packets distributed. If, hypothetically, we decided by law to exclude the text of an e-mail from the domain of inspection as a matter of law, that would simply draw a road map for malicious actors as to where to hide their malware.

To be sure, there is a good argument from necessity: if the private sector efforts fail to secure the network then the government must step in. And, that argument from necessity *might* possibly convince the courts that government monitoring of content on the Internet falls into that limited class of cases where some form of special needs allows for derogation from the Fourth Amendment's particularity and warrant requirements. If the program were couched in an administrative fashion without criminal sanction, it might pass constitutional muster.[14]

But, even if lawful, such a program would require the resolution of a number of difficult and challenging policy questions: Should a government-operated Internet inspection system be run by the military or by the civilian organs of government? How would it be structured legislatively to protect privacy and civil liberties? What would be the legitimate and illegitimate uses of the personal data examined and how long would that data be retained? And, perhaps most importantly, what would be the oversight mechanism that would be used to ensure that the program was operated lawfully and within its authorized parameters? The American public will be especially leery of any program that collects personally identifiable information and subjects it to automated computer analysis.[15] In the end, the policy questions may prove intractable.

THE INTERNET "KILL SWITCH"

In some debates, the discussion of federal authority asks whether or not the president could order a private sector actor to disconnect from the Internet in time of emergency. Government lawyers believe they already have that authority under Section 706 of the Telecommunications Act of 1934. Others think the law is ambiguous and seek to make the power explicit—allowing the president to declare a cyber emergency, for instance.

Needless to say, civil libertarians and ISPs are opposed to that sort of power. Right now, the scope of the president's emergency authority to kill connections to the Internet is an unclear muddle.

MANAGING EXTERNALITIES—THE ROLE OF GOVERNMENT IN FOSTERING PRIVATE SECTOR CYBERSECURITY

In the last chapter, we also saw how many uses of cybersecurity goods have externalities—both positive and negative ones. Traditionally, the government can address these externalities by subsidizing those with positive effects while minimizing negative effects through taxation, regulation, or the imposition of liability. There are, as we've noted, good reasons to be suspicious of any government effort to deal with externalities—both because of problems of regulatory capture and, in the cyber context, the inability of the government to react nimbly enough to evolving cyber threats. But, there are, as well, reasons to think that the private sector cannot organize for its own self-defense and that the government's reliance on the private sector for its own connectivity demands its engagement.

Whatever the limits of the theoretical model, there is little doubt that, as a practical matter, some government engagement with the private sector is inevitable. The recent proposals from the Obama Administration and Congress signal a heightened interest in affirmative government action and make legislation distinctly more probable. What might a government program look like?[16]

Nudging the Market: Incentives, Subsidies, and Disclosures

One alternative, worthy of consideration, is for the government to do as little as possible to nudge the markets toward more effective cybersecurity.[17] In this model, instead of, say, having the government create standards, the breach of which might result in liability, it ought to be more feasible for the government (in partnership with industry) to develop a set of recommended best practices for cybersecurity. If it did so, it is possible that an independent certification industry would develop and that insurance rates would follow compliance with those standards.

The Obama Administration's legislative proposal of May 2011 appears to be an effort in this direction, but it is so convoluted that it shows how difficult the process of nudging the market really can be. Under the Administration's proposal,[18] the DHS would begin to take a significant regulatory role in managing cyberspace security in the private sector. Working with industry, the DHS would identify certain core critical-infrastructure operators (presumably these would include both the ISPs and certain critical functions like the electric grid). Once they were identified, the DHS would work with the critical infrastructure sectors to develop a priority list of the most important cyber threats and vulnerabilities for those operators.

Using those priority lists, the infrastructure operators then would be required to develop their own plans for implementing the agreed on frameworks as a way of addressing cyber threats. The implementation efforts would be assessed by a third-party, commercial auditor. Some operators would also be required to report on their efforts to the Security and Exchange Commission and certify that their plans are sufficient (on the theory, one supposes, that inadequate cybersecurity also poses a financial risk of loss to investors). Third-party auditors responsible for assessing compliance would provide reports to the providers and the DHS. If the DHS decided that a security framework adopted by a critical infrastructure sector was not adequate, the DHS would be authorized to work with the National Institute of Standards and Technology (NIST) to mandate a modified framework. Finally, the DHS would be authorized to publicly identify critical infrastructure providers whose plans it deemed inadequate.[19]

All of which is far more confusing than it is illuminating. This proposal creates a regulatory complex that will be difficult to effectively administer. It would enshrine a structure of prioritization and regulatory development that would, inevitably, be far behind the technological curve of threats in cyberspace. And, in the end, in order to give its nudges coercive effect, the proposed law holds out the prospect that the federal government will wind up dictating standards of security to a private industry that is far more nimble and innovative than the government ever can be.

Liability and Insurance: Unleash the Lawyers

Consider next the question of liability under the tort law for harms caused by the products being sold. One can imagine the development of a liability rule that would require service providers to pay for any harm caused by their failure to take reasonable protective actions. This would force software manufacturers and ISPs to change the products they provide and/or raise their prices as a way of accounting for these negative external effects.

Such a structure would have much theoretically to recommend it. Liability for tortious wrongs is a comparatively efficient method of modifying private sector behavior.[20] For one thing, it does not require the government to set a constantly changing standard of conduct. Instead, the law simply requires that a provider take reasonable precautions and leaves the articulation of what constitutes a reasonable precaution to the development of the common law.

More importantly, the creation of a liability system often naturally leads to the development of an insurance system against liability. The insurance function allows for a further spreading of risk in a way that fosters broad private sector responsiveness. And, with enough data, insurance companies routinely and relatively efficiently price the comparative costs and benefits of preventative actions, requiring cost-effective measures as a condition of insurance. Indeed, in maturing markets, insurance companies often take the lead in setting reasonable standards of care—much as they did with the development of building and fire codes in the late 19th century.

But, it may be exceedingly difficult to get from here to there. Insurance pricing is not feasible without both standards against which to measure conduct and liability that arises from failure to meet those standards. In the cyber domain, neither is currently available. There are no generally accepted cyber-security standards and there is no generally applicable liability system in place to account for failures to meet those standards.[21] Despite the growth of some private sector standard-setting initiatives, private sector actors are likely to be very unwilling to voluntarily create standards that lead to liability where none currently exist. As a result, the only sure way to create liability would be for the government to step in to set liability standards or force industry to do so. Any such effort would also be fraught with political risk.

Regulation and Taxation

A more intrusive step down the road would be to develop a traditional regulatory model of mandatory standards for cybersecurity. This would (as already noted) raise significant questions about the government's ability to define the standards appropriately. It would also raise the routine problem of operationalizing regulatory mandates in a complex technical area. Even cyber-sophisticated governments like in Estonia have been shut down because they did not know how to address threats and vulnerabilities and create doctrine about risk. How then are we to define the parameters to deal with these threats that could be mandated for the private sector?

The final means by which the government can incentivize private sector activity is, of course, the tax code. If we tax an output or provide a tax credit/incentive for an expenditure, we create a financial incentive to act—one that history has shown to be fairly powerful in its ability to shape behavior. Though many believe that using the tax code to incentivize conduct can have unintended and undesirable consequences and that our record of using the tax code for incentives is poor, it nonetheless remains a tool by which our government has frequently sought to modify private actor conduct. In this case, for example, Congress might consider a tax credit for qualifying expenditures on security systems as a way of pushing the private sector towards more security-conscious decisions. In this way, we might subsidize positive behavior (or, conversely, tax activities with negative externalities). Here, too, problems of government competence to regulate will, of course, arise.

Protected Networks

One critical difficulty in combating cyber intrusions is, as we've noted before, the prevalence of anonymity on the Internet. This anonymity is inherent in the structure of the Internet and, in the long run, can only be changed by modifications to the existing Internet protocols established by the Internet Engineering Task Force (IETF).[22] While the entire Internet might be better protected by the development of identification protocols, the IETF's institutional resistance to such structural changes (as well as the commitment of many Internet participants to a vision of Internet anonymity and freedom) makes this highly unlikely.

What is more likely, however, is that the economic incentives will drive the market to create walled gardens (a club good) with restricted membership. While these would have the virtue of greater security, they would come at the cost of limiting access to the World Wide Web of information now available on the Internet—in effect, limiting the very factors that make the Internet of such great value. In the near term, we are more likely to see some modified efforts that will try to create the effects of a walled garden without so decisively limiting access. These will include, for example, a continued effort by the federal government to develop and foster the use of trusted identities. We may also see some cyber service providers moving to set different terms and conditions of service for different classes of customers. All of these actions are likely to be voluntary in nature, with users agreeing to sacrifice unlimited access in the name of security. Any mandate in this area that smacks of a national identification requirement to access the Internet will meet fierce political opposition and will likely be nearly impossible to achieve.

* * *

In World War II, as the German bombs fell on British factories, the government did not require each factory to build its own anti-aircraft defense system, complete with fighters, radar, anti-aircraft guns, and fire and medical emergency responders. Rather, the collective defense of the national war-making capacity was left in the hands of the Churchill government, who saw the protection of the factors of military production as an obligation of the national defense establishment.[23] And yet, today, when we face a similar sort of threat (at least in so far as cyber threats, like airpower, can act at a distance in relatively short time frames), the idea of making the national government exclusively responsible for providing for national cybersecurity seems a bit quaint, and utterly impractical. We can't imagine government "cyber fighters" deployed on the Internet; nor can we envision a government-sponsored data backup and recovery system.

Perhaps, what we are experiencing is a systematic failure of analogies. Cyberspace is like airpower, but it really isn't. The responsibility of ISPs to manage the content on the Internet and screen for malicious software may be no more than the obligation that a highway operator has to screen traffic on the highway (i.e., none at all). Or, maybe ISPs operating the Internet are like airplane operators and other public carriers who can (or should) control access to their systems and exclude those who pose a threat. Whichever analogy you choose defines your answer to a host of policy questions relating to the obligations of the public and private sectors.

In truth, the only answer is to say that cyberspace is unique unto itself. And, the best way to correctly approach fundamental policy questions about the division of authority between government and private actors is to begin with a fundamental analysis of first principles.

Those economic principles suggest that there is a clear, but limited, domain within which government action is both appropriate and required—the domain of fostering the sharing of cybersecurity information. As for the rest of the bundle of cybersecurity goods, we face a wicked problem: private sector actions will, doubtless, create externalities that the market cannot account for and that cannot be effectively managed by a self-organizing private sector. But, the prospect of government action to correct for those externalities raises the same traditional problems of regulatory capture that attend any government endeavor. More fundamentally, precisely because cyberspace is so unique, in the rapidity and path-breaking nature of change in the domain, we face the almost intractable problem of creating policy too slowly for it to be of any utility.

16
Chapter

Protecting America's Critical Infrastructure

In the State of Washington, wind power is increasingly being used to generate electricity.[1] That's, obviously, a fundamentally good thing. But, the electric utilities sometimes have a small problem—during storms, the wind turbines generate too much power, more than the system can use. The oversupply of electricity might, in a worst case scenario, overwhelm the grid and cause a blackout. To guard against this prospect, the power authorities have taken the smart grid concept and turned it on its head.

Typically, the idea behind a smart energy grid is that in times of high demand the energy company can regulate the power consumption of its customers, reducing energy use by modifying cooling tower temperatures for example and shifting energy usage by commercial consumers to nonpeak times, if needed. Smart grid technology, managed through the Internet, evens out the peaks and valleys of electricity demand by consumers and lets producers plan for a more regular and constant generating schedule.

In Washington, the Bonneville Power Authority reverses that paradigm. When the wind turbines create too much supply, the Authority offloads the excess power into the hands of volunteer customers. It might, for example, raise the temperature in a customer's water heater or heat ceramic bricks in an electric space heater. These systems are, in effect, thermal sinks, and when the crisis passes, they can return the stored energy to the grid. In other words, instead of smoothing the peaks and valleys of demand, the Authority evens out the variations in supply.

These energy storage systems are operated at a distance. They are turned on and off through remote communications enabled by Internet technology. It's a wonderful technology—and yet a vulnerable one. For whenever any control system gets linked to the Internet, we gain remote access—and so do those who might want to hack the system to disable, disrupt, degrade, or destroy it (the four horrible "d's" of computer hacking). Though it is mildly speculative, the Bonneville system opens up the more than merely theoretical possibility for action at a distance that goes down to the consumer level. Where other systems intrusions have been at the wholesale level (like, say, Stuxnet), imagine the consequences if a cyber intrusion could affirmatively affect the ceramic bricks in your personal space heater. The mind boggles.

IS IT OR ISN'T IT?

We need to be careful in determining exactly when a cyber intrusion has occurred. On November 8, 2011, officials in Springfield, Illinois, reported that cyber hackers had gained remote access to the city's water utility, possibly from a Russian IP address. Newspapers around the country reported the incident, sometimes in breathless tones.

Less than 20 days later, the DHS finished a review of the computer logs for the utility and concluded that there was no evidence of a hacker intrusion. It was a contractor who remotely accessed the system from Russia, accidentally causing the damage.

Or, maybe the utility is racing to conceal a vulnerability? In cyberspace, we can never be sure, can we?

The Bonneville system, like all utility systems is operated by a Supervisory Control and Data Acquisition (SCADA) system. The vulnerability of SCADA systems has been known for some time. In 2007, a DHS experiment known as the Aurora test,[2] confirmed that intrusions into SCADA systems were capable of having real-world effects. In that case, a diesel generator was burned out and destroyed. And, of course, the Stuxnet virus in Iran, with which this book opened, is exactly the same thing—an intrusion on a system that, at least in Iranian eyes, was a piece of critical infrastructure.

The prospects of further SCADA attacks should heighten everyone's concern. Indeed, the Department of Energy Inspector General recently concluded that there were cyber shortcomings in more than one-third of the smart grid projects that got federal funding, ranging from incomplete strategies to improperly vague plans of response.[3] The threats and weaknesses in the system "may expose the . . . systems to an unacceptable level of risk." And, SCADA systems run virtually every utility and manufacturing plant in America (indeed, around the globe). We can imagine any number of worst case scenarios, ranging from blackouts to floods, at the hands of cyber hackers. We need to build a better cyber policy for the protection of critical infrastructure.

But, what does such a policy look like? Earlier we discussed what economic principles tell us—and they tell us that mostly we should let the market drive the answer. But, what answer is that? If we could conceive of the right infrastructure protection policy, what would it be?

Put another way, the dominant model today seems to be one of sitting back and hunkering down in defense behind firewalls and antivirus programs and intrusion protection systems. While those strategies certainly have their uses, we are entitled to ask whether the private sector ought not to be looking in a different direction for guidance.

MEDICAL MODELS

One way to approach a model of private sector cybersecurity is to become resigned to reality; to recognize that "stuff happens" is not just a mantra for the disaffected and unhappy. Rather, it's a truism of the world and it's a particular truism for the cyber domain. What this means is that, for better or worse, failure is inevitable. A cybersecurity strategy that is premised on the possibility of a perfect defense and 100 percent protection against attacks is a practical impossibility (it may even be a theoretical impossibility, though that is a more debatable proposition).

Rather, our principal planning should be based on the premise that at least some attacks will succeed; that is, that with a near-100 percent degree of certainty, we should prepare to fail. There are many systems like that which would serve as a good model for emulation. The electric grid, for example, is not designed to work 100 percent of the time; everyone knows that blackouts can occur both because of manmade errors and as a result of natural disasters. The principal goal of the electric grid management paradigm is to provide for the rapid restoration of power. That means many back-ups to replace systems taken offline and an effective repair system for fixing the grid when it gets broken. (Of course, we sometimes think that the repair system is less effective than it might be, but that is a critique of the implementation of the model, not the model itself.)

One particularly intriguing way to think about cybersecurity is to use as a mental model our medical/public health care system. Not the flawed aspects of it in terms of insurance and coverage, but the basic structure. In many ways, cybersecurity maps very well onto the healthcare system.[4] Just as we never expect everyone to remain perfectly healthy, we should never expect every computer system to remain free of malware. The similarity of the metaphor even extends to the names we use for computer malware—virus and infection, for example.

The implications in the design of a system that begins from a premise of failure are significant. As in the medical system, our first set of rules would deal with disease or infection prevention. In the healthcare world, these are often simple steps related to personal hygiene—washing your hands, drinking clean water, and the like. Likewise, in the cyber domain, good cyber hygiene is a strong candidate for success in limiting the number of infections—good passwords, regularly changed, are like washing your hands. Making sure that you think before you click on a suspect hot link to avoid a malware infection is a lot like boiling your water before you drink it (or not drinking water that you suspect is unsafe). Just as wide swathes of disease can be prevented through simple cleanliness, many cyber infections can be readily prevented through simple equivalent steps.

The next part of the analogy is vaccination. Almost every American has gotten his or her required vaccinations before going to school. As a result, smallpox has been effectively eradicated and cases of polio are in steep decline. We can readily imagine using the same concept in relation to computer malware; indeed the programs that are most likely to be employed are, quite deliberately, called antivirus programs, evoking the medical construct. For the private sector response, one could imagine a public relations campaign to encourage the use of up-to-date antivirus and maybe even an insurance and/or liability system for encouraging the adoption of the requirement generally. Alternatively, the private sector could deploy a health certification function to validate whether a system you are in communication with is using the best available antiviral technology.[5] Depending on how serious you consider the problem to be, one could even imagine a mandatory vaccination model (one that would, obviously, require governmental mandates) as a condition of access to the web.

We can take the medical model still further. For example, in the medical system when a disease outbreak does occur, our healthcare system reacts by doing two things: it floods resources to the site of the infection to combat it (send Cipro, for example, to those exposed to anthrax) and it quarantines those who have been exposed to the disease so that they can't spread the infection by exposing others to it (as, for example, when students who are ill are sent home from school). The cybersecurity model can also map onto this structure—as malware discovery and resolution resources are flooded to the infected system to remove the infection and the compromised computer server is often taken offline until it is fixed.

We can see something of how this works in the Anonymous attack on the security consultancy Stratfor in late 2011. Stratfor provides open source intelligence on national security risks around the globe. Its paying subscribers receive e-mail briefings on a daily basis (as do others who subscribe to a free information update system). When Anonymous hacktivists penetrated the system and stole all of the e-mail information (and some credit card information as well, apparently),[6] Stratfor was obliged to close its website for several weeks while working to resolve the security vulnerabilities. Only after they were confident (whether their confidence is justified remains to be determined) that the intrusion by Anonymous had been scrubbed was the website re-launched.

Finally, to complete the model, we can think of some of the other aspects of a public health system that might have echoes in the cyber domain: cyber research is much like medical research; we need excess hospital bed capacity to deal with epidemic infections and we need something similar in the cyber domain; and just as the Centers for Disease Control tracks the outbreaks of various diseases, we need to think of the US-CERT system (the DHS component that collects and distributes information about new cyber viruses that have been discovered) as the cyber equivalent of the CDC.

Perhaps, most importantly, however, the conceptualization of cybersecurity as an analog to public health brings with it a fundamental sea-change in our thinking. We would recognize that an effort to prevent all cyber intrusions is as unlikely to succeed as an effort to prevent all disease. Computer systems, like people, *will* get infected. The goal is to prevent those infections that are preventable, cure those that are curable, and realize that when the inevitable illness happens, the cyber system, like the economic system, must be constructed to continue operating. Resiliency in computer systems, like resiliency in staffing, is essential.

To be sure, this public health construct is not the be all and end all of analogies. There are plenty of ways in which it does not map well onto cybersecurity. What, for example, is the medical equivalent of a permanent wipe of a computer memory? And, what is the cyber equivalent of running out of hospital beds in an emergency? Still, the public health model is a very useful way of thinking about cybersecurity.

RESILIENCY

Most particularly, the medical model starts us thinking about one of the most significant questions we can in the cyber context: What does it mean to be resilient? Or, to put it more prosaically, the Department of Defense is defending an immense cyber system (with more than 7 million computers!). How do we insure that it continues to operate even when under attack and even when some aspects of that attack succeed?

In brief, it means that the systems are robust, adaptable, and capable of rapid response and recovery. Or, as Franklin Kramer of the Atlantic Council recently noted,[7] resiliency means a multiplicity of techniques and mechanisms:

- Diversity—The creation of cyber systems with multiple forms of programming in architecture so that any single form of attack is not successful against all systems.
- Redundancy—The frequent creation of snapshots or checkpoints of data and systems in a known and stable operation so that critical systems can be readily restored. To the extent restoration is not feasible, the

development of external backup systems is necessary so that compromised operating systems can be replaced.

- Integrity—The development of tests and structures so that systems are maintained in modules that make tampering with them more difficult to achieve and more evident when they do occur.
- Isolation/segmentation/containment—The creation of a system architecture where intrusions can be compartmentalized when discovered. In that way, the infected portion of the system can be isolated so that a single failure will not cascade across the system.
- Detection/monitoring—Advanced persistent threats can be resident, unobserved within a cyber system for a long time. Malicious activity within the system will often be infrequent and difficult to detect. So persistent and pervasive internal monitoring is necessary to give a better sense of when and how intrusions are occurring.
- The principle of least privilege—Many intrusions are by insiders who take advantage of access to install malicious software. In addition to better personnel screening, one effective answer is to insure that the people given access to a system get the least amount of privileged access necessary to achieve their purposes.
- Distributedness and moving target defense—If targets are concentrated in a single place and protected by an unchanging defense, a malicious intruder has a fixed target against which to plan. If you distribute targets widely and vary the defense, the system will be better able to frustrate an attack. In addition, this sort of protocol enhances the ability to quickly adapt to new forms of attack.
- Randomness, unpredictability, and deception—Along the same lines, as with any competition between parties, the introduction of variability into the mix makes a successful attack more difficult to achieve.

Taken together, these various tactics create a more resilient system—one that is not immune to failure but is capable of operating even when subject to intrusion or attack.

PRIVATE WAR?

Laws like the Neutrality Act and the Logan Act prohibit private actors from waging war or negotiating with foreign powers on behalf of the United States. Naturally, that's considered a government function.

So what is a company to do if an attack against its infrastructure is coming from a state-sponsored attacker? Does it rely on the government? Or will its efforts to defend itself violate the law? In fact, if it fires back and the conflict escalates, will the first shot in the first cyber war be fired by a private company?

A HYBRID—CREATING A PUBLIC–PRIVATE PARTNERSHIP

To close out this discussion of infrastructure protection, let's consider one final possible model. Perhaps the time has come to consider a different organizational structure for cyber defense, for which the author offers this novel idea:[8] We might think about whether or not we should formalize the public–private partnership necessary for cyber defense by creating a Congressionally-charted, nonprofit corporation (akin to the American Red Cross and the Millennium Challenge Corporation). One might notionally call it the Cybersecurity Assurance Corporation or CAC.[9]

This potential organizational adaption would address many of the concerns that have frustrated the purely private or public responses. It would eliminate the first mover economic problem by federalizing the response. And, it would allow greater maintenance of the security of classified information within the ambit of a government corporation. As a corollary, the quasi-public nature of the CAC might (if appropriate legal structures were adopted) provide a forum in which defense-related private sector information could be shared without fear of compromise or competitive disadvantage. Thus, the CAC would provide a secure platform that allowed the government and the private sector to fully utilize our information assurance capabilities and call on both public and private resources.[10]

Indeed, the premise is that with the proper incentives, private sectors actors can self-organize to achieve tasks.[11] It is simply the case that the current economic structures of cyber security do not provide those incentives. One significant benefit of the CAC structure would be to change the incentive structure to provide a secure, noncompetitive forum where collaboration could be fostered.

At the same time, the quasi-private nature of the organization would provide greater assurance that legitimate concerns for privacy and government overreaching were suitably addressed. The centralization of the effort would allow for a unified and continuous audit of privacy compliance. The maintenance of a private sector control structure would further insulate against misuse and abuse by governmental authorities. And, the absence of return on investment concerns would allow the organization to focus on privacy protection and network integrity.

By far, the most important requirement will be the drafting of an institutional charter clearly delineating the authorities and responsibilities of the CAC. What, after all, will the CAC actually do and how will it do it? At a minimum, one expects that the CAC will serve as a centralized information sharing system for threat information, much as Information Sharing and Analysis Centers (ISACs) do now (the ISACs are discussed in the next chapter), but with a greater capacity to marry that information to government-derived data and, potentially, with the capacity to anonymize and redistribute threat information more successfully than ISACs currently do. Indeed, the expectation is that, because of its particular authorities, the CAC will be able to achieve greater sharing than under current structures. If we judge that it cannot, then the entire enterprise is not worth the effort.

In addition, the CAC could also be authorized to conduct the following additional functions: incident review and reporting, threat assessment and analysis, and the operation of intrusion detection and prevention systems. Of course, the devil is in the detail: current owners of networks will be unwilling to delegate the responsibility for intrusion protection to the CAC unless they see a significant benefit from the collectivization of a security response. Again, if the CAC cannot achieve that objective, the enterprise is without benefit. But, as this book has argued earlier, the current model of complete reliance on private incentives to create the optimal level of intrusion detection and prevention has, plainly, not worked. The potential inherent in a CAC structure provides a halfway house that, if successful, will eliminate the natural instinct of the federal government to fully federalize a response.

The initial charter will then need to identify the means by which the CAC can achieve its objectives. Will it have, for example, authority to define security standards and best security practices? Will it have regulatory authority to create and mandate private sector compliance? Will participation in its intrusion and detection activities be voluntary or mandatory? Will it be authorized to collect fees or reimburse expenses incurred by its private sector partners? And, given the privacy sensitivities, under what rules will the CAC be authorized to cooperate with U.S. government authorities?

Many additional practical questions would, of course, need to be answered regarding the development of the CAC. One should not, of course, think that the creation of such a structure will be easy. It would require Congressional authorization, after all. Of equal significance, the start up costs of the CAC will require a Congressional appropriation and the long-term funding needs will have to be addressed through some sort of fee mechanism. These are not modest challenges to the development of the CAC structure.

THE ISRAEL–PALESTINE CYBER "WAR"

One final, real world example (albeit from outside the United States) gives a good flavor of the difficulties and challenges in defining conflict in cyberspace, in defending critical infrastructure, and in determining the proper role of a government in protecting private sector assets. It arises in the always challenging Middle East in the context of the long-running conflict between Israel and its neighbors.

The incident began with a simple intrusion. A hacker who goes by the name oxOmar (who says he is a 19-year old living in Saudi Arabia) stole and posted the credit card information of thousands of Israelis. An Israeli hacker (calling himself oxOmer—a play on oxOmar's name) then stole Saudi credit card numbers and published them. Showing some restraint, he refrained from publishing the security codes.

So far, the war seemed little more than a minor semi-criminal skirmish. But, in January 2012, oxOmar upped the ante.[12] Coordinating with a Palestinian hacker group under the name Nightmare, he plotted a DDoS attack on two Israeli websites of symbolic significance—El Al, the national airline, and the Tel Aviv stock exchange. The attacks (which were praised by Hamas leaders as opening up a new front in the resistance against Israel) were of modest success. Access was blocked for a few hours at most.

But, as a demonstration of a proof of concept, the attacks were far more powerful. They once again demonstrated the asymmetric possibilities of cyber conflict and the challenges of a proportionate response against an anonymous enemy. At the same time, they forced the Israeli private sector and the government to recognize the need to redouble their efforts to defend critical infrastructure while, again, emphasizing that often some of the most important pieces of the economy are beyond the protection of the cyber military.

In this one episode, the challenges of protecting critical infrastructure were clearly defined, as was the concept that the private sector infrastructure has public benefits and effects. The incident also demonstrated the need for better private sector resiliency—providing the United States with a concrete lesson in the need for better coordination.

17
Chapter

The Organization
of the United States
Government

A few years ago, the Central Intelligence Agency (CIA) working cooperatively with Saudi Arabia set up a honey pot website[1] to attract jihadi sympathizers. By all reports, the website served as a useful intelligence gathering tool, giving the unseen CIA and Saudi observers insights into the activities and interests of the terrorists who frequented the site. By 2008, however, it had become apparent that some were using the website to make operational plans to infiltrate jihadists into Iraq where they would join the insurgency, potentially threatening the lives of American troops. The National Security Council (NSC) convened a group of representatives from the Department of Defense (DoD), CIA, Department of Justice (DOJ), the Office of the Director of National Intelligence (ODNI), and the NSA to consider the matter. Eventually, over the CIA's objections, a DoD team from Joint Functional Component Command—Network Warfare (JFCC-NW) (the predecessor of U.S. CyberCommand)—took down the website. Their actions caused collateral effects as far away as Germany, and disappointed our Saudi collaborators.[2]

The incident illuminates a host of definitional and policy issues and challenges in the cyber realm, many of which are considered in other chapters of this book. But, equally clear from this anecdote are the challenges we face from the lack of any effective, purpose-built, standing organizations or processes within the U.S. government for developing policy or making decisions about cyber attacks and cyber defense. Rather, as this particular event makes clear, critical decisions that may set a precedent are frequently made in an ad hoc manner often without the benefit of either the time or the inclination for a broader and comprehensive consideration of the policy implications of the decisions.

The organizational deficit is two-fold: It is, first and foremost, a lack of structures for the *making* of a comprehensive policy and a lack of organizational cohesiveness in driving solutions forward in a way that includes all relevant stakeholders. It is, secondarily, a lack of adequate structures for *implementing* the policy decisions that have been made and for auditing our success (or failure) in doing so. This organizational deficit is not for a lack of effort. For more than 10 years, various Executive boards, agencies, and working groups have struggled to create a cohesive framework for cyber decision-making.

Yet, today, most observers would agree that the United States has yet to develop a stable solution. As two well-regarded observers recently noted:

> [W]e also developed on an *ad hoc* basis over the last two decades various organizational structures in response to the cyber threat. Yet those infrastructure protection boards and cyber commissions typically lacked leadership, had no real authority, and were often made up of individuals who did not have combined expertise in national security, cyber security, policy, and law.
>
> Meanwhile, the private sector, owners of most of our critical cyber infrastructure, pursued an unstructured response to the threats, relying in the first instance on government systems for cyber security.[3]

A number of legitimate reasons explain why we have yet to develop these structures and processes. There are, first, several unique challenges inherent in deterring or preventing cyber attacks. These include the well-known attribution problem, the dependence of the civilian economy and military capability on information technology, and the difficulty in distinguishing between attack and exploitation. More prosaically, despite the proliferation of boards and commissions, we simply have not paid enough sustained attention to the problem: organizational structures for the U.S. government to support our cyber deterrence activities have developed organically, over the past 20 years, through episodic and often reactive attention, rather than the product of a concerted policy-making process.

Then, too, by virtue of the nature of the cyber intrusions we have experienced, our organizational efforts have focused systematically on defensive measures rather than on offensive ones. As a consequence, though our organizational structures for cyber defense are incomplete and lack coherence, with gaps and overlaps in responsibility and authority that have yet to be resolved, our structures for controlling attack/response mechanisms are even more immature and have yet to evolve to permit consideration of a "whole of government response" that would bring to bear all aspects of government power.

The lack of coherence is magnified because existing structures tend to conflate two distinct operational functions—those of policy decision-making and those of implementation. The function of setting cyber policy and deciding a course of action will typically rest with governmental authorities. However, in the cyber domain (unlike, say, the nuclear domain), aspects of the implementation of those decisions will affect private sector actors who deploy their own defensive mechanisms and whose networks may be used to deliver a cyber response. The complex interaction between civilian, governmental, and military organizational structures for both offensive and defensive operations requires simplification.

In this chapter, we review the history of existing American structures and processes within the Executive Branch and examine the role of nonexecutive structures in the Legislative and Judicial branches of government. From this background, the next chapter proceeds to a consideration of several particularly challenging questions relating to cyber policy and organization.

Some government structures (like those intended to foster cyber resilience) have a relatively long history (in cyber terms); others (like those relating to cyber attack) are almost nonexistent and just recently developed. Let's examine the existing federal structures and how they came to be.

CYBER DEFENSE AND RESILIENCE

Though conceptually distinct, the U.S. government has treated cyber defense and resilience functions as interrelated, and developed structures that seek to address both aspects of deterrence/denial through a single set of mechanisms.

Early Efforts

President Clinton made the first significant U.S. effort to address cyber defense and resilience issues with the issuance of Presidential Decision Directive (PDD)-63 in May 1998.[4] The directive noted the potential vulnerability of American infrastructure (ranging from transportation to water systems) and set forth a process for the development of an infrastructure assurance plan to protect critical assets. Notably, the directive treated cyberspace as a *mode* by which threats to infrastructure would be propagated and did not identify cyberspace, itself, as a critical infrastructure asset. Each sector of the economy was to identify its vulnerabilities and propose remedies for them. The directive called for development of response plans to minimize the damage of attacks on infrastructure and reconstitution plans for restoring capabilities rapidly.[5]

PDD-63 also devised a coordination structure that has, in effect, become the model for all succeeding cyber defense and resilience activities. Within the federal government, each economic sector was associated with a lead agency that would have the principal responsibility for coordinating activities with the private sector and developing the federal plans. As one might expect, these designations followed the regulatory functions of then-existing federal agencies: Treasury was the lead for banking activities, HHS for public health, Energy for electric power, and so on.[6] These agencies would appoint senior officials to serve as Sector Liaisons who would, in turn be coordinated by a National Coordinator for Security, Infrastructure Protection and Counter Terrorism who would, himself, be a subordinate of the national security advisor (i.e., part of what today we would call the National Security Council). The work of this federal organization would be supplemented by the appointment of a board of prominent nonfederal leaders (infrastructure providers and state and local officials) who would provide advice under the auspices of the National Infrastructure Assurance Council (NIAC), a board that continues to exist today.[7]

ISACs

As a direct result of PDD-63, the U.S. government fostered the creation of sector-specific Information Sharing and Analysis Centers (ISACs). The purpose of the ISACs, as the name suggests, is to enable the sharing of information, within each sector, about threats and vulnerabilities to that sector. Since 1998, ISACs have been created in many of the critical infrastructure sectors (e.g., Financial Services; Real Estate; and Electricity). Most notably, an Information Technology ISAC was one of the first created. The current reach of the ISACs to the various critical infrastructures is extensive. When considered collectively, the individual private/public sector ISACs possess an outreach and connectivity network to approximately 85 percent of the U.S. critical infrastructure.

The ISAC structure is intended to: provide each sector with 24/7 information sharing/intelligence capabilities; allow the sector to collect and analyze threats based on its own subject matter analytical expertise; and coordinate with the government on sector-specific impacts. The efforts have been moderately successful in disseminating information, but complaints from the industry continue to arise that the government is not effectively using private sector expertise to leverage its capabilities,[8] and does not (often for classification reasons) adequately share threat information in the cyber domain.[9]

Recent Developments

President Bush sought to advance the Clinton initiative, and gave voice to the first National Strategy to Secure Cyberspace.[10] For the first time, the strategy recognized that cyberspace was a separate infrastructure in its own right, worthy of protection because of its inherent value (rather than, as before, because it provided a means by which attacks on other infrastructure could occur). The principal noteworthiness of the strategy, for purposes of this inquiry, lay in its call for the development of a public–private architecture for responding to national cyber incidents.[11]

This recognition of the uniqueness of cyberspace as an independent infrastructure was confirmed in Homeland Security Presidential Directive (HSPD)-7, which defined critical infrastructure as "both physical and cyber-based" assets so vital to the United States that the incapacity or destruction of such systems and assets would have a debilitating impact on American interests.[12] HSPD-7 sought to define the coordinating role of the DHS in protecting cyber assets, directing the DHS Secretary to "maintain an organization to serve as a focal point for the security of cyberspace. The organization will facilitate interactions and collaborations between and among Federal departments and agencies, State and local governments, the private sector, academia and international organizations. To the extent permitted by law, Federal departments and agencies with cyber expertise, including but not limited to the Departments of Justice, Commerce, the Treasury, Defense, Energy, and State, and the Central Intelligence Agency, will collaborate with and support the organization in accomplishing its mission."[13]

As the laundry list of involved agencies makes clear, the coordinative function on cybersecurity issues is a daunting task. The challenge is magnified when one considers the multivariate nature of the tasks that comprise a government-wide approach to cybersecurity. In January 2008, President Bush adopted a Comprehensive National Cybersecurity Initiative (CNCI), portions of which were declassified by President Obama in 2010. The CNCI identifies 12 broad cybersecurity initiatives, ranging from increased cyber education and cyber domain situational awareness to a call for the development of a comprehensive cyber deterrence strategy. All but three of these initiatives are fairly characterized as requiring efforts of cyber defense and/or cyber resilience.[14]

The complexity of the coordination task was highlighted by the principal recommendation of President Obama's Cyber Space Policy Review, a comprehensive review of American cyber policy undertaken at the start of the Obama Administration.[15] Recognizing the difficulty of coordinating so many initiatives in so many agencies, the Review called for the appointment of a White House-level policy coordinator (colloquially knows as a Cyber Czar) who would anchor leadership on cyber issues within the White House.[16] Indeed, the need for leadership was so palpable that the Review's first chapter was entitled "Leading from the Top." Responding to this call, in December 2009, President Obama appointed Howard Schmidt as the first Special Assistant to the President and Cybersecurity Coordinator.

The Cybersecurity Coordinator's powers remain, however, consultative and coordinative rather than directive and mandatory. As the Review made clear, the coordinator does not (and was not intended to) have any operational authority or responsibility, nor the authority to make policy unilaterally. Rather, the coordinator is intended to act through the normal interagency process to harmonize and coordinate policy across interagency boundaries.[17] Here too, as the CNCI's task-list makes clear, the predominant effort for the coordinator has been in the realms of cyber defense and cyber resilience.

CYBER ATTACK AND NON-CYBER RESPONSE

The U.S. military has moved aggressively to establish doctrine and structures for the control of military operations in cyberspace. The Army, for example, has developed a concept of operations and a set of capabilities requirements for military action in cyberspace.[18] Likewise, the Navy has created a Fleet Cyber Command and reactivated the 10th Fleet for cyber warfare.[19] Similarly, the Air Force has designated its existing Space Command as the locus for its cyberspace mission and begun inculcating its Airmen with the need to be Cyber Wingmen.[20]

To coordinate these sometimes disparate efforts, on June 23, 2009, the Secretary of Defense issued a memorandum creating a new command, the U.S. Cyber Command, within the structure of our military forces. More particularly, the Secretary created Cyber Command as a sub-unified command subject to the authority of the commander of the U.S. Strategic Command.[21] As detailed in section 18.d(3) of the DOD Unified Command Plan, the U.S. Cyber Command (USCC) is tasked with securing American freedom of action in cyberspace and mitigating the risks to national security that come from its dependence on cyberspace. It is, therefore, the home of both offensive and defensive military cyber missions of all sorts. A catalog of its missions includes:

- integrating cyberspace operations and synchronizing cyber war fighting effects across the global environment;
- supporting civil authorities and international organizations in cyberspace activities;[22]
- directing global information grid operations and defense;
- executing full spectrum military cyberspace operations;
- de-conflicting offensive cyberspace operations;
- providing situational awareness of cyberspace operations, including indications and warnings; and
- providing military representation to U.S. and international agencies on cyberspace matters.

In short, Cyber Command serves as a broad-based, comprehensive locus for U.S. military cyberspace operations, with significant impact on nonmilitary civilian operations. And, consistent with existing joint doctrine, the commander of Cyber Command will, generally, have the freedom to select and approve specific courses of action to achieve the mission objectives set by his superiors.[23]

It is, of course, difficult to develop a concrete sense of what USCC actually will do. The Command did not become operational until October 2010. It was only in May 2010 that its first nominated commander was confirmed by the Senate. Since then, the Command has been deeply engaged in developing its strategic vision—the result in 2011 was two documents: a broad-based strategy and a narrower statement of how and when offensive cyber operations can be undertaken.

The broad strategy (the *Department of Defense Strategy for Operating in Cyberspace*)[24] is comprehensive in one sense—it takes a wide and holistic view of the problem. But, it is narrow in another sense—it focuses almost exclusively on defensive measures. Thus, the strategy began by explaining why the DoD had chosen to consider cyber a domain separate from the land, sea, and air. It then went on to develop new defensive operating concepts to protect DoD networks and systems, while touting partnerships between the DoD and other government agencies, the private sector and international partners. These are, indeed, worthwhile objectives. But, as General James Cartwright (retired Vice-Chairman of the Joint Chiefs of Staff) put it in an interview, the all-defense/no-offense perspective of the *Strategy* was incomplete: "We've got to step up the game; we've got to talk about our offensive capabilities and train to them; to make them credible so that people know there's a penalty to this. . . . You can't have something that's a secret be a deterrent." And, as Cartwright added, the *Strategy* needs to make clear that there is a right of self defense, "because otherwise everything is a free shot at us and there's no penalty for it."[25]

Some of General Cartwright's concerns may, however, have been answered by the more recent and narrower DoD statement on its offensive cyber policy. In the *Department of Defense Cyberspace Policy Report*,[26] the DoD made clear that the United States "reserves the right to respond using all necessary means to defend our Nation . . . from hostile acts in cyberspace [which] may include significant cyber attacks directed against the U.S. economy."[27]

But, even this declaration leaves some ambiguity: what, after all, is a significant cyber attack? One assumes that the current spate of cyber espionage intrusions (mainly from China) is not an attack, so even this declaratory policy leaves an open question regarding a response to these less significant intrusions. Even more problematic, since cyber espionage looks just like a cyber attack coming in, distinguishing them based on the end result may be unduly passive. To that end, the United States needs a policy (likely broader than a military response) that engages all of the instruments of government power (diplomacy, law enforcement, economic sanctions, etc.) in responding to small-scale cyber espionage intrusions.

As these policies get developed, Cyber Command remains, ironically, a bit of a virtual command as of early 2012. The most that can be said is that it appears to be quite flexible in its scope. The authorizing documentation provides DoD with ample ability to develop within Cyber Command any number of cyber-related missions. With respect to cybersecurity matters, it is likely in the end that the limitations on the scope of activity in Cyber Command will be more in the nature of resources and external competition with other U.S. government agencies, rather than inherent limitations in its authorities. In short, we have a new Cyber Command, but the policy and doctrine that will define its objectives remain to be better defined. We can, however, expect a significant investment of effort and resources in the Command's development as it grows over the next few years.

The military is not, of course, the only U.S. governmental institution that would be responsible for a cyber response. The dynamics of the domain will necessarily involve other governmental agencies in any cyber action. After all, the Internet is a uniquely borderless domain.[28] Thus, any effective strategy will necessarily require a governmental organization and process that enables international engagement. While one could, in theory, imagine a situation in which all of our cyber responses were enabled by military-to-military interactions, the prospects for such a scenario are dim. Rather, one can readily anticipate that international engagement will require engagement across the domain of diplomacy, law enforcement, and infrastructure protection, with a necessarily wide variety of international interlocutors.

Likewise, our government's cyber capabilities are not only useful as a cyber response measure. They may well play a role when kinetic military strikes would be viewed as too drastic or disproportionate, or even as a response to diplomatic disagreements, both overtly and covertly. And, of course, these capabilities can and will be used as a tool to supplement more traditional military operations to disable an enemy's command and control structures. We have only begun our efforts to build the structures necessary to direct these multiple missions.[29]

18
Chapter

Challenging Questions of
Policy and Organization

We have, in earlier chapters,[1] discussed the unique aspects of cyberspace that make policy challenging to develop. The difficulties of attributing an attack to a particular actor are well-documented. Likewise, the independence (or purported quasi-independence) of certain cyber actors from state sponsors further complicates the equation of attribution, and the surreptitious nature of some intrusions often makes attacks difficult to perceive (and thus respond to).

But, the particular challenges for conceptions about the organization and processes of the U.S. cyber policy lie not in these difficulties, for they are more technological than organizational. They will likely not be resolved by a decision on how the government and private sector are organized. Put another way, it is hard to imagine how an organizational change in the U.S. government would increase (or decrease) our ability to resolve the attribution question on a routine basis.

Rather, it is useful to consider difficulties that particularly give rise to organizational challenges in our defense of cyberspace. Given the uncertainties surrounding the cyber realm and its rapidly mutating nature, no effort can identify, much less address, all of the salient organizational challenges. A few, however, are notable.

RISK ASYMMETRY

It is a relatively uncontroversial assessment of the current state of affairs to say that, in the cyber domain, the risk to the United States is asymmetric. Our nation, with its highly technology-dependent systems,[2] is comparatively more vulnerable to cyber attack than are many of our nation-state peer adversaries. Our comparative vulnerability is also significantly greater than that of many nonstate actors.

We have yet, however, to internalize the implications of this asymmetry for deterrence organization and policy. Our conception of deterrence is effected by memories of the Cold War, where the threat and response were relatively symmetric. We assumed that a nuclear attack would merit a nuclear response.

But, there is no reason to believe that a cyber attack of any form *necessarily* requires a directly proportionate cyber response. Indeed, given the reality of asymmetric cyber reliance by our adversaries, the implication is that our response to a cyber attack should not be confined to a cyber response. While it is likely (indeed, almost certain) that a cyber-based response will form a portion of any deterrent strategy, it is equally likely (indeed, also equally certain) that our actions will engage the full panoply of U.S. governmental authority—ranging from economic sanctions to diplomatic endeavors, to espionage, to criminal prosecution and even to noncyber kinetic military responses as the circumstances may require.

In a recent speech on Internet freedom, Secretary of State Clinton emphasized this point, suggesting the broad scope of potential U.S. responses to cyber threats: "States, terrorists, and those who would act as their proxies must know that the United States will protect our networks. Those who disrupt the free flow of information in our society or any other pose a threat to our economy, our government, and our civil society. Countries or individuals that engage in cyber attacks should face consequences and international condemnation. In an Internet-connected world, an attack on one nation's networks can be an attack on all. And by reinforcing that message, we can create norms of behavior among states and encourage respect for the global networked commons."[3]

And yet, at this juncture, the structures for a coordinated whole-of-government response to cyber threats and for the delivery of a noncyber response are immature. A recent GAO study made clear that the White House has retained fairly tight control over the development of any deterrence strategy, assigning responsibility for the task directly to the National Security Council (rather than, say, assigning it to a DoD/State working group for development).[4] But, as the vignette that opened chapter 17 (in which we noted the difficulties of coordinating a decision to disrupt a jihadi website) makes evident, the White House–coordinated structures have yet to develop a doctrine for the expression of cyber policies.

What is necessary is a structure and organization that will allow the entire panoply of governmental responses to be considered. These will range across the entire domain of federal activity (often requiring international cooperation) and could include (and this is just a sampling of possibilities):[5]

- *Public exposure and shaming*—The United States might, for example, publicize data and information identifying cyber intrusions and countries whose weak or ineffective civil justice system permits or fosters illegal activity.

- *Diplomatic condemnation*—We could work to develop international norms of behavior, including cooperation in the suppression of cyber intrusions, and then use diplomatic processes to develop shaming techniques that might modify state actor behavior.
- *Economic sanctions*—One can readily imagine a role for economic sanctions in response to cyber intrusions. For example, the United-States could impose retributive tariffs on noncooperative countries. More aggressively, it might boycott or blacklist products from countries known to introduce malicious hardware into COTS technology, and seek to convince other nations to adopt similar sanctions.
- *Cyber sanctions*—Sometimes cyber acts will beget cyber sanctions. If a country persists in misusing Internet domain name directories, for example, international organizations might, in turn, limit or restrict the development of new domains within that country. More extreme sanctions (for example, bandwidth throttling) are also conceivable.
- *Financial punishments and criminal sanctions*—Administrative, civil, and criminal sanctions may be available in situations where an actor (or an intermediary) may be readily identified. In traditional conceptions of deterrence theories, these sorts of sanctions are considered effective as a response to malfeasant individual conduct.
- *Expulsion from international organizations*—In conjunction with any of these sanctions, the United States might, in significant cases, consider suspending or expelling a country from relevant international organizations as a sanction for its activities (or those within its borders).
- *Espionage and other covert responses*—Naturally, one response to covert cyber activities will be covert activities by America. Indeed, it may well be that covert cyber activities will be a critical enabler for the effective implementation of other whole-of-government responses, providing essential intelligence to enhance effective targeting of the response.
- *Cyber intrusions or attacks*—Of course, the fact that other responses are possible does not mean that a cyber response is inappropriate. It may often be the case that a like-for-like cyber response will be deemed to have the maximum deterrent effect while achieving proportionality.
- *Kinetic military attacks*—And, finally, there is no reason to suppose that a cyber attack with kinetic or near-kinetic effects on American targets must, necessarily, be responded to with an equivalent cyber response. It is at least plausible to consider the possibility that a traditional kinetic response will be the more proportionate and responsible one.

Our organizational structures and processes ought to be designed to accommodate and foster the consideration of these various options. Contrast that with our nuclear deterrence structures, which were principally intended to verify that an attack had been launched and allow the president the opportunity to respond, if he deemed it necessary. Indeed, one of the lessons from our experience with nuclear deterrence is that often the lens through which response actions can be taken needs to be broadened (as it was, for example, in our response to the Cuban missile crisis). In the cyber domain, the need to institutionalize that broadening of response will likely be even greater. Our structures must provide for a less focused response and allow for the consideration of all feasible action options. Instead of narrowing the structure and focusing on a single decision, the cyber response structure must be necessarily more diffuse, lest we run the risk of conceiving of the cyber domain in predominantly military terms and thus militarizing a fundamentally civilian environment.

There are, of course, likely to be costs to this broadening. Most notably, it risks frustrating decision-making altogether. But, if the structures and processes are properly defined and well-led, that challenge can be overcome. And, the virtues of a whole-of-government response will likely outweigh the costs associated with a more complex decision-making process.

FEDERAL "COMPETITION"

Given the many challenges faced by the federal government, it is unsurprising that some see a continuing lack of adequate coordination at the federal level in our cyber resilience and, particularly, defense activities. As the GAO reported in 2010, though several coordinating groups exist at the White House, agencies continue to have "overlapping and uncoordinated responsibilities for cybersecurity activities."[6] To the extent the lack of coordination is discussed publicly, the perception is that there is an ongoing fight for control of the domestic cybersecurity effort, pitting the National Security Agency against the Department of Homeland Security.

The perception of, at best, a lack of coordination and, at worst, continuing conflict over control of the cybersecurity mission is only exacerbated by acts that at least on the surface suggest a continuing dissonance. An example was the announcement by the NSA, in October 2009, that it was breaking ground on a new facility in Utah to provide "intelligence and warnings related to cybersecurity threats, cybersecurity support to defense and civilian agency networks, and technical assistance" to the DHS. In November 2009, the DHS opened its own new facility, the National Cybersecurity and Communications Integration Center, in Arlington, Virginia. This facility will "house the National Cyber Security Center, which coordinates cybersecurity operations across government, the National Coordinating Center for Telecommunications, which operates the government's telecommunications network, and the United States Computer Emergency Readiness Team, which works with industry and government to protect networks and alert them of malicious activity."[7]

The two new facilities are, at least on the surface, somewhat duplicative (both, for example, purport to have a warning and alert function and both also anticipate assisting civilian networks in protecting themselves against attack) and indicative of a continuing need for strategic-level cyber coordination.

Duplicative effort and the waste it entails are not the only risks posed by uncoordinated federal activity. There may well be instances where the division of responsibility impedes essential information sharing of threat signatures (as the discussion of the ISACs in the previous chapter suggests). There may also be occasions where the comparative lack of transparency at the NSA precludes effective oversight and control of executive activity by the legislative branch and the public.[8]

But, perhaps most significantly, the lack of coordination reflects an inability to bridge a cultural gap between the operational environment of the private sector and that of the national security environment. To be sure, the DHS as an institution does not fully reflect the robust, competitive private sector environment of Silicon Valley. But, allowing the NSA or Cyber Command to have the predominant role will, inevitably, bring a more militarized or intelligence-focused perspective to the problem than would be the case if the civilian DHS agency had a primary role. Thus, it matters significantly which agency is assigned as the lead for protecting civilian networks. As Rod Beckstrom (former Director of the DHS National Cybersecurity Center) noted, which agency leads the cybersecurity effort makes a difference because an "intelligence culture is very different from network operations or security culture."[9]

To some degree, the dissonance between DHS and NSA activities is a product of a significant disparity in their resources and expertise. As the DHS Inspector General recently reported, DHS/US-CERT lacks both the authority to compel other federal agencies to follow its recommendations and the staff to adequately conduct operations.[10] The NSA, by contrast, is well-funded and staffed and has, within the domain of its own operations, ample authority to act—authority that has only been enhanced by the creation of Cyber Command. Indeed, despite the DHS's statutory authority and responsibility for protecting civilian infrastructure, it appears that it is the NSA (and not the DHS) that has begun a program, called Perfect Citizen, to detects cyber assaults on private infrastructure.[11] Though details of this new program are hazy,[12] it appears possible that the program will conflict with or duplicate programs operated by the DHS. It may also presage an effort by the NSA and the Pentagon to exert more control over civilian networks generally.

Sadly, reports of a general dissonance between the DHS and the NSA continue almost unabated. In late 2011, for example, the White House thwarted NSA attempts to seek legislation that "would have required hundreds of companies that provide such critical services as electricity generation to allow their

Internet traffic to be continuously scanned using computer threat data provided by the spy agency." More generally, the White House has told the NSA to
stand down and stop seeking greater authority to protect domestic networks.[13]

Though we've painted a bit of a grim picture so far, all is not hope-
less. Indeed, late in 2010, the DHS and the NSA adopted a Memorandum of
Understanding relating to cooperation against cyber threats.[14] The agreement
provides a clear mechanism through which the DHS can request assistance
from the NSA to address particular cyber threats. The agreement also provides
a mechanism for the converse—DHS assistance to NSA—but one suspects that
type of assistance will be relatively rare. And, while a cooperative mechanism
now exists, the agreement only nods at joint planning and execution efforts.

Meanwhile, at present, the White House cyber coordinator lacks the authority to de-conflict these competing structures. His role, avowedly, lacks
any authority over operational decisions or budgetary priorities. The result,
beyond the perception of conflict, is confusion among the public and likely the
creation of gaps and overlaps in authorities and responsibilities.[15]

THE POLICY "FORD SEDAN"

In an earlier chapter, we discussed the assumption of rapidity, that is, the
belief that a response to a cyber attack might have to occur immediately. For
reasons discussed then, that assumption may be wrong and there may be time
to assess and respond to a cyber attack with some greater thought.

But, if we broaden the lens a bit and ask about an assumption of rapidity
not for military response but, rather, for the development of policy, the reality
flips. It is often the case that the pace of events in cyberspace is so quick that
policy cannot keep up.[16] The problem, here, is a structural one, rather than
a systematic substantive challenge, and is more common whenever technological change needs to be accounted for. Put simply, policy is made through
policy-making institutions and our institutions are bounded by existing processes and inherent limitations. In a world in which notice and comment rulemaking[17] takes 18–24 months[18] to complete—during which time, the average
processing speed of computer chips will have doubled—our system for making policy is ill-suited to the task.[19]

Any number of examples of this phenomenon could readily be cited, but
the recent revolutionary movements in the Middle East are a particularly good
example of the accelerating pace of events enabled by cyberspace. The Internet gives nonstate actors the ability to communicate rapidly and organize
(to, in effect, have an organic command and control system) that begins to
rival that of sovereigns.

Consider this: On January 25, 2011, the people of Egypt took to the streets
in a day of rage, protesting the rampant poverty, unemployment, and government corruption seen throughout the country. The young rebels in the crowds

used social media to mobilize the people. One Facebook page dedicated to a protest, for instance, had more than 80,000 followers.[20] Through exchanges with Tunisian protesters, they learned how to reduce the effects of tear gas on their eyes by putting "vinegar or onion under your scarf."[21] The origins of the resistance lay even more deeply in social coordination. Bloggers in Egypt tried to organize local strikes against the government, and they, in turn, energized youthful bloggers in Tunis.

The governments in the Middle East were slow to respond and did so with little subtlety. One day after the revolt in Egypt started, Facebook, Twitter, Gmail, and YouTube were shut down, and the cell phone company Vodaphone suspended service. The day after that, Egypt's four main ISPs cut off international access to their customers.[22] While the government claimed it was not responsible for killing the Internet, efforts seemed targeted specifically to quell the uprising. A few days later, the government apparently gave up, restoring service.[23]

Within a few short weeks, Mubarak had been ousted from his Presidency and Egypt began a transition to some new form of government, though the final resolution of the Egyptian crisis has yet to be determined. Social media services have come back online, and appear to be a continuing part of the effort to transform the country. And, Egypt may only be the start of a larger phenomenon. As one leader in Egypt, Walid Rachid, said: "Tunis is the force that pushed Egypt, but what Egypt did will be the force that will push the world." He and others in his movement dream of sharing their experiences with similar youth movements in Libya, Algeria, Morocco, and Iran.[24] As of the day this chapter was drafted, Libya had changed governments, and strife continued to rage in Bahrain and Syria—the ultimate result remains unknown.

These unfolding events are a vivid example of how the cyber domain creates social change at a dizzying pace—in this case, to quite literally challenge a sovereign government backed by law enforcement and military power. Not only were the Middle Eastern nations unable to adapt, but one has a clear sense that our own policy-making in the United States was left behind the curve of events. For weeks, as the democracy movement grew, America was slow to respond, leaving many to wonder if our diplomacy was too little, too late.[25] To be sure, the shock of change in the Middle East might have overwhelmed our decision-making even at a slower pace, but there can be little doubt that the cyber-infused rapidity of events made the job significantly more challenging.

For another example, consider the Obama Administration's recent comprehensive cybersecurity legislative proposal.[26] This proposal was, itself, the product of many years work, dating back to the Bush Administration. Within the Obama Administration, it was more than two years in the crafting—something to be expected given the complexity of the topic and the significant equities at issue.

But the very slowness of that process was, quite possibly, the downfall of the proposal. Some of it was outdated even before it was proposed: For example, the Administration draft relies heavily on authorization for the deployment of an intrusion detection and prevention system.[27] But, cyber experts are generally of the view that intrusion systems are becoming out of date.[28] Indeed, as of the date this chapter was drafted, Congress had yet to pass any cyber legislation in response to the president's submission—and prospects for a successful response were dim, with the legislation being shelved in early August 2012.

In short, our hierarchical decision-making structures remain dominant and operate far too slowly to catch up with the pace of cyber activity. Our policy-making apparatus can't respond to the pace of cyberspace innovation. To repeat an apt phrase from our earlier discussion, the government is using a Ford sedan policy making system to manage the cyberspace Porsche system.[29]

In the end, then, the issue of rapidity seems to look in two directions at the same time. On the one hand, we need structures in place that slow down our responses in time of crisis and allow the time for mature consideration lest we overreact to a situation in haste. On the other hand, as is often the case when technological change is at hand, some of our long-term policy-making structures are so slow-moving that we risk being left behind, caught up in a mode of thought (built when sovereign states acted in a kinetic world) that no longer reflects the dominant reality of our new systems.

* * *

It seems clear that at this juncture our governing structures are not yet well developed and do not facilitate the adoption of coherent policies, much less permit their successful implementation. To a very real degree, our failure to adopt a rational structure is a reflection of the medium with which we are dealing. The cyber domain is a nonhierarchical interconnected web of systems; we should be little surprised that our efforts to impose a hierarchical system of order on a fundamentally disordered structure have, to date, met with less than complete success.

But, that does not mean that we should not try. Indeed, despite the difficulty, we must. If we are to maintain the utility of the web as a tool of communication and control, we necessarily must adopt some form of hierarchy to protect the cyber domain. The task, though simply stated, is a daunting one.

19

Chapter

The "Borderless" International Internet

Cyberspace is a domain without distinct borders where action at a distance is the new reality. In effect, almost every computer in America is a potential border entry point. This reality makes international engagement on cybersecurity essential.

Even more notably, the sheer scale of the network demands a global approach. The Internet is as large a human enterprise as has ever been created. More than 2 billion users send more than 88 quadrillion e-mails annually, and they register a new domain name with the Internet Corporation for Assigned Names and Numbers (ICANN) every second of every day. The scope of the Internet is as broad as the globe and that makes the scope of the Internet governance question equally as broad—who sets the rules for the Internet and what rules they set is a question that can only be answered on an international basis.

This then, is a fundamental question—perhaps THE fundamental question—of cyber conflict today: How does a fractured international community respond to the phenomenon of the Internet? One has the clear sense that 40 years ago, when the Internet was born, the various sovereign nations of the world didn't think much of the innovation. By and large, they systematically ignored it and let it grow on its own with its own relatively unstructured set of governing authorities. And then sometime in the last 10 years, the nations of the world looked up and suddenly recognized that the Internet had become this immense entity—possibly the largest human enterprise in existence—and that it had a vast influence and power. The Internet could be used to change governments and spread culture; it could run nuclear power plants and fight a war. With that realization, sovereign nations became quickly and intensely interested in the Internet. The result is a trend toward the re-sovereignization of cyberspace or what Chis Demchack and Peter Dombrowski of the Naval War College call the "Rise of a Cybered Westphalian Age,"[1] that is, an age in which sovereign nations control the Internet.[2]

And so, the question is: Who will run the Internet? Will it be separate sovereign countries? Will it be the UN? Or a set of nongovernmental organizations like ICANN and the Internet Engineering Task Force? For America this question poses a problem. Some think it is critical that our engagement occur in a manner that is protective of American interests and maintains American freedom of action. By contrast, some (including the Obama Administration) advocate a general approach that favors the development of multilateral norms to preserve the openness of the Internet, while relying on supra-national organizations to manage cybersecurity problems. The choice is of truly profound significance—perhaps more so than any other question addressed in this book.

THE RISE OF SOVEREIGNS

Nobody owns the Internet. We've seen throughout this book how sovereign nations around the globe have allowed the Internet to grow without significant control or regulation. Rather, technical standards are set by the IETF and limited substantive regulation of the Internet (e.g., the creation of new top level domain names and the like) is done by ICANN. ICANN was, originally, a quasi-American corporation chartered by the Department Commerce, but it has been spun off as a nonprofit international organization.

On a nation-state level, this is slowly changing. Some countries have responded to this reality by attempting to cut themselves off from the Internet or censor traffic arriving at their cyber borders. The most notorious example is China's attempt to construct a Great Firewall to keep Internet traffic out of the country.[3] China conducts an active effort to suppress adverse news on the Internet, with more than 300,000 Internet monitors engaged in the process.[4] As a result, the recent unrest in the Middle East seems to be unable to find traction in China. The instinct to regulate is not, however, limited to authoritarian regimes. Even liberal Western countries like Australia have proposed restrictions on Internet traffic, albeit for on the surface more legitimate reasons, such as limiting the spread of child pornography.[5]

Or, consider another example from a relatively small nation, Belarus. According to the Library of Congress[6] on December 21, 2011, the Republic of Belarus published Law No. 317-3. The law imposes restrictions on visiting and/or using foreign websites by Belarusian citizens and residents. It also requires that all companies and individuals who are registered as entrepreneurs in Belarus use only domestic Internet domains for providing online services, conducting sales, or exchanging e-mail messages. In addition, the owners and administrators of Internet cafes or other places that offer access to the Internet might be found guilty of violating this law and fined and their businesses might be closed if the users of Internet services provided by these places are found visiting websites located outside of Belarus and if such behavior of the clients was not properly identified, recorded, and reported to the authorities. Talk about a Westphalian response to the borderless Internet!

The impetus for greater control has also led a number of nations to call for a UN organization (the International Telecommunications Union [ITU]) to exert greater control over the operation of the Internet. Likewise, some nations have urged greater international control over the content of the Internet. Indeed, Russia and China have begun advocating for the adoption of an international treaty to govern conflict in cyberspace—a Cyberspace Geneva Convention, if you will. Critical to their draft proposals are the adoption of cyber conflict norms about targeting (about which more in the following text), married to an international standard that allows each nation to manage its domestic Internet however it pleases (in effect, giving international law approval to domestic Internet censorship).

Indeed, according to Demchack and Dombrowski, this development is inevitable:

> A new "cybered Westphalian age" is slowly emerging as state leaders organize to protect their citizens and economies individually and unwittingly initiate the path to borders in cyberspace. Not only are the major powers of China and the United States already demonstrating key elements of emerging cybered territorial sovereignty, other nations are quickly beginning to show similar trends. From India to Sweden, nations are demanding control over what happens electronically in their territory, even if it is to or from the computers of their citizens.
>
> This process may be meandering, but . . . it was inevitable, given the international system of states and consistent with the history of state formation and consolidation. As cyberspace is profoundly manmade, no impossible barriers hinder the growth of national borders in cyberspace. They are possible technologically, comfortable psychologically, and manageable systemically and politically.[7]

That prospect certainly reflects the reality of the issue from the perspective of nations, but it may not reflect the intent of the broader Internet community. We can be sure of resistance to this trend.

INTERNET ACCESS AS A HUMAN RIGHT

One way to think of that resistance is to ask: do human beings have a fundamental right to have access to the Internet? How you view the question may very well drive your assessment of the right structures for the international governance of the Internet. Indeed, if you think access is a fundamental right, you will be unalterably opposed to the new cybered Westphalia.

Vinton G. Cerf, thinks the answer is clearly "no,"[8] and he ought to know. After all, Cerf is one of the fathers of the Internet and currently serves as the Chief Internet Evangelist for Google—he is one of the grand old men of the network (if any endeavor that is barely 40 years old can be said to have a grand old man). According to Cerf, the right way to think about technology is as an enabler of rights—not as the right itself. Human rights "must be among the things we as humans need in order to lead healthy, meaningful lives, like freedom from torture or freedom of conscience. It is a mistake to place any particular technology in this exalted category, since over time we will end up valuing the wrong things." After all, 150 years ago having a horse might have been an essential enabler; 50 years ago, a car. The Internet, like any technology, is a means to an end—not the end itself.

Others disagree. For example, the United Nations Special Rapporteur on the Promotion and Protection of the Right to Freedom of Opinion and Expression, is of the view that a complete denial of access to the Internet is a violation of international law: "[C]utting off users from Internet access, regardless of the justification provided, [is] disproportionate and thus a violation of article 19, paragraph 3, of the International Covenant on Civil and Political Rights."[9] The Rappoteur views the denial of Internet access as an unacceptable means of controlling freedom of expression and limiting dissent. Set against the backdrop of the Arab Spring, there is a certain force to his concerns.

In the end, the disagreement may not matter. Most would admit that the Internet is an exceedingly powerful enabler of freedom. Those who design the Internet, and those who manage it, ought to do so cognizant of the great force they have unleashed—and that it can be used for good or ill. One way to think about the Internet as human right issue is to simply ask whether those designing the Internet's architecture (like the IETF) might not owe a duty of care to the general world population to take greater steps to make the Internet impervious to malware and viruses.

DATA SOVEREIGNTY

The Westphalian image is one of conflict, rather than cooperation. Already, we can see how it will play out in cyberspace. Consider just one issue: In a wide, interconnected world, data and applications run on servers. Those servers, though connected to a borderless web, all reside somewhere physically. Who controls them and the data they contain?

The real estate sales mantra ("location, location, location") is equally relevant to critical aspects of distributed computing services. While the location of a data storage center may be irrelevant to many operations and applications, the physical location of a piece of data or information is often critical in determining which sovereign nation controls that data. Indeed, if information is power, then the location of information may determine who exercises power in cyberspace. The trend toward cloud systems—and the lack of any consensus on the rules that govern them—is a paradigmatic example of the breakdown in international governance.

International and national institutions need to come to grips with these challenges (often the issue is spoken of as one of data sovereignty, that is, which sovereign controls the data). The question of control is not a new one—issues of data sovereignty have been around since the first bits and bytes of data were transferred to a cheaper offshore data storage facility. But, the transition to a broader Internet-based model has greatly exacerbated the problem. When a customer uses cloud data storage, for example, it outsources data storage requirements to a third party via the Internet. The service provider owns the equipment and is responsible for housing, running, and maintaining it. Those servers can be anywhere—in the United States, in Europe, in Russia, or in a smaller third-world country.

When the customer is a private sector company, the transition to cloud storage and processing services creates difficult jurisdictional issues. Whose law is to be applied? The law of the country where the customer created the data? The law of the country (or several countries) where the server(s) are maintained? Or, the law of the home country where the data storage provider is headquartered? At a minimum, customers need to exercise caution and get concrete legal advice before transferring data offshore.[10]

There is, today, no international standard that governs the question of data sovereignty. Nor is any institution (say, the United Nations) likely to sponsor an agreement of this nature in the near future. Rather, disputes about the control of data are resolved on a case-by-case basis often turning on geography and/or economic factors. The fundamental factor that is likely to determine the resolution of a dispute is the physical location of the server. For example, when the United States recently began seeking banking data from Swiss banks for tax collection purposes, the critical factor was that the Swiss banks had to have a physical presence in the United States in order to be effective in the international financial marketplace.

For government data on overseas servers, the issues are made even more difficult to assess by the addition of national security concerns. Even if one could gain legal assurance (perhaps through contractual arrangements or international agreements) as to the integrity of data maintained in cloud servers offshore, that legal protection would not prevent or protect against intrusions and exploitations by foreign espionage agencies.

To be sure, the potential for intrusion and exploitation exists wherever the cloud data servers are located. If we have learned anything from recent intrusions like Operation Shady RAT, Byzantine Hades, and the penetration of

RSA, it is that American-based servers are not immune from attack. But, the vulnerability to intrusion is increased significantly when the data repository is offshore. The potential for the exploitation of an insider threat increases whenever non-American staff has access to American data. Local cybersecurity capabilities of the cloud server's host country and its ISPs may be weaker than they are domestically. Nondomestic cloud servers will be outside of the protective umbrella we are attempting to create through public–private partnerships here in the United States. Perhaps most worrying, we can never know what the potential is for foreign espionage overseas nor discount the potential that peer-competitor nations like Russia and China will be more successful in targeting offshore cloud data servers.

The lesson here is that the Internet has a real world physical presence with its fiber optic transmission lines and server farms. Every data storage facility is located somewhere. And, when that "somewhere" is not in the United States, American companies and its government run the risk that the data stored overseas will be subject to the sovereign control of the country where the data is located. That's probably tolerable and manageable for a private company. It is less tolerable and manageable for federal, state, and local governments. If, as some say, geography is destiny, principles of good governance and caution require U.S. governments to control their own destiny.

AN INTERNATIONAL STRATEGY

Given the limitations of a Westphalian-based policy, it is not surprising that the Obama Administration has pursued a multilateral approach to international cyber issues. The recently released *International Strategy for Cyberspace*[11] points toward the creation of an "open, interoperable, secure, and reliable" communications and information architecture (surely, a positive goal) through building and sustaining norms of international behavior. The strategy goes further in articulating the norms it seeks to foster (freedom, privacy, respect for property, protection from crime, and the right of self-defense), but one may be forgiven in thinking that these norms are articulated at too high a level of generality; and unlikely to find great acceptance in many nations that value neither privacy nor freedom.

The limits of this sort of strategy are best exemplified by how the strategy addresses the problem of cyber crime. We saw, in chapter 7, how limited the effectiveness of the Cybercrime Convention has been. And yet, the principal goal of the new strategy for addressing cyber crime is to harmonize criminal law internationally by expanding accession to the Convention. If there were a realistic prospect that criminal havens, like Russia and China, would both join the convention and also implement it aggressively, this policy would likely be effective. But, in the absence of that prospect, the promise of a multilateral policy seems a bit empty.

CYBER WARFARE CONVENTION

Consider how the multilateral impulse has begun to drive negotiations over a cyber warfare convention. For years, the United States resisted Russian blandishments to begin negotiations over a cyber warfare convention, akin to the chemical warfare convention. The Russian model would outlaw certain types of cyber attacks (say, on civilian targets, like electric grids) as out of bounds. At its core, this seems a reasonable objective.

The principal American objection has been that a cyber treaty, unlike a ballistic missile treaty, is inherently unverifiable. In other words, in a world where weapons cannot be identified and counted and where attribution is difficult, if not impossible, how could any country be assured that others were abiding by the terms of the agreement?

Beyond verifiability, there is a question of enforceability. Those who are skeptics of a cyber warfare convention point, for example, to the provisions of the 1899 Hague Convention, which prohibited the bombardment of civilian targets.[12] Needless to say, the commitment to withhold bombing of civilian targets did not survive the World War II Blitz of London and the firebombing of Dresden (not to mention the nuclear targeting of Hiroshima and Nagasaki). There is, it is argued, therefore good reason to doubt that a prohibition on targeting, say, electric grids, would be sustainable in a truly significant conflict.[13] Notwithstanding these concerns, in 2009, the United States abandoned its position and agreed to discussions with Russia.[14]

As Jack Goldsmith of Harvard points out, in addition to the inherent inability to verify or enforce any cyber-disarmament treaty, the treaty would greatly limit America's freedom to act offensively in support of its own sovereign interests.[15] To be sure, we would be bound to restrain the NSA's operations in a host of ways to abide by the treaty's requirements. In addition, we would have to clean up our own house. In a 2010 survey by McAfee, the computer security company, more information technology experts around the world expressed concern about the United States as a source of computer network attacks than about any other country.[16] And so, we would likely be obliged to take steps to monitor the domestic Internet (and reign in our own hacker community) in compliance with our treaty obligations that would be a civil libertarian nightmare.

More significantly, the proposed treaty comes with some baggage. Non-Western states view the cyber domain less as a means of communication and more as a means of control—a viewpoint they want to import into any global treaty. Consider the International Information Security agreement among the Shanghai Cooperation Organization nations (China, Kazakhstan, Kyrgyzstan, Russia, Tajikistan, and Uzbekistan). Under the agreement, state security and state control over information technologies and threats are permitted. In the view of the SCO nations, the major threats to their own sovereignty are the dominant position in the information space of Western nations and the "dissemination of information harmful to the socio-political systems, spiritual, moral, and cultural environment of the States."[17]

INTERNET FREEDOM

And that leads to another consideration—America's interest in Internet freedom. We are often conflicted in that view, since freedom to use the Internet for political purposes often comes at the cost of decreased security on the network. But by and large we have come to see freedom of expression on the Internet as a fundamental good. That's why Secretary of State Hillary Clinton emphasized that "Those who disrupt the free flow of information in our society or any other pose a threat to our economy, our government, and our civil society."[18]

Indeed, as a symbol of our view that freedom of expression is critical, the United States is leading efforts to develop the technology for a shadow Internet—one that can be deployed independent of the main backbone of the network. If successful this new technology would, in effect, create an Internet in a suitcase and would enable dissidents to avoid the censorship of repressive authoritarian countries. To quote Secretary of State Hillary Rodham Clinton again: "We see more and more people around the globe using the Internet, mobile phones and other technologies to make their voices heard as they protest against injustice and seek to realize their aspirations. . . . There is a historic opportunity to effect positive change, change America supports. . . . So we're focused on helping them do that, on helping them talk to each other, to their communities, to their governments and to the world."[19]

In short, one aspect of the new multilateral policy calls for the development of norms that are squarely at odds with those espoused by repressive governments. In that context, finding an international consensus is likely to prove very difficult.

THE INTERNATIONAL TELECOMMUNICATIONS UNION

So, if the Westphalian model leads to conflict and if the multilateral model involves disagreements that can't be squared, why not go the whole hog and create an international institution to run the Internet? Alas, that option, too, is problematic.

For years, the architecture of the Internet has been defined by two NGO organizations—IETF and ICANN. Both are nonpartisan and professional and their policy-making is highly influenced by nations that are technologically reliant on the Internet and have contributed the most to its development and growth. As a consequence, America has an influential role in those organizations.

Many in the world see this as problematic. The International Telecommunications Union (the ITU dates back to 1865 but is now a part of the UN) has been proposed as a better model for Internet governance. Transferring authority to the ITU (or a similar organization) is seen as a means of opening up the control of the Internet into a more conventional international process that dismantles what some see as the current position of global dominance of U.S. national interests. In the ITU, like most UN institutions, a one nation/one vote rule applies—a prospect that would certainly diminish Western influence on Internet governance.

Indeed, some argue that giving the ITU a role in Internet governance is no different from the role that the World Customs Organization has in setting shipping standards, or the International Civil Aviation Organization has in setting aviation traffic rules. To some degree that may be true. The IETF is an inefficient means of setting binding international technical standards.

On the other hand, aviation communications frequency requirements and standard shipping container sizes are not fraught with political significance in the same way that the Internet has become. Rather those institutions succeed precisely because they manage the mundane, technical aspects of a highly specialized industry. They would be ill-suited to provide broadly applicable content regulation for a world-girding communications system. Thus, some fear that a transition to the ITU would run the risk of politicizing an already contentious domain even further.

At bottom, however, the preference for ICANN over the ITU is not just about national interests. It is also, more fundamentally, about the contrast between ICANN's general adherence to a deregulated market-driven approach and the turgid, ineffective process of the international public regulatory sector. Recall the Ford policy sedan issue that we earlier addressed with respect to the American policy making apparatus. The problem will, if anything, be exacerbated in the international sphere. Given the scale of the problem, it is likely that the mechanisms for multinational cooperation are too cumbersome, hierarchical, and slow to be of much use in the development of international standards. Acceptable behavior on the Internet mutates across multiple dimensions at a pace that far outstrips the speed of the policy-making apparatus within the U.S. government already—and the international system is immeasurably slower. Indeed, some are reasonably concerned that there is no surer way to kill the economic value of the Internet than to let the UN run it.

Thus, though there is a real intellectual appeal to the idea of an international governance system to manage an international entity like the Internet, the prognosis of a cybered Westphalian age is almost certainly more realistic. We are likely to see the United States make common cause with trustworthy allies and friends around the globe to establish cooperative mechanisms that yield strong standards of conduct while forgoing engagement with multilateral organizations and authoritarian sovereigns.

Part IV

The Future and Beyond

And so, we come to the end of our exploration of conflict in the cyber domain. We've examined the fundamental nature of the problem, reviewed some of the practical issues that bedevil our response and taken a look at first principles. In this final section, we try to put it all together.

First, in chapter 20, we do a little crystal ball gazing. One thing we know for sure about the cyber domain is that it's a lot like the weather in Kansas—if you don't like it now, just wait a bit and it will change. Indeed, change is the only certainty, but how we change is the $64,000 question. Here, we offer a few educated guesses about what the future might hold.

And then, in the final chapter, we try to sum up what we've learned, distilling the lessons of the book into a few basic truths. Our premise is that, no matter what the future holds, if we understand the true nature of conflict in the cyber domain we should be fairly well grounded in any future scenario. Of course, only time will tell . . .

20

Chapter

What the Future Holds

Who knows what the future of the Internet holds? Anyone attempting to answer the question must do so with a healthy degree of humility. We really do not know what we don't know. The entire future of our engagement with the cyber domain is precisely what former Secretary of Defense Donald Rumsfeld meant when he spoke of "unknown, unknowns." And in that way the cyber domain is not unique. Experts routinely misunderstand trends and their predictions about the future are often wrong. Indeed, expert predictions are often no more accurate than random guesses.[1] Yet, because we are hardwired with an aversion to uncertainty, we seek foreknowledge. But, we rely on those predictions at our peril.[2]

In the classic science fiction novel *Marooned in Real Time,* published in 1986, author Vernor Vinge imagined the prospects for the human race as computer processing power continued to increase exponentially, while data storage costs became, conversely, exponentially less. In the end, he posits a Singularity of some sort where the increased capacity for connection and analysis on a global scale through the cyber domain triggers a fundamental, indescribable change in human nature.[3] Though one suspects that such a transformative change in our society is unlikely (at least in the near term), the developments in cyber technology are guaranteed to bring about changes in ways that are impossible to predict.

So what can we see in the future? Notwithstanding a quite reasonable fear of error, here are a few thoughts ranging in order from near-term to longer-term trends.

CLOUD COMPUTING

Cloud Computing is the new thing. Everyone is rushing to it—the new Federal Cloud Computing Strategy isn't called "Cloud First" for no reason.[4]

Indeed, the reasons to like the cloud are obvious. Cloud systems allow significant economies of scale. Using them is often cheaper and more efficient at the same time.

The *cloud* is really a name for a variety of services. The fundamental thing that links all of them is that instead of being resident on a user's laptop or tower system the services are provided by cloud service providers, whose servers are connected to the consumer through the Internet. The types of services available are as broad as we can conceive:

- Software-as-a-Service (SaaS): On-demand software and its associated data are accessed directly from the cloud purveyor by users using a thin client (i.e., a small processer with little or no memory storage capacity).
- Platform-as-a-Service (PaaS): The consumer is given the ability to deploy onto the cloud infrastructure consumer-created or acquired applications created using programming languages and tools supported by the cloud service provider.
- Infrastructure-as-a-Service (IaaS): Essentially a turnkey outsourcing of hardware, software, data storage, application development, and other fundamental computing resources to a third party cloud service provider via the Internet.
- Cloud Storage-as-a-Service (CSaaS): A business model in which a large company rents out data storage space on their servers to another company or individual.

All of these services share a common theme: the consumer does not manage or control the underlying cloud infrastructure including network, servers, operating systems, or storage, but has access to his data or applications on an as-needed basis from the cloud service provider.

The other variable is the identity of the cloud service provider. While we often think of the cloud as a public cloud—that is, a cloud owned by a third-party service provider who sells cloud services to the general public—that is not the only cloud structure we can conceive. It is possible to have an internal or private cloud within a consumers' organization. And, a community cloud can be owned by several organizations in support of a specific community of some form. In general, however, the trend is toward the public cloud—both because it is more efficient and because it is cheaper. For example, late in 2011 Congress decided to compel certain Federal agencies (like the Department of Defense)[5] to use commercial cloud services instead of in-house private clouds.

The cloud will also bring with it some real potential security benefits. Increasingly, multiple systems are running in a cloud environment and those systems may run on multiple machines. Under many circumstances, this will mean that it is more difficult to construct malware that has machine level effects. When malware attempts to execute in the cloud context, it does so on software that emulates a hardware device, rather than on the hardware itself. This often limits or modifies the malware's capacity for harm.

What this means is that cyber attacks may be significantly harder to accomplish in a cloud-oriented system. By its nature, the cloud permits the creation of systems with different trust levels at different tiers of interaction. At the client level, where most individuals and applications operate, the user has only a limited set of permissions and access. Hence, the capacity for malfeasance is potentially limited by the structure of the system. To put it colloquially, a gamer in Worlds of Warcraft is inherently incapable of corrupting the game.

But, this also creates greater potential for catastrophic vulnerabilities that will need to be guarded against. Security works at the client level in cloud systems precisely because the cloud system owner is, in effect, god. Thus, a successful attack at this next higher level (say, through malware that works on the cloud system) will have even worse consequences—one may not even know if the system has been compromised. Of equal concern is the challenge of identifying a trustworthy god. Cloud computing may make human factors issues less frequent, but the effects of a security compromise may be much greater. Who would we trust to be the electrical grid god?

Another consequence of the trend toward cloud computing is that the cloud makes anonymity much easier to achieve. This is so not because anonymization techniques are better in the cloud. Rather, it is because information is not held in a single discrete location; it is often divided up and stored in parts on many different servers. One may readily foresee significant challenges in adapting place-specific concepts of American constitutional protections in the Fourth Amendment to a context where the place to be searched and the thing to be seized simply don't exist in any single identifiable way. Indeed, in response to this conundrum the government may decide to mandate some form of guaranteed responsiveness. If cloud owners can't pull the information necessary for government intervention, governments around the globe may adopt CALEA-like mandates (of the kind we discussed in chapter 12) for the cloud.[6] In any event, the trend towards cloud computing will exacerbate the problem of attribution, not ameliorate it.

Finally, at a meta level, the promise of the cloud comes with a real risk—one that, perhaps, we have not yet come to grips with. Today's cloud system uses thin clients—simple interfaces like Google's Chromebook system—with minimal independent computing power. All of the data, software, and operating systems, and processing resources are stored in the cloud, managed by a cloud system administrator.

If that sounds familiar, it should. We are, quickly, recapturing the system configuration of the early 1980s, when dumb terminals (little more than a screen and a keyboard) connected to a mainframe maintained by a systems administrator. The administrator made the resource allocation decisions, prioritized work, and controlled access to the processing systems. So the translation is clear: thin client = dumb terminal; cloud = mainframe.

That centralized system of control is fundamentally authoritarian. Today's Internet structure empowers individuals. On a laptop, an individual can have more processing power and data storage capacity than imaginable. From that laptop, one can link to the web and communicate with anyone. The laptop owner can choose his own software, save his own data, and innovate as and when he pleases. Of course, with that power comes real risk—the laptop user is also responsible, in the end, for his own security system and the integrity of his own programs. But, for many, that cost is worth the benefit—independence is a valuable commodity.

In a cloud system or the old mainframe system, the user makes none of those decisions. The software is provided by the system administrator, who stores the users data and controls what new innovations are made available. That's a fundamentally authoritarian model where the individual loses much of the independence that has made the web a fountain of innovation and invention.

In a liberal western democracy, perhaps that is not a problem—after all, American users don't have to choose Google as their cloud provider if they don't want to, or, for that matter, move to cloud services at all. But, in more authoritarian states, the trend toward the cloud will make citizens even less able to control their own destiny. China will love the cloud structure for those very reasons.

The Internet empowered the liberty of dissent; we should be concerned that the cloud may take it away. What we are likely to see, however, is greater cloud use around the globe—with adverse effects on freedom under authoritarian systems.

INFORMATION MANAGEMENT

Another likely future trend will be better, re-engineered information management systems and requirements. Because secrets will become increasingly harder to protect and information will be more ubiquitous, one can anticipate an effort by actors to limit or eliminate the necessity of maintaining secrecy in the first instance.

Most private sector actors are just beginning to apply this new structure and modify their behavior accordingly. Currently, many protect all the information that they have equally. But increasingly they are coming to recognize that this is both unnecessary and costly. A restructuring of their information management systems should, broadly speaking, recognize three different categories of information:

- Information currently collected but which need not be. For example, retailers will come to recognize that they often do not need to collect the financial information of their clients. A token of some form that authenticates identity will be more than adequate to insure payment. If financial information is not collected in the first instance, protecting it becomes unnecessary.
- Information necessary to run the entity's operation but which has no external use. This category would include, for example, marketing information or stock ordering and pricing data. Here, the data is of limited use outside the entity, hence it is an unlikely target for theft, except perhaps by a competitor. The principal questions will be issues of backup and resiliency to maintain continuity, with security issues secondary.
- The crown jewels—intellectual property and other proprietary information whose disclosure would damage the institution. Properly identified, this volume of data is much smaller and therefore protection is much more manageable.

VIRTUAL WORLDS

Consider another novel phenomenon: The development of seemingly independent virtual realities where real-world actors can interact online in created worlds. Like cloud computing, the development of virtual worlds holds both peril and promise.

The ambit of virtual worlds includes sophisticated games, like World of Warcraft and systems that mimic the real world, complete with economic and social interactions, such as Second Life (a world where, quite literally, you can create an avatar and live a second life—complete with job, family, finances, and social activities). These worlds are distinct from traditional cybersystems and in many ways defy our ability to monitor actions that occur in them. The simplest of these virtual worlds, Facebook, has more than 900 million active users and would, if it were a real-world population, be the third largest nation-state in the world, trailing behind only China and India in size. Some of the more complex systems are also growing impressively large—Maple Story[7] has more than 92 million users.

Of equal note, some of these second worlds are designed with deliberate real-world connections. Thus, for example, consider the mixed reality world (linking the real world and the virtual) that the government creates for its own benefit when it uses virtualization to control predators in the Afghanistan/Pakistan region whose real-world consequences are quite deadly. If only for its use as a kinetic force-projection mechanism, the virtual world is one of critical national security interest.

Indeed, given the degree to which virtual worlds seek to simulate the real world, we should not be surprised that we face all the same sorts of potential for criminal or other malevolent behavior in these second environments. Already we see sophisticated securities frauds that have virtual world consequences. Second Life has, reportedly, had its first instance of bank fraud. EVE Online, another social interaction construct, has had several well-publicized bank frauds. And, China has legislated government control over virtual currencies in response to virtual world operators issuing their own currencies and allowing them to be used in the real world.[8]

But, the challenges of the virtual world are most relevant when they overlap into the physical world. The interactive nature of the virtual world makes it an ideal place for spear-fishing—using an official-looking request to secure personal information—increasing the likelihood that individuals will be unwittingly recruited to act against their own interests or, depending on what they disclose, against the interests of their country, company, or organization.

Thus, the nature of the virtual world risk arises from a systematically greater inability to control information. In the virtual world (even more than the physical one), the distinction between operational information and data security is disappearing. This will have the real-world consequence of making us vulnerable to attacks on information systems and things we operate. The difference, one should hasten to add, is not one of kind but of degree—the virtual world fosters a degradation of security.

Other risks arise from other interactions between the virtual world and real-world events. National security threats may arise, for example, when digital virtual currencies are traded in a virtual world in a manner that effectuates the real world transfer of funds for purposes of money laundering. It is, in effect, an unregulated system of exchange (much like black market money changers are in the real world). Because the core of most virtual worlds is a real functioning economy (even if only offering trade in digital magical weapons), the situation is ripe for manipulation of the system. This is particularly the case because very little real world law applies directly in the virtual world (beyond, perhaps, the confines of contractual agreements between the users and the providers) and any application of real-world law is fraught with challenges.[9]

In short, the growth of participation in virtual worlds has not created any new and different cybersecurity threats, but it has clearly enhanced the capacity to commit real-world crime already and may augment the capacity to commit real-world terror, espionage, or war.

A NEW INTERNET

One way of thinking about the problems of cybersecurity is that they are, fundamentally, inherent in the structure of the Internet and its original design.

The Internet was built without authentication as a protocol and so any security functionality is, by definition, an add-on function. That's why, for example, the DNSSEC protocols we discussed in chapter 6 have taken so long to develop and will take even longer to fully deploy; they aren't a built-in part of the original protocols.

So, why not have a new Internet? Start over again with a structure that has greater security provisions built-in from the beginning? While it is nearly impossible to imagine that the existing Internet will ever disappear, it is quite plausible to imagine that a series of alternate Internets might be created.

This is particularly likely to be tried by those whose primary concerns sound in the security domain rather than in the freedom or privacy sphere. Indeed, U.S. Cyber Command head General Keith Alexander, has already floated the concept of a .secure network for critical services, such as banking, that would be walled off from the public Internet. Access to .secure could be limited to those whose identity and authority to access it are authenticated by some credential. As General Michael Hayden, the former head of the CIA put it, "we need a more hardened enterprise structure for some activities and we need to go build it. . . . All those people who want to violate their privacy on Facebook—let them continue to play."[10]

These sorts of gated communities are, it seems, inevitable, and may not be limited to a .secure network. Given the challenges to security in a cloud computing world and the dim prospects for effective international cooperation, some portions of the system will take on an almost Wild West character. To combat this, some anticipate the development of segmented gated communities all over the system. Entrance to these systems will be carefully monitored and available only to trusted participants who agree to give up their anonymity to some degree and allow strong attribution of their actions.

These trusted communities will not, of course, be pervasive. They will only be successful to the extent that strong intrusion detection and behavior monitoring technologies are developed. But, given the vulnerabilities that exist in the unregulated cyber domain, one can fully anticipate that some users will, in the long run, gravitate to a more secure, albeit more isolated, domain.

This trend will mean, naturally, that users will move away from the current vision of a singular Internet and net neutrality. But, such trusted networks already exist (e.g., America's Secret and Top Secret classified networks).[11] One possible future will see the recreation of walled gardens, like those that were developed when AOL was first exploring Internet access.

In the end, however, one suspects that the trend to walled gardens will be limited. They may very well become prominent in authoritarian countries; China is already a near walled garden behind the Great Firewall and other authoritarian political systems like Iran are following suit. But, within the broader, more liberal, Western democracies, one suspects that their utility will be limited. There will be certain specialized areas (like the military and the financial networks) where it will be welcome, but the basic problem is that the entire concept contradicts the fundamental value of the Internet. It is an engine of change and innovation precisely because of its globe-spanning, go anywhere, do anything nature. Those who cower inside walls of their own making are likely to be safer, but in the brutal competition of technological innovation it is inevitable that they will fall behind.

QUANTUM COMPUTING

Finally, let's play completely outside the box for just a few minutes. The entire structure of the Internet (and thus all of the power and all of its danger) is tied to the technology that undergirds it—the integrated silicon chip. That chip, at the heart of every computer, is the physical mechanism that creates the 1s and 0s of binary code and drives the Internet. What if that weren't the basis for Internet computing anymore?

That's a scary and revolutionary thought. But, it is also sort of like thinking "What if we had something that went faster than the horse and buggy?" without knowing precisely what that "something" might be. You can imagine how great a paradigm shift it would be, even if you don't know precisely what the "it" actually is.

We may (just may) be standing on the threshold of such a change.[12] Physicists have developed the concept of a quantum computer—that is, one whose operations are based on theories of quantum physics in the same way that our current crop of computers are based on the operation of classical physics laws. In quantum physics, for example, it is possible for a particle to be in two places simultaneously and to be entangled with other particles and affect their activity instantaneously—what Einstein called "spooky action at a distance."

The transformation that would come from a quantum computer is quite stunning. In a classic computer, each bit of data can be either a 1 or a 0. In a quantum computer, the qubit (short for quantum bit) can be either a 1, or a 0, or *both* 1 and 0 at the same time. And, when qubits are entangled with each other, they can, in theory, share information instantaneously—in effect, enabling all the entangled qubits to work on a single problem simultaneously like some massive set of connected classical computers.

If ever realized, these quantum computers would make the power of contemporary computers look puny by comparison—much as the car (or spaceship) leaves the horse and buggy behind. Because of the indefinite nature of a qubit's state, a 2-qubit system could compute four values at once; a 3-qubit system, eight; a 4-qubit system, 16, and so on.[13] One practical example of what this power entails: As we saw in chapter 12, current encryption programs based on large prime number multiplication are amazingly robust and difficult to break. Yet, theoretical physicists have shown that for a quantum computer the factoring of a large prime number and the breaking of prime number encryption codes would be trivial. Recently a quantum computer successfully factored the number 15, suggesting that the theoretical capacity to break prime number encryption may eventually become reality.[14]

Nor are these developments merely theoretical. At Oxford and Yale, theoreticians have built 4- and 8-qubit large computing chips. When they get up to roughly 50 qubits, the power will match that of a contemporary laptop. Entrepreneurs in Singapore and Canada are working on the question. Google has been looking into quantum computing for more than three years. When will a large quantum computer be built? It's impossible to know—possibly never. But, if one is produced, well, then this whole book will become instantly outdated.

21
Chapter

Concluding Thoughts

Hardly a day passes in Washington without a legislative proposal or media story about cybersecurity. In the three years before this writing alone, President Barack Obama crafted a new cyberspace policy, appointed a so-called Cyber Czar, and submitted a comprehensive legislative proposal to Congress. Competing Senate cyber bills clamored for attention on the floor of the chamber during the last session of Congress. Turf wars between the Department of Homeland Security and the National Security Agency were widely reported. The Deputy Secretary of Defense announced a new Cyberstrategy 3.0, and a United States Cyber Command was created at the Pentagon. Still, risks abound. Nobody quite knows who unleashed the Stuxnet cyber attack against Iranian nuclear facilities (although the United States is strongly implicated) and a classified cyber war game is reported to have (hypothetically) brought down the entire New York City electric grid. In the end, billions of dollars in federal funding hang in the balance; not to mention the vast and immeasurable consequences that cybersecurity has on the privately owned critical infrastructure in America.[1]

The tumult of policy confusion is substantial, even by Washington standards. As this book draws to a close, it is useful to step back a bit from all of the issues we've considered and all of the manifestations of cyber conflict that we've examined and think about some fundamental principles that ought to guide policy and legislation effecting the Internet and cybersecurity. Since, as Aristotle said, the nature of the thing "is the thing itself," any examination should be based on what is known about the current nature of the Internet and cyberspace. Here are 11 truths about cyberspace that emerge from what has been covered in this book.

CYBER ATTACKS ARE INDIRECT

The cyber domain is basically an incorporeal network of information. It transmits bits of information (essentially 1s and 0s) across geographic boundaries at amazing speeds, allowing access to information at a distance. With access to information often comes control. Through cyberspace, nation-states can perpetrate espionage, industrial spies can steal trade secrets, criminals can steal money, and militaries can disrupt command-and-control communications.

These are real and powerful dangers. But, the cyber domain, while connected to physical and kinetic reality, is not that reality itself. Real-world effects are collateral to cyber effects rather than their immediate and direct product. To be sure, that condition is likely to be temporary. Now that cyber attacks like the recent Stuxnet malware have demonstrated that a virus can, at least in theory, shut down a nuclear reactor or disable an electrical grid, the prospect of serious, second-order, physical effects in the real world is significant. But, the reality of large-scale cyber attacks remains, thankfully, somewhere down the road—it isn't here yet.

CYBERSPACE IS EVERYWHERE

The Department of Homeland Security has identified 18 sectors of the economy as the nation's critical infrastructure and key resources. As one would expect of a comprehensive list, it covers everything from transportation to the defense industrial base. It also includes energy, financial systems, water, agriculture, and telecommunications.

The remarkable thing is that virtually all of the sectors now substantially depend on cyber systems. Even those activities most solidly grounded in the physical world—such as manufacturing or food production—have become reliant on computer controls and access to the World Wide Web of information. Manufacturing systems are controlled by computer systems operated at a distance through virtual connections; farmers use global positioning system (GPS) tracking, satellite data, and just-in-time ordering to maintain their operations. The list goes on.

THE INTERNET DESTROYS TIME AND SPACE

The fundamental characteristic of the Internet that makes it truly different from the physical world is that it lacks any boundaries. It spans the globe and it does so near-instantaneously. There is no kinetic analog for this phenomenon—even the most global-spanning weapons, like missiles, take 33 minutes to reach their distant targets.

This creates a profound challenge for American policy because the reality is that cybersecurity is an international issue. Significant instances of espionage have originated overseas. Some countries, such as Russia and Ukraine, have become known as safe havens for cyber criminals. It can be anticipated that if there ever is a cyber war, America's enemies will launch their attacks from overseas sites that, initially, are beyond U.S. control.

Some countries, notably China, have responded to this reality by attempting to cut themselves off from the Internet or censor traffic arriving at their cyber borders. But such strategies are, in the end, bootless. In the long run, they will prove ineffective, and to the extent they are effective, they cut countries off from the benefits of the Internet. The salient feature of the cyber domain is precisely its ability to accumulate and integrate large bodies of information over long distances in an instant. Any country that erects effective cyber borders is systematically agreeing to forgo those benefits, to its own detriment. While that might be feasible for a totalitarian state, it will never work for America.

THE WESTPHALIAN AGE LOOMS

One of the critical questions that lies ahead of us is the nature of Internet governance. Today, for the most part, rules about the borderless Internet domain are set by nonprofit international organizations. The IETF sets the protocols for Internet transmissions. The ICAAN runs the addressing system of assigning Domain Names. Neither is accountable to any sovereign nation.

That state of affairs is being challenged. Powerful sovereign nations, recognizing the importance of the Internet, seek to exert control—often at cross-purposes to each other. Formal international bodies, like the UN and the ITU seek a role in setting the ground rules for Internet conduct. Meanwhile, informal groups devoted to the concept of Internet freedom battle to maintain the Internet as outside of the Westphalian nation-state structure.

Where the contest will end is anybody's guess. Perhaps the IETF and ICAAN will retain their authority. Perhaps the UN and the ITU will take control. But, the strength of the sovereign nation system suggests that the most likely result is some formal nation-state control of the Internet—a prospect that we face with some trepidation.

ANONYMITY IS A FEATURE, NOT A BUG

One of the critical challenges in cyberspace is the problem of anonymity. Because it is often difficult, if not impossible, to identify who is acting at a distance—it took one sophisticated group nearly a year to identify who hacked the Dalai Lama's network and even then they were not 100 percent certain of their conclusion—espionage, theft, and intrusions are often impossible to attribute to a particular actor. How can any nation, company, or individual adequately respond if it is not possible to identify the source of the problem?

This predilection for anonymity is inherent in the structure of the Internet. As originally conceived, the cyber domain serves simply as a giant switching system, routing data around the globe using general Internet protocols. It embeds no other function (like identity or verification of delivery) into the protocols. The simplicity of this system is, to a large degree, the cause of its pervasiveness. Because it is so simple to use and add content, the cyber domain is readily expandable. It is the minimalist nature of Internet protocols that made this particular Internet into The Internet.

All of which means that regardless of whether anonymity is good (it protects political speech) or bad (it allows hackers to hide), it is here to stay. One can imagine, of course, the creation of so-called walled gardens or gated communities on the Internet—sites to which access is strictly controlled, or where users must identify themselves to access a particular portion of the Internet. There already are many classified networks or corporate-only servers that are isolated niches separate from the public Internet. One can also imagine a rule requiring assured identities, where access to the Internet requires identification. But, outside of totalitarian regimes that, too, is unrealistic.

MAGINOT LINES NEVER WORK
IN THE LONG RUN

In the aftermath of World War I, the French built a strong, immobile defensive system along their border with Germany—the Maginot Line. Everyone knows what happened next: at the beginning of World War II, the Germans simply went around the line and France quickly fell.

In many ways, cybersecurity is in the midst of its Maginot Line period. Governments, companies, and other users hunker down behind firewalls and deploy virus protections and intrusion-detection systems in a principally passive defensive effort. Like the Maginot Line, America's current system of firewalls is rather ineffective. Billions of dollars in theft occur each year. Terabytes of data are stolen. And, there is no sense at all of how many intrusions go undetected each day. In short, the offense is stronger than the defense and that means that U.S. reliance on passive defenses is as doomed as the French were in 1940.

Counteracting that vulnerability will require the development of active defenses that, instead of merely standing guard at Internet system gateways, look beyond those gateways to assess systems patterns and anomalies. With that sort of information, cybersecurity could transition from detecting intrusions after they occur to preventing intrusions before they occur.

FROM 85 TO 90 PERCENT OF U.S. GOVERNMENT TRAFFIC TRAVELS OVER NONGOVERNMENT NETWORKS

As a corollary to the idea of active defenses (and to the conception that the cyber domain is pervasive), any policy needs to recognize that huge swathes of essential government activity involve communications via networks that are predominantly operated by the private sector. Much as steel factories were essential to the construction of battleships, Internet communications companies have become an essential component of effective government activity. This is yet another reason why any active defenses must, inevitably, be deployed on nongovernment networks. In other words, the best defenses (whether government or private) must operate in the private-sector domain.

This concept is highly controversial, and rightly so. The specter of a government-operated intrusion-prevention system operating on the private-sector Internet is a daunting one for civil libertarians. Relying on private-sector systems is, in many ways, problematic in its operational effectiveness (for some relatively convincing economic reasons) and will not give the government the assurance of effectiveness that it requires.

But, the need for active defenses operating in the private sector cannot really be denied without, again, wishing for a cyber domain that simply is not the one that exists today. Who should operate the defensive systems is a much more difficult question, but the need for an active defense is clear. That means that whoever operates the systems must be subject to strict oversight and scrutiny. There must be an effective means of protecting the privacy and personal liberties of innocent users of the cyber domain.

THERE IS A LEGITIMATE ROLE FOR GOVERNMENT

There is a legitimate—indeed necessary—government role in protecting the Internet against theft, espionage, and cyber attacks. Just as there is a role for government law enforcement to protect tangible private property, there is a role in protecting cyberspace properties. In part, this is because of externalities by which the security failure of one network affects others outside the network. There is also a national security component which necessitates a vigilant federal role. But, by far the greatest role for the government is as a facilitator—of information sharing and of technological innovation.

NSA DOES IT BETTER THAN DHS

It seems near inevitable that the federal government will play a role in providing solutions to the cybersecurity problem, if only because it must do so for its own benefit, irrespective of private-sector needs. The question then arises as to which federal agency to entrust with that task, and there is currently a brutal turf war battle between those who favor a civilian governmental role, mostly through the DHS, and those who favor a military role, principally the NSA and U.S. Cyber Command. The cultural difference between these approaches is vast and the stakes behind the resolution of this turf war are high.

In theory, the answer is easy: the strong preference should be for a civilian response for what is, after all, a predominantly civilian network. But, the hard truth is that the civilian side of the government lacks the expertise and manpower to effectively do the job—which is why the DHS has announced its plan to hire 1,000 new cyber experts. But, until these new experts are on board (and finding and hiring that many will be a long process), civilian defenses will have to rely on existing expertise that lies predominantly within the NSA.

NO DEFENSE WILL EVER BE
100 PERCENT PERFECT

Indeed, the only certainty is the uncertainty of the efficacy of any protective cyber systems. No matter how well constructed, the cyber domain is sufficiently dynamic that their defeat is inevitable. Someday, somewhere, a cyber attack or intrusion will succeed in ways that one can only imagine, with consequences that one cannot fully predict.

It follows that a critical component of any strategy is to plan for the inevitable instances in which the country's defenses fail. This means the creation of incentives and structures that encourage the development of a resilient cyber network that can contain any intrusion and rapidly repair any damage. Some analysts have suggested that this means the United States should think of cyber viruses much like one does of public health in the real world. Some computers will inevitably get sick. To deal with this possibility, the United States should (to carry the analogy forward) have policies that call for widely distributing known vaccines, quarantining sick computers, and swarming resources to the site of the infection to cure those who are ill.

HARDWARE ATTACKS ARE EVEN HARDER
TO PREVENT THAN SOFTWARE ATTACKS

One little noticed and poorly understood aspect of cybersecurity is the degree to which American cyber hardware is manufactured overseas. As the Defense Science Board has noted, virtually all of the chips that Americans use in the innards of their computers are constructed offshore.

This is a significant vulnerability. But as a panel of the Defense Science Board recognized (and, indeed, recommended), the U.S. government must continue to purchase commercial goods. It is simply untenable to suppose that the United States will ever forgo the economic benefits of a globalized purchasing system. Yet such a system carries inherent risks.

Both private-sector and public-sector strategies to eliminate those risks are nonexistent and those required to mitigate it seem to be mostly nibbling around the edges. The steps that the U.S. government is currently taking to enhance supply chain security cannot eliminate the risks to cyber assurance posed by the use of commercial systems. The dispersed nature of the cyber domain only serves to exacerbate the international character of the problem and render it seemingly insoluble.

* * *

These truths reflect a fair assessment of the reality of cyberspace conflict today. But, the single and most fundamental principle to which we must adhere is a sense of humility about anyone's understanding of cyberspace. We must be aware that the cyber domain is a dynamic environment that changes constantly.

Today, people use the Internet in ways they did not imagine just five years ago (witness the growth of social networks and the development of Internet communications protocols like Skype), much less a few months ago (as with WikiLeaks and the subsequent cyber hacktivist attacks). So, anything that the United States or the international community does in terms of legislation or regulation must emphasize flexibility and executive discretion over mandates and legislative proscriptions. It is quite possible that today's great idea for Internet security will kill tomorrow's essential application.

As the White House, Congress, and the American public address cybersecurity concerns (as we surely must), they should all bear in mind as a guiding principle the wisdom of Hippocrates: "First, do no harm."

Notes

CHAPTER 1

1. A T-shirt slogan, available from www.thinkgeek.com.

2. A useful history of the invention of the integrated circuit chip is to be found in T.R. Reid, *How Two Americans Invented the Microchip and Launched a Revolution* (Random House, 2001).

3. Nassim Taleb, "The World in 2036," *The Economist,* November 22, 2010. Oddly enough, Taleb's sentiment echoed the words of Theodore Roosevelt, roughly 100 years earlier: "Over the whole earth the swing of the pendulum grows more and more rapid, the mainspring coils and spreads at a rate constantly quickening, the whole world movement is of constantly accelerating velocity." Theodore Roosevelt, *The Works of Theodore Roosevelt,* vol. 14 (Memorial Edition, 1923–26), 274–75, quoted in Edmund Morris, *Colonel Roosevelt* (Random House, 2010).

4. Statistics regarding worldwide Internet usage are compiled by Internet World Stats, http://www.Internetworldstats.com/stats.htm.

5. This phenomenon is common in the development and use of many new technologies and is well described in Stewart Baker, *Skating on Stilts: Why We Aren't Stopping Tomorrow's Terrorism* (Hoover, 2010).

6. The initiative was announced in National Security Presidential Directive 54/ Homeland Security Presidential Directive 23 on January 8, 2008. Much of the directive remains classified. An unclassified version is available at http://www.whitehouse.gov/cybersecurity/comprehensive-national-cybersecurity-initiative.

7. *Cyber Space Policy Review: Assuring a Trusted and Resilient Information and Communications Infrastructure,* May 29, 2009, http://www.whitehouse.gov/assets/documents/Cyberspace_Policy_Review_final.pdf.

8. Albert Einstein to Franklin Delano Roosevelt (August 2, 1939), http://media.nara.gov/Public_Vaults/00762_.pdf. It is sometimes said that the letter was written for Einstein by Professor Leo Szillard, whose theoretical work lies at the core of nuclear chain reactions.

9. Ronald Clark, *Einstein: The Life and Times* (Avon, 2001), 752.

10. A video of the interview from 1965 (NBC, "The Decision to Drop the Bomb") is available at http://www.youtube.com/watch?v=P6ncKNqfxk0.

11. Many of the details of the Stuxnet worm required extended analysis to uncover. They are well described by Ralph Langer, "Cracking Stuxnet: A 21st Century Cyber Weapon" *TED* (March 2011), http://www.ted.com/talks/ralph_langner_cracking_stuxnet_a_21st_century_cyberweapon.html. The details in the paragraphs that follow are derived from Mr. Langer.

12. Yaakov Katz, "Stuxnet May Have Destroyed 1,000 Centrifuges at Natanz," *Jerusalem Post,* December 24, 2010, http://www.jpost.com/Defense/Article.aspx?id=200843.

13. Yaakov Katz, "Stuxnet Virus May Have Set Back Iran's Nuclear Program by 2 Years," *Jerusalem Post,* December 15, 2010, http://www.jpost.com/IranianThreat/News/Article.aspx?id=199475.

14. Symantec, W32.Stuxnet Dossier (February 2011), http://www.symantec.com/content/en/us/enterprise/media/security_response/whitepapers/w32_stuxnet_dossier.pdf.

15. Houman Shasar, *Esther's Children* (Jewish Publication Society of America, 2002), 432.

16. William J. Broad, John Markoff, and David E. Sanger, "Stuxnet Worm Used against Iran Was Tested in Israel," *New York Times,* January 15, 2011, http://www.nytimes.com/2011/01/16/world/middleeast/16stuxnet.html?_r=1&nl=todaysheadlines&emc=tha2.

17. David E. Sanger, "Obama Order Sped Up Wave of Cyberattacks Against Iran," *New York Times,* June 1, 2012, https://www.nytimes.com/2012/06/01/world/middleeast/obama-ordered-wave-of-cyberattacks-against-iran.html?_r=1&pagewanted=all.

18. Zelkja Zorz, "Israel General Claims Stuxnet Attacsk as One of His Successes," http://www.net-security.org/secworld.php?id=10596.

19. Jeffrey Carr, "Did the Stuxnet Worm Kill India's INSAT-4B Satellite?" *Forbes,* September 29, 2010, http://blogs.forbes.com/firewall/2010/09/29/did-the-stuxnet-worm-kill-indias-insat-4b-satellite/.

20. Christopher Williams, "Stuxnet Virus 'Could Be Adapted to Attack the West'," *The Telegraph,* July 27, 2011, http://www.telegraph.co.uk/technology/news/8665487/Stuxnet-virus-could-be-adapted-to-attack-the-West.html.

21. Gazprom produces much of the oil and gas that fuel Western Europe, http://www.gazprom.com/.

22. Duqu may not be that significant. The antivirus firm Sophos notes that unlike Stuxnet—which was targeted at a very limited number and type of SCADA systems—Duqu is indiscriminate and runs on any system it infects, which makes it little more than an annoying keylogger attack, and not a targeted cyber weapon. See Paul Ducklin, "Duqu Malware Spurs New Stuxnet-Style Conspiracy Theory," October 20, 2010, http://nakedsecurity.sophos.com/2011/10/20/duqu-virus-spurs-new-stuxnet-style-conspiracy-theory/.

CHAPTER 2

1. Mikko Hypponen, "Fighting Viruses, Defending the Net," *TED* (July 2011), http://www.ted.com/talks/mikko_hypponen_fighting_viruses_defending_the_net.html.

2. Jason Ukman, "Anonymous Claims it Obtained Military Data in Breach of Booz Allen Systems," *Washington Post,* July 11, 2011, http://www.washingtonpost.com/blogs/checkpoint-washington/post/hacker-group-claims-it-obtained-military-data-in-breach-of-booz-allen-systems/2011/07/11/gIQAqadL9H_blog.html.

3. Grant Cluley, "Bastille Day Malware Spammed out to French Computer Users," *Naked Security,* July 12, 2011, http://nakedsecurity.sophos.com/2011/07/12/bastille-day-malware-spammed-out-to-french-computer-users/.

4. "Syria's Cyberwar against Dissidents," AEP, July 11, 2011, http://news.ninemsn.com.au/article.aspx?id=8271489.

5. Ed Pilkington, "Phone Hacking Spotlight Falls on Former News International Boss, Les Hinton," *Guardian* (London), July 8, 2011, http://www.guardian.co.uk/media/2011/jul/08/phone-hacking-scandal-les-hinton.

6. David G. Post, *In Search of Jefferson's Moose: Notes on the State of Cyberspace* (Oxford University Press, 2009), http://jeffersonsmoose.org/.

7. Solomon Moore, "Ship Accidents Sever Data Cables off East Africa," *Wall Street Journal,* February 28, 2012, http://online.wsj.com/article/SB10001424052970203833004577249434081658686.html?mod=googlenews_wsj.

8. Remarks on the Department of Defense Cyber Strategy, July 14, 2011, http://www.defense.gov/speeches/speech.aspx?speechid=1593.

9. The facts of this case are drawn from the official case report, *United States v. Robert Tappan Morris,* 928 F.2d 504 (2d Cir., 1991).

10. *Live Free or Die Hard* (20th Century Fox, 2007), http://www.imdb.com/title/tt0337978/.

11. This short section is derived from a blog post: Rosenzweig, "The Incredible Scale of the Internet," *The Foundry,* January 3, 2012 (Heritage Foundation), http://blog.heritage.org/2012/01/03/the-incredible-scale-of-the-internet/.

12. Gus Lubin, "Incredible Things that Happen Every 60 Seconds on the Internet," *Business Insider,* December 26, 2011, http://www.businessinsider.com/incredible-things-that-happen-every-60-seconds-on-the-internet-2011-12.

13. Matt Raymond, "How Big Is the Library of Congress," February 11, 2009, http://blogs.loc.gov/loc/2009/02/how-big-is-the-library-of-congress/.

14. Stacy Cowley, "Unprofitable Demand Media Files for IPO," CNNMoney.com, August 8, 2010, http://money.cnn.com/2010/08/06/technology/demand_media_ipo/.

15. Thomas Hobbes, *Leviathan,* ch. 13, para. 9 (1651). I am not, of course, the first to offer this analogy. Others have, more colorfully, likened action in cyberspace to the Wild West of America's frontier. Michael Fertik and David Thompson, *Wild West 2.0* (Amacom, 2010).

16. See, for example, *US-CERT Monthly Activity Report* (April 2011), http://www.us-cert.gov/press_room/monthlysummary201104.pdf.

17. Michael Barrett, Andy Steingrubel, and Bill Smith, *Combatting Cybercrime: Principles, Policies and Programs* (April 2011), https://www.paypal-media.com/assets/pdf/fact_sheet/PayPal_CombatingCybercrime_WP_0411_v4.pdf.

18. IC3, *2010 Internet Crime Report*, http://www.ic3.gov/media/annualreport/2010_IC3Report.pdf. The IC3 is a cooperative enterprise of the FBI, the Bureau of Justice Assistance, and the National White Collar Crime Center.

19. Department of Justice Inspector General, "The Federal Bureau of Investigation's Ability to Address the National Security Cyber Intrusion Threat," April 2011, http://www.justice.gov/oig/reports/FBI/a1122r.pdf.

20. William J. Lynn III, "Defending a New Domain: The Pentagon's Cyberstrategy," *Foreign Affairs*, September–October 2010.

21. "The Cost of Cyber Crime," *Detica*, February 14, 2011, http://www.detica.com/uploads/press_releases/THE_COST_OF_CYBER_CRIME_SUMMARY_FINAL_14_February_2011.pdf.

22. Elinor Mills, "Study: Cybercrime Costs Firms $1 Trillion Globally," *CNet News*, January 28, 2009, http://news.cnet.com/8301–1009_3–10152246–83.html.

23. Norton, *2011 Cybercrime Report*, http://us.norton.com/content/en/us/home_homeoffice/html/cybercrimereport/.

24. "The Cost of Cyber Crime."

25. "Cost of Cyber Crime Is Not Science Fiction, Says Detica," *Information Age*, May 4, 2011, http://www.information-age.com/channels/security-and-continuity/company-analysis/1621903/cost-of-cyber-crime-is-not-science-fiction-says-detica.thtml.

26. Government Accountability Office, "Cybercrime: Public and Private Entities Face Challenges in Addressing Cyber Threats" (GAO-07-705, June 2007). These figures are also broadly consistent with the estimate of $140 billion annual losses made by Ferris Research, as reported in "Cybersecurity: Where Is the Security?" May 12, 2010, http://www.milesstockbridge.com/pdfuploads/640_Miles_Cyberspace_092410.pdf. Phishing is the colloquial phrase used to define efforts to trick the unwary to voluntarily disclose their identity and passwords.

27. "2011 Cost of Data Breach Study," March 2012 (Ponemon Institute).

28. Eric Engleman and Chris Strohm, "Cybersecurity Disaster Seen in U.S. Survey Citing Spending Gaps," *Bloomberg*, January 31, 2012, http://www.bloomberg.com/news/2012–01–31/cybersecurity-disaster-seen-in-u-s-survey-citing-spending-gaps.html.

29. This is an immense amount of data. A petabyte is roughly 1,000 terabytes and the storage capacity to hold that much data must have cost several hundreds of thousands of dollars.

30. *Combating Robot Networks and Their Controllers* (Unclassified Version 2.0), May 6, 2010, http://www.scribd.com/doc/51938416/Botnet-Analysis-Report-Final-Unclassified-v2–0. One of the authors of the report, Rafal Rohozinski, gave a colloquial talk on this study to the St. Galen Symposium, http://www.youtube.com/watch?v=DpRYXRNWka0&feature=youtu.be.

31. Christopher Drew and Verne G. Kopytoff, "Deploying New Tools to Stop the Hackers," New York Times, June 17, 2011, http://www.nytimes.com/2011/06/18/technology/18security.html?_r=1&scp=1&sq=hackers%20symantec&st=cse.

32. A recent comprehensive study commissioned by the European Network and Information Security Agency reached much the same conclusion when surveying the academic literature in Europe. See Ross Anderson, Rainer Bohme, Richard Clayton, and Tylenr Moore, *Security Economics and the Internal Market*, § 4.2 (ENISA 2007).

33. The draft language is contained in sections 101 and 106 of the Administration's May 2011 proposal, http://www.whitehouse.gov/sites/default/files/omb/legislative/letters/Law-Enforcement-Provisions-Related-to-Computer-Security-Full-Bill.pdf. Data breach laws do exist in 48 of the 50 states, but there is no central repository of this information.

34. See *Regulatory Framework for Electronic Communications in the European Union* (December 2009), 55, http://ec.europa.eu/information_society/policy/ecomm/doc/library/regframeforec_dec2009.pdf.

35. "Tracking GhostNet: Investigating a Cyber Espionage Network, Information Warfare Monitor," March 29, 2009, http://www.scribd.com/doc/13731776/Tracking-GhostNet-Investigating-a-Cyber-Espionage-Network.

36. Overview by the U.S.-CCU of the Cyber Campaign against Georgia in August 2008 (August 2009), http://www.registan.net/wp-content/uploads/2009/08/US-CCU-Georgia-Cyber-Campaign-Overview.pdf.

CHAPTER 3

1. Dhruv C. Katoch, "Bam-i-Duniah (Roof of the World): A Future Conflict Scenario," *CLAWS Journal* (Summer 2010): 153.

2. Eric Schmitt and Thom Shanker, "U.S. Debated Cyberwarfare against Libya," *New York Times,* October 17, 2011, http://www.nytimes.com/2011/10/18/world/africa/cyber-warfare-against-libya-was-debated-by-us.html?_r=1&hp.

3. David A. Fulghum, Robert Wall, and Amy Butler, "Israel Shows Electronic Prowess," *Aviation Week,* November 25, 2007, http://www.aviationweek.com/aw/generic/story.jsp?id=news/aw112607p2.xml&headline=Israel%20Shows%20Electronic%20Prowess&channel=defense.

4. Ian Black, "Cyber-Attack Theory as al-Qaida Web Sites Close," *Guardian* (London), October 21, 2008, http://www.guardian.co.uk/world/2008/oct/22/alqaida-terrorism-internet.

5. "Unclassified Statement of James R. Clapper before the United States Senate," Select Committee on Intelligence, January 31, 2012, http://intelligence.senate.gov/120131/clapper.pdf.

6. "FBI Director Says Cyber Threats Will Surpass Threats from Terrorists," *ABC News,* February 1, 2012, http://federalcrimesblog.com/tag/national-intelligence-director-james-clapper/.

7. Department of Defense, "Strategy for Operating in Cyberspace" (July 2011), http://www.defense.gov/news/d20110714cyber.pdf.

8. Siobhan Gorman and Julian Barnes, "Cyber Combat: Act of War," *Wall Street Journal,* May 31, 2011, http://online.wsj.com/article/SB10001424052702304563104576355623135782718.html.

9. Ellen Nakashima, "List of Cyber-Weapons Developed by Pentagon to Streamline Computer Warfare," *Washington Post,* June 1, 2011, http://www.wash ingtonpost.com/national/list-of-cyber-weapons-developed-by-pentagon-to-stream line-computer-warfare/2011/05/31/AGSublFH_story.html.

10. We discuss these legal questions in more detail in the next chapter.

11. Jeffrey Carr, *Inside Cyber Warfare* (O'Reilly, 2010), 17.

12. "Overview by the U.S.-CCU of the Cyber Campaign against Georgia in August of 2008," August 2009, http://www.registan.net/wp-content/uploads/2009/08/US-CCU-Georgia-Cyber-Campaign-Overview.pdf.

13. "Project Grey Goose, Phase II Report: The Evolving State of Cyber Warfare," (March 20, 2009), 15–17, http://www.scribd.com/doc/13442963/Project-Grey-Goose-Phase-II-Report.

14. Department of Defense, "Strategy for Operating in Cyberspace," 2.

15. David E. Sanger, "America's Deadly Dynamics with Iran," *New York Times,* November 6, 2011, http://www.nytimes.com/2011/11/06/sunday-review/the-secret-war-with-iran.html?ref=opinion.

16. If it was an Iranian response, it also violated other international conventions, including the prohibition on targeting diplomats.

17. *United States Army Functional Concept for Fires,* 10 (TRADOC Pam 525-3-4, October 13, 2010).

18. Dmitri Alperovitch "Revealed: Operation Shady RAT," (August 2011), 3, http://www.mcafee.com/us/resources/white-papers/wp-operation-shady-rat.pdf.

19. Ellen Nakashima, "U.S. Accelerating Cyberweapon Research," *Washington Post,* March 19, 2012, http://www.washingtonpost.com/world/national-security/us-acceler ating-cyberweapon-research/2012/03/13/gIQAMRGVLS_story.html?hpid=z6.

20. Nakashima, "U.S. Accelerating Cyberweapon Research."

21. "The Dangers of Getting Picked Up in a Parking Lot," *Signal Online,* August 2011, http://www.afcea.org/signal/articles/templates/Signal_Article_Template.asp?articleid=2702&zoneid=326.

22. Unclassified Statement of James R. Clapper before the U.S. Senate, Select Committee on Intelligence, January 31, 2012, http://intelligence.senate.gov/120131/clapper.pdf.

23. Department of Defense, *Annual Report to Congress: Military and Security Developments Involving the People's Republic of China* (2010), 16.

24. "Google Defends against Large Scale Chinese Cyber Attack: May Cease Chinese Operations," *TechCrunch,* January 12, 2010, http://techcrunch.com/2010/01/12/google-china-attacks/.

25. Ellen Nakashima, "Chinese Leaders Ordered Google Hack, U.S. Was Told," *Washington Post,* December 5, 2010, http://www.washingtonpost.com/wp-dyn/content/article/2010/12/04/AR2010120403347.html. The author maintains an active security clearance and, accordingly, has not read the underlying classified cables.

26. "Special Report: In Cyberspy vs. Cyberspy, China Has the Edge," *Reuters,* April 14, 2011, http://www.reuters.com/article/2011/04/14/us-china-usa-cyberespio nage-idUSTRE73D24220110414.

27. Michael Joseph Gross, "Enter the Cyber-Dragon," *Vanity Fair,* September 2011, http://www.vanityfair.com/culture/features/2011/09/chinese-hacking-201109?printable=true.

28. David Winder "Did China Hack the F35 Lightning II Strike Fighter?" April 21, 2009, http://www.daniweb.com/news/story220469.html.

29. Alperovitch, "Revealed: Operation Shady RAT," 3.

30. Jeremy Kirk, "'Night Dragon' Attacks from China Strike Energy Companies," *Network World,* February 10, 2011, http://www.networkworld.com/news/2011/021011-night-dragon-attacks-from-china.html.

31. "U.S.–China Economic and Security Review Commission" (November 2010), 252, http://www.uscc.gov/annual_report/2010/annual_report_full_10.pdf.

32. Siobhan Gorman, "Electricity Grid in U.S. Penetrated By Spies," *Wall Street Journal,* April 8, 2009, http://online.wsj.com/article/SB123914805204099085.html.

33. Richard Clarke, "China's Cyberassault on America," *Wall Street Journal,* June 15, 2011, http://online.wsj.com/article/SB10001424052702304259304576373391101828876.html.

34. Siobhan Gorman, "Chinese Hackers Hit U.S. Chamber," *Wall Street Journal,* December 21, 2011, http://online.wsj.com/article/SB1000142405297020405840457710541568535300.html.

35. Joseph Menn, "Microsoft Says Hacking Code Could Have Leaked," *Reuters/ Chicago Tribune,* March 16, 2012, http://www.chicagotribune.com/business/sns-rt-us-microsoft-securitybre82f1dl-20120316,0,6125896.story.

36. Testimony of Paul K. Martin, Inspector General, NASA, before the House of Representatives Committee on Science, Space and Technology, Subcommittee on Investigations and Oversight, "NASA Cybersecurity: An Examination of the Agency's Information Security," February 29, 2012, http://oig.nasa.gov/congressional/FINAL_written_statement_for_%20IT_%20hearing_February_26_edit_v2.pdf.

37. Michael Riley and Dune Lawrence, "Hackers Linked to China's Army Seen From EU to D.C.," *Bloomberg,* July 26 2012, http://www.bloomberg.com/news/2012-07-26/china-hackers-hit-eu-point-man-and-d-c-with-byzantine-candor.html.

38. Krebs on Security, "Who Else Was Hit by the RSA Hackers?" October 24, 2011, http://krebsonsecurity.com/2011/10/who-else-was-hit-by-the-rsa-attackers/#more-11975.

39. "RSA: Nation-State Responsible for SecureID Breach," October 11, 2011, http://www.computerworlduk.com/news/security/3310032/rsa-nation-state-responsible-for-securid-breach.

40. Krebs on Security, "Who Else Was Hit."

41. Matthew Robertson and Helena Zhu, "Slip-Up in Chinese Military TV Show Reveals More Than Intended," *Epoch Times,* August 21, 2011, http://www.theepochtimes.com/n2/china-news/slip-up-in-chinese-military-tv-show-reveals-more-than-intended-60619.html.

42. Ellen Nakashima and Jason Ukman, "Chinese Cyberwar Video Goes Missing," *Washington Post,* August 25, 2011, http://www.washingtonpost.com/blogs/checkpoint-

washington/post/chinese-vanish-cyberwar-video-that-caused-stir/2011/08/25/gIQA
AK8edJ_blog.html?tid=sm_twitter_washingtonpost.

43. Gross, "Enter the Cyber-dragon."

44. Nicole Perlroth, "Electronic Security a Worry in an Age of Digital Espionage," *New York Times,* February 10, 2012, sec. Technology, https://www.nytimes.
com/2012/02/11/technology/electronic-security-a-worry-in-an-age-of-digital-espio
nage.html.

45. This quote from the *Liberation Army Daily* of June 16, 2011, based on an English translation report available at: "China Cyberwar Strength Must Be Boosted to
Counter Pentagon is Threat: Top Military Newspaper," *Huffington Post,* June 16, 2011,
http://www.huffingtonpost.com/2011/06/16/china-cyber-war-strength-pentagon-
threat_n_878024.html.

46. "China Confirms Existence of Elite Cyber-Warfare Outfit the 'Blue Army,'"
Fox News, May 26, 2011, http://www.foxnews.com/scitech/2011/05/26/china-confirms-
existence-blue-army-elite-cyber-warfare-outfit/#ixzz1bFssUtkn.

47. Bryan Krekel, Patton Adams, and George Bakos, "Occupying the Information
High Ground: Chinese Capabilities for Computer Network Operations and Cyber
Espionage," Northrop Grumman, U.S.–China Economic and Security Review Com-
mission, March 2012, http://www.washingtonpost.com/r/2010–2019/WashingtonPost/
2012/03/08/National-Security/Graphics/USCC_Report_Chinese_Capabilities_for_
Computer_Network_Operations_and_Cyber_%20Espionage.pdf.

48. Government Accountability Office, "Defense Department Cyber Efforts," May
2011, 2–3, http://www.gao.gov/new.items/d1175.pdf.

49. Government Accountability Office, "Defense Department Cyber Efforts."

50. The details here are all derived from Eric Schmitt and Thom Shanker,
Counterstrike: The Untold Story of America's Secret Campaign against Al-Qaeda
(Macmillan, 2011).

CHAPTER 4

1. This chapter is derived in part from *National Security Threats in Cyberspace*
(American Bar Association and National Strategy Forum, 2009), a workshop
publication for which I was the Rapporteur.

2. Ellen Nakashima, "Pentagon: Cyber Offense Part of U.S. Strategy," *Washington
Post,* November 16, 2011, http://www.washingtonpost.com/national/national-security/
pentagon-cyber-offense-part-of-us-strategy/2011/11/15/gIQArEAlPN_story.html.

3. See *Security News Daily,* May 17, 2011, http://www.securitynewsdaily.com/
obama-reserves-right-nuke-hackers-0801/.

4. *Department of Defense Cyberspace Policy Report* (November 2011), http://www.
defense.gov/home/features/2011/0411_cyberstrategy/docs/NDAA%20Section%20
934%20Report_For%20webpage.pdf.

5. Jack Goldsmith, "Can We Stop the Global Cyber Arms Race?" *Washington
Post,* February 1, 2010, http://www.washingtonpost.com/wp-dyn/content/article/
2010/01/31/AR2010013101834.html.

6. John Markoff and Thom Shanker, "Halted '03 Iraq Plan Illustrates U.S. Fear
of Cyberwar Risk," *New York Times,* August 2, 2009, http://www.nytimes.com/2009/
08/02/us/politics/02cyber.html.

7. Eric Schmitt and Thom Shanker, "U.S. Debated Cyberwarfare against Libya," *New York Times,* October 17, 2011, http://www.nytimes.com/2011/10/18/world/africa/cyber-warfare-against-libya-was-debated-by-us.html?_r=1&hp.

8. Ellen Nakashima, "Pentagon Is Debating Cyber-Attacks," *Washington Post,* November 6, 2010, http://www.washingtonpost.com/wp-dyn/content/article/2010/11/05/AR2010110507464.html.

9. For those interested in an extended discussion of the Title 10/Title 50 distinction—its history and import—I recommend Robert Chesney, "Military-Intelligence Convergence and the Law of the Title 10/Title 50 Debate," *Journal of National Security Law and Policy* 5 (2012): 539, http://papers.ssrn.com/sol3/papers.cfm?abstract_id=1945392.

10. "CIA Chief Panetta: Obama Made 'Gutsy' Decision on Bin Laden Raid," *PBS Newshour,* May 3, 2011, http://www.pbs.org/newshour/bb/terrorism/jan-june11/panetta_05–03.html.

11. 50 U.S.C. § 413b(e).

12. Ellen Nakashima, "Pentagon Is Debating Cyber-Attacks."

13. "Advanced Questions for Lieutenant General Keith Alexander," USA Nominee for Commander, United States Cyber Command in Hearings before the United States Senate Armed Services Committee (April 13, 2010), 25, http://www.washingtonpost.com/wp-srv/politics/documents/questions.pdf; see also William J. Lynn III, "Defending a New Domain: The Pentagon's Cyberstrategy," *Foreign Affairs* 97 (September/October 2010): 103 (the U.S. military must "respond to attacks as they happen or even before they arrive").

14. Remarks of Kim Taipale, Duke University Center on Law, Ethics and National Security (April 2010), http://www.law.duke.edu/lens/conferences/2010/program.

15. Martin Libicki, *Cyberdeterrence and Cyberwar* (RAND, 2009), 62.

16. Tom Blau, "War and Technology in the Age of the Electron," in *Defense Security Review* (London 1993), 94, 100.

17. Nelson Schwartz and Louise Story, "When Machines Take Control," *New York Times,* May 7, 2010, B1.

18. Gregory S. McNeal, "The U.S. Practice of Collateral Damage Estimation and Mitigation," November 9, 2011, http://ssrn.com/abstract=1819583.

19. Stewart Baker, "Cyberwar, Lawyers, and the U.S.: Denial of Service," September 30, 2011, http://www.foreignpolicy.com/articles/2011/09/30/denial_of_service?page=0,1.

CHAPTER 5

1. Portions of this chapter first appeared as Paul Rosenzweig, "Lessons of WikiLeaks: The U.S. Needs a Counterinsurgency Strategy for Cyberspace," *Back-grounder* 2560 (May 2011) (The Heritage Foundation), and also appeared as part of a longer paper: Paul Rosenzweig, "Making Good Cybersecurity Law and Policy: How Can We Get Tasty Sausage?" *I/S: A Journal of Law and Policy for the Information Society* 8 (2012): 393.

2. Ravi Somaiya and Alan Cowell, "WikiLeaks Struggles to Stay Online after Cyberattacks," *New York Times,* December 3, 2010, http://www.nytimes.com/2010/12/04/world/europe/04domain.html?_r=1&ref=world.

3. John F. Burns and Ravi Somaiya, "Cyberattackers Focus on Enemies of WikiLeaks's Assange," *New York Times,* December 8, 2010, http://www.nytimes.com/2010/12/09/world/09wiki.html?ref=todayspaper. Joby Warrick and Rob Pegoraro, "WikiLeaks Avoids Shutdown as Supporters Worldwide Go on the Offensive," *Washington Post,* December 8, 2010, http://www.washingtonpost.com/wp-dyn/content/article/2010/12/08/AR2010120804038.html?hpid=moreheadlines.

4. Ashlee Vance and Miguel Helft, "Hackers Defend WikiLeaks, Testing Online Speech," *New York Times,* December 8, 2010, http://www.nytimes.com/2010/12/09/technology/09net.html?_r=1&hp.

5. Ravi Somaiya, "WikiLeaks Mirror Sites Appear by the Hundreds," *New York Times,* December 6, 2010, http://www.nytimes.com/2010/12/06/world/europe/06wiki.html?_r=1&ref=world.

6. Christopher Walker, "A Brief History of Operation Payback—WikiLeaks," *Salon.com,* December 9, 2010, http://www.salon.com/news/feature/2010/12/09/0.

7. The sovereign states were not, of course, mere bystanders. Dutch police have arrested one suspected member of Anonymous. Tim Hwang, "WikiLeaks and the Internet's Long War," *Washington Post,* December 10, 2010, http://www.washingtonpost.com/wp-dyn/content/article/2010/12/10/AR2010121002604.html?hpid=opinionsbox1. And, nobody can be certain that the counterattacks on AnonOps.net were not state-authorized or state-initiated.

8. Nicole Perlroth and John Markoff, "Attack on Vatican Web Site Offers View of Hacker Group's Tactics," *New York Times,* February 26, 2012, https://www.nytimes.com/2012/02/27/technology/attack-on-vatican-web-site-offers-view-of-hacker-groups-tactics.html.

9. Michael Isikoff, "Hacker Group Vows 'Cyberwar' on U.S. Government, Business," March 8, 2011, http://www.msnbc.msn.com/id/41972190/ns/technology_and_science-security.

10. The manifesto was posted as a YouTube video, "Anonymous to the Governments of the World," April 25, 2010, http://www.youtube.com/watch?v=gbqC8BnvVHQ.

11. The video declaration is available at http://planetsave.com/2012/02/28/anonymous-declares-war-on-united-states-government/. The transcript includes the following: "Our time for democracy is here. Our time for real change is here. This is America's time, to have its own revolution. Therefore, Anonymous has decided to openly declare war on the United States government. This is a call to arms. We call upon the Citizens of the United States to stand beside us in overthrowing this corrupted body and call upon a new era. Our allegiance is to the American people, because they are us, and we are them."

12. Scott Shane, "FBI Admits Hacker Group's Eavesdropping," *New York Times,* February 3, 2012, https://www.nytimes.com/2012/02/04/us/fbi-admits-hacker-groups-eavesdropping.html?_r=1.

13. See Abe Greenwald, "The Return of Anarchism," *Commentary* (March 2011), 32.

14. "A Message to Anonymous from #Team Black Hat" (December 2011), https://www.youtube.com/watch?v=PkHhx_Hk3c0&feature=player_embedded#! For another report of internal divisions in Anonymous, see "ITAC Blog, Trouble in Paradise for Hacker Group Anonymous?" March 23, 2011, http://itacidentityblog.com/trouble-in-paradise-for-hacker-group-anonymous.

15. The use of numbers and other symbols to replace letters is a common motif for computer hackers and other sophisticated users. The language is called "leet." Here, the number 3 stands for an E (reversed, of course) and 5 stands for S.

16. Ryan J. Reilly, "'Homeless Hacker' Lawyer: DDoS Isn't an Attack, It's a Digital Sit In," http://idealab.talkingpointsmemo.com/2011/09/homeless-hacker-lawyer-ddos-isnt-an-attack-its-a-digital-sit-in.php; see also "Anonymous: Police Made 'Sad Mistake' in Arresting DDoS Attack Participants," January 28, 2011, http://www.pcmag.com/article2/0,2817,2376861,00.asp#fbid=XSjjh1UUgg3.

17. Quoted in Stephani Ward, "Crime or Protest?" *ABA Journal* 11 (November 2011), http://www.abajournal.com/magazine/article/crime_or_protest_hacking_groups_pose_nettlesome_legal_issues/.

18. Somini Sengupta, "For Suspected Hackers, a Sense of Social Protest," *New York Times,* July 26, 2011, sec. Technology, http://www.nytimes.com/2011/07/26/technology/for-suspected-hackers-a-sense-of-social-protest.html?scp=1&sq=hacker%20anonymous%20sit%20in&st=cse.

19. "Interpol: 25 Suspected Anonymous Hackers Arrested In New Crackdown," *Huffington Post,* February 28, 2012, http://www.huffingtonpost.com/2012/02/28/interpol-anonymous-hackers_n_1306630.html.

20. Somini Sengupta, "Arrests Sow Mistrust inside a Clan of Hackers," *New York Times,* March 6, 2012, https://www.nytimes.com/2012/03/07/technology/lulzsec-hacking-suspects-are-arrested.html.

21. Chad Bray, "FBI's 'Sabu' Hacker Was a Model Informant," *Wall Street Journal,* March 8, 2012, http://online.wsj.com/article_email/SB10001424052970204603004577269844134620160-lMyQjAxMTAyMDAwOTEwNDkyWj.html?mod=wsj_share_email.

22. Esther Addley and Jason Deans, "WikiLeaks Suspends Publishing to Fight Financial Blockade," *Guardian* (London), October 24, 2011, http://www.guardian.co.uk/media/2011/oct/24/wikileaks-suspends-publishing.

23. "Counterinsurgency," *FM* (December 2006), 3–24, http://www.fas.org/irp/doddir/army/fm3–24.pdf.

24. Michael S. Schmidt, "F.B.I. Director Warns about Terrorist Hacking," *New York Times,* March 7, 2012, https://www.nytimes.com/2012/03/08/us/fbi-director-warns-about-terrorist-hacking.html.

25. In 1648 the Peace of Westphalia established the system of national sovereignty that continues to govern international relations to this day. Issues directly related to international questions are discussed in Chapter 19.

26. U.S. Army Field Manual 3–24 at 1–2.

27. The Office of the President, "National Security Strategy" (May 2010), 27.

28. The Office of the President, "National Security Strategy," 28.

29. *United States of America v. John Doe 1, John Doe 2 . . . and John Doe 13,* U.S. District Court of Connecticut, April 23, 2011, 7, http://www.wired.com/images_blogs/threatlevel/2011/04/Coreflood-47_Dec-Briana-Neumiller.pdf.

30. *United States of America v. John Doe 1, John Doe 2 . . . and John Doe 13.*

31. I first heard this idea from a former student of mine, an Air Force JAG officer, Michael Hopkins, to whom credit is due.

32. Thom Shanker and Eric Schmitt, "U.S. Military Goes Online to Rebut Extremists," *New York Times,* November 17, 2011, http://www.nytimes.com/2011/11/18/world/us-military-goes-online-to-rebut-extremists.html?_r=1&ref=world.

33. Jenna Wortham, "Web Site Will Shut Down to Protest Antipiracy Bills," *New York Times,* January 17, 2012, https://www.nytimes.com/2012/01/18/technology/web-wide-protest-over-two-antipiracy-bills.html?_r=1&hp.

34. The official announcement of the indictment, with links to the actual text, is here: http://www.justice.gov/opa/pr/2012/January/12-crm-074.html.

PART II

1. Only the Shadow knows for sure what evil lurks, but we can be confident that lurk it does and always will.

CHAPTER 6

1. WHOIS Review Team, "Final Report (Draft) Executive Summary," December 5, 2011, http://www.icann.org/en/reviews/affirmation/whois-rt-draft-final-report-exec-summary-05dec11-en.pdf.

2. "Tracking GhostNet: Investigating a Cyber Espionage Network, Information Warfare Monitor," March 29, 2009, http://www.scribd.com/doc/13731776/Tracking-GhostNet-Investigating-a-Cyber-Espionage-Network.

3. Siobhan Gorman, "US Homes In on China Spying," *Wall Street Journal,* December 13, 2011, http://online.wsj.com/article/SB10001424052970204336104577094690893528130.html.

4. "National Strategy for Trusted Identities in Cyberspace" (April 2011), http://www.whitehouse.gov/sites/default/files/rss_viewer/NSTICstrategy_041511.pdf.

5. Michael Wines, "China Expands Microblog Identification Program," *New York Times,* January 18, 2012, https://www.nytimes.com/2012/01/19/world/asia/china-expands-program-requiring-real-name-registration-online.html?_r=1.

6. *McIntyre v. Ohio Elections Commission,* 514 U.S. 334 (1995).

7. Marc Rotenberg, "Planning for the Future of Cyber Attack Attribution," hearing before the House of Representatives Committee on Science and Technology and Subcommittee on Technology and Innovation 2, July 15, 2010, http://scholarship.law.georgetown.edu/cgi/viewcontent.cgi?article=1106&context=cong (citing Trina K. Kissel, "License to Blog: Internet Regulation in the People's Republic of China," *Indiana International and Comparative Law Review* 17 [2007]: 229).

8. A much better, delightful, introduction to the IETF is "The Tao of the IETF" (2012), https://www.ietf.org/tao.html.

9. The problem of international governance of the Internet is discussed more fully in Chapter 19.

10. Somini Sengupta, "Hacker Rattles Internet Security Circles," *New York Times,* September 11, 2011, http://www.nytimes.com/2011/09/12/technology/hacker-rattles-internet-security-circles.html?scp=3&sq=iran%20hacker&st=cse.

11. "Internet Security: Duly Notarised," *The Economist,* September 4, 2011, http://www.economist.com/blogs/babbage/2011/09/internet-security?fsrc=scn/tw/te/bl/dulynotarised.

12. Gregg Keizer, "Hackers Steal SSL Certificates for CIA, MI6, Mossad," *Computerworld,* September 4, 2011, http://www.computerworld.com/s/article/9219727/Hackers_steal_SSL_certificates_for_CIA_MI6_Mossad.

13. Steve Bellovin, "SMBlog: Comments on the National Strategy for Trusted Identities in Cyberspace," July 11, 2010, http://www.cs.columbia.edu/~smb/blog/2010–07/2010–07–11.html.

CHAPTER 7

1. Ian Traynor, "Russia Accused of Unleashing Cyberwar to Disable Estonia," *Guardian* (London), May 17, 2007, http://www.guardian.co.uk/world/2007/may/17/topstories3.russia.

2. 18 U.S.C. § 1030.

3. I learned a great deal about the Russian Business Network from and was pointed to some of the sources referenced in this section by a presentation given by Mr. Rob Wile, a graduate student in my Summer 2011 class at Medill School of Journalism, Northwestern University.

4. Peter Warren, "Hunt for Russia's Web Criminals," *Guardian* (London), November 14, 2007, http://www.guardian.co.uk/technology/2007/nov/15/news.crime.

5. This story and others are presented in the deeply detailed study of the RBN: VeriSign, "The Russian Business Network: Rise and Fall of a Criminal ISP," in *Cyber Fraud: Tactics, Techniques and Procedures*, ed. James Graham (CRC Press, 2009), 171–207.

6. "U.S.GovernmentTakesDownCorefloodBotnet—KrebsonSecurity,"April2011, http://krebsonsecurity.com/2011/04/u-s-government-takes-down-coreflood-botnet/.

7. 18 U.S.C. §§1345, 2531.

8. See *United States Supplemental Memorandum in Support of Preliminary Injunction (United States v. Does 1–13)* (D. Ct.), April 23, 2011, 3.

9. There is some doubt as to the authenticity of this letter, but it is too amusing not to cite, especially since the underlying jurisdictional issue was quite real. See Clyde Barrow to Henry Ford, April 13, 1934, http://texashideout.tripod.com/ford-letter.html.

10. The treaty was first adopted in 2001, http://conventions.coe.int/Treaty/en/Treaties/Html/185.htm.

11. These hypotheticals come from a letter to Senators Leahy and Grassley from a group of concerned activists. The author was a member of that group. See "Letter to Sens. Leahy & Grassley," August 3, 2011, https://www.cdt.org/files/pdfs/CFAA_Sign-on_ltr.pdf.

12. The Lori Drew case is well summarized in Paul Rosenzweig and Brian Walsh, eds., *One Nation under Arrest* (Heritage Foundation, 2010), ch. 8.

13. Most notably, we have come to understand Chinese research that examines the possibility of creating a cascading failure in American electrical grids. See Jian-Wei Wang and Li-Li Rong, "Cascade-based Attack Vulnerability on the US Power Grid," *Safety Science* 47 (2009): 1332, http://www.docstoc.com/docs/30535594/Cascade-Based-Attack-Vulnerability-on-the-US-Power-Grid%E2%80%9D.

14. 18 U.S.C. §1030(a)(2)(C).

15. It is notable, for example, that the private sector efforts to track the Chinese intrusion into the Dalai Lama's computer system (known as GhostNet) were conducted by a Canadian company. If an American company had done the work, it would likely have violated federal law.

16. See Joshua Phillipp and Matthew Robertson, "China Fights a War without Firing a Gun," *Epoch Times,* May 4, 2011, http://www.theepochtimes.com/n2/china-news/china-fights-a-war-without-firing-a-gun-55649.html; and "China's Cyber Threat a High-Stakes Spy Game," *KQED News,* November 27, 2011, http://www.kqed.org/news/story/2011/11/27/76386/chinas_cyber_threat_a_highstakes_spy_game?source=npr&category=technology. According to Jim Lewis of the Center for Strategic and International Studies, this example is but one of a hundred.

17. Office of the National Counterintelligence Executive, *Foreign Spies Stealing US Economic Secrets in Cyberspace,* October 2011, http://www.ncix.gov/publications/reports/fecie_all/Foreign_Economic_Collection_2011.pdf.

18. Office of the National Counterintelligence Executive, *Foreign Spies,* i.

CHAPTER 8

1. This chapter is derived from a prior essay published in Harvey Rishikof, Stewart Baker and Bernard Horowitz, eds., *Patriots Debate: Contemporary Issues in National Security Law* (ABA Publishing, 2012).

2. "Legality of Intrusion Detection System to Protect Unclassified Computer Networks in the Executive Branch," DOJ, Office of Legal Counsel (August 2009), http://www.justice.gov/olc/2009/legality-of-e2.pdf; "Legal Issues Relating to the Testing, Use, and Deployment of an Intrusion Detection System (Einstein 2.0) to Protect Unclassified Computer Networks in the Executive Branch," DOJ, Office of Legal Counsel (January 2009), http://www.justice.gov/olc/2009/e2-issues.pdf.

3. The qualification "current" is critical. In *United States v. Jones,* No. 10-1259 (January 23, 2012), http://www.supremecourt.gov/opinions/11pdf/10-1259.pdf, several justices of the Supreme Court suggested they might reconsider the third-party doctrine discussed in text. If they choose to do so in the future some of the analysis in this chapter will be dated.

4. 425 U.S. 435 (1976).

5. 442 U.S. 735 (1979).

6. See, e.g., Stephen J. Schulhofer, "The New World of Foreign Intelligence Surveillance," *Stanford Law and Policy Review* 17 (2006): 531, 546 (calling the reasoning of these cases "exceptionally strained"). Others think the doctrine makes sense. See, e.g., Orin S. Kerr, "The Case for the Third-Party Doctrine," *Michigan Law Review* 107 (2009): 561. As noted, although the Supreme Court may reconsider the doctrine, it has not yet done so.

7. See the OLC opinions in note 2.

8. *O'Connor v. Ortega,* 480 U.S. 709 (1987) (government employee has privacy expectation in the contents of his desk at work).

9. Ellen Nakashima, "NSA Allies with Internet Carriers to Thwart Cyber Attacks against Defense Firms," *Washington Post,* June 17, 2011, http://www.washingtonpost.com/national/major-internet-service-providers-cooperating-with-nsa-on-

monitoring-traffic/2011/06/07/AG2dukXH_story.html. The regulations governing this program are DoD-DIB Voluntary Cyber Security and Information Assurance, 77 Fed. Reg. 27615 (May 11, 2012), http://www.gpo.gov/fdsys/pkg/FR-2012-05-11/pdf/2012-10651.pdf.

10. David Ignatius, "Department of Internet Defense," *Washington Post*, August 12, 2011, http://www.washingtonpost.com/opinions/department-of-internet-defense/2011/08/12/gIQAPQcxBJ_story.html.

11. The precise extent and nature of this voluntary feedback is unclear from official records. DoD says only that companies are "asked to report network incidents." According to the recent Privacy Impact Assessment (PIA), published by the Department of Homeland Security, "The [ISP] may, with the permission of the participating DIB company, also provide some limited information about the incident to U.S.-CERT sufficient to capture the fact of occurrence. U.S.-CERT may share the fact of occurrence information with DoD pursuant to existing U.S.-CERT procedures in an effort to increase DoD's understanding of the threats to their critical assets that reside within the DIB companies' networks and system. The [ISPs] may voluntarily choose to send U.S.-CERT information related to cyber threat indicators or other possible known or suspected cyber threats." *PIA for Joint Cybersecurity Services Pilot*, January 13, 2012, http://www.dhs.gov/xlibrary/assets/privacy/privacy_nppd_jcsp_pia.pdf.

12. Ellen Nakashima, "Cyber Defense Effort Is Mixed, Study Finds," *Washington Post*, January 12, 2012, http://www.washingtonpost.com/world/national-security/cyber-defense-effort-is-mixed-study-finds/2012/01/11/gIQAAu0YtP_story.html.

13. To finish the picture however, we need to acknowledge that there is some real doubt that the DIB Pilot, even in its current form, is worth the effort. Though theoretically a sound investment, a recent Department of Defense review of the program suggests that it has been of only limited utility. In particular, of the 52 malicious incidents identified during the course of the program, only two of them were identified based on NSA threat data that the companies did not already have themselves. See Ellen Nakashima, "Cyber-Defense Program Gets Review," *Washington Post*, January 13, 2012, http://www.washingtonpost.com/world/national-security/cyber-defense-effort-is-mixed-study-finds/2012/01/11/gIQAAu0YtP_story.html.

14. *Michigan Dept. of State Police v. Sitz*, 496 U.S. 444 (1990). The limitation to noncriminal sanctions is likely a critical distinction that bears on the constitutionality of any program. *City of Indianapolis v. Edmond*, 531 U.S. 32 (2000) (disapproving checkpoint drug searches).

15. For example, an Illinois statute, (625 Ill. Compiled Stat. § 5/11–501.1, Ill. Rev. Stat, ch. 95 1/2, 11–501.1 (1981)), provides that any person who drives an automobile in that state consents to take a breath-analysis test when requested to do so by an officer as incident to an arrest for driving while intoxicated. Other states have similar laws.

CHAPTER 9

1. This chapter originally appeared in a slightly different form as part of Paul Rosenzweig, "Privacy and Counter-Terrorism: The Pervasiveness of Data," *Case Western Reserve Journal of International Law* 42 (2010): 625.

2. For an overarching history of the transition from human intelligence to U-2 spy planes and, eventually, to satellites, see generally Tim Weiner, *Legacy of Ashes: The History of the CIA* (Doubleday, 2007).

3. Law enforcement electronic interceptions are generally governed by Title III of the Omnibus Crime Control and Safe Streets Act of 1968, Pub. L. No. 90-351, 82 Stat. 197 (codified in scattered sections of 5, 18, and 42 U.S.C.), and intelligence interceptions are governed by the Foreign Intelligence Surveillance Act of 1978, Pub. L. No. 95-511, 92 Stat. 1783 (codified as amended in scattered sections of 50 U.S.C.).

4. An article by William Safire instigated a significant political controversy. See William Safire, "You Are a Suspect," *New York Times*, November 14, 2002, A35. It led directly to the creation of a blue-ribbon panel, the Technology and Privacy Advisory Committee and, eventually, to the cancellation of the Total Information Awareness program. The final report of the Technology and Privacy Advisory Committee is available at http://www.defense.gov/news/Jan2006/d20060208tapac.pdf.

5. See, e.g., Scott Shane and Eric Lipton, "Passengers' Actions Thwart a Plan to Down a Jet," *New York Times*, December 27, 2009, A1.

6. See Linda Null and Julia Lobur, *The Essentials of Computer Organization and Architecture*, 2nd ed. (Jones and Bartlett, 2006), 26.

7. A petabyte is 1000^5 bytes, an exabyte is 1000^6 bytes, and a yottabyte is 1000^8 bytes.

8. Samuel J. Palmisano, "Thoughts on the Future of Leadership," September 20, 2011, https://www.ibm.com/smarterplanet/us/en/leadership/stories/pdf/prepared_remarks.pdf.

9. Though the original statement may be apocryphal, many have quoted it since, including McNealy himself. See, e.g., Matt Hamblen, "McNealy Calls for Smart Cards," *Computer World*, October 12, 2001, http://www.computerworld.com/s/article/64729/McNealy_calls_for_smart_cards_to_help_security.

10. See, e.g., *Kyllo v. United States*, 533 U.S. 27 (2001) (the use of thermal imagining outside the home without a warrant is an illegal search when it is used, even indirectly, to reveal activity taking place within the home).

11. *United States Department of Justice v. Reporter's Comm. for Freedom of the Press*, 489 U.S. 749, 762 (1989).

12. See *Reporter's Comm. for Freedom of Press v. United States Department of Justice*, 816 F.2d 730, 732 (D.C. Cir. 1987).

13. *Reporter's Comm. for Freedom of the Press*, 489 U.S., 764.

14. I learned this from discussions with ChoicePoint's CEO Derek Smith and other industry practitioners. See also Ralph M. Stair and George W. Reynolds, *Fundamentals of Information Systems* (Course Technology, 2003), 362 (discussing Experian's collection of public records from government databases).

15. Stephanie Clifford, "Online Ads Follow Web Users, and Get Much More Personal," *New York Times*, July 30, 2009, A1; Natasha Singer, "You for Sale: Mapping, and Sharing, the Consumer Genome," *New York Times*, June 16, 2012, https://www.nytimes.com/2012/06/17/technology/acxiom-the-quiet-giant-of-consumer-database-marketing.html?_r=1&adxnnl=1&pagewanted=all&adxnnlx=1343927034-y5RxqLygbEY59fw4079WvQ.

16. Peter Steiner, "On the Internet, Nobody Knows You're a Dog," *New Yorker*, July 5, 1993, 61 (image).

17. See Clifford, "Online Ads Follow Web Users."

18. Peter Baker and Carl Hulse, "Obama Hears of Signs that Should Have Grounded Plot," *New York Times*, December 30, 2009, A1.

19. For a useful description of NORA, see Martha Baer, Katrina Heron, Oliver Morton and Evan Ratliff, *Safe: The Race to Protect Ourselves in a Newly Dangerous World* (HarperCollins, 2005), 340–45.

20. Simson Garfinkel, "A Powerful Grasp on the Nonobvious," *CSO* 5 (August 2006), 30.

21. A summary of the al-Banna case can be found in Stewart A. Baker and Nathan A. Sales, "Homeland Security, Information Policy, and the Transatlantic Alliance," in George Mason University Law and Economics Research Paper Series 09-20 (March 2009), http://ssrn.com/abstract=1361943. See also Charlotte Buchen, "The Man Turned Away," *PBS Frontline*, October 10, 2006, www.pbs.org/wgbh/pages/frontline/enemywithinh/reality/al-banna.html.

22. For a more thorough description of the ATS, see Paul Rosenzweig, "Targeting Terrorists: The Counterrevolution," *William Mitchell Law Review* 34 (2008): 5083, 5086–90. See also Privacy Act of 1974, Notice of Privacy Act System of Records, 72 Fed. Reg. 43,650–02, August 6, 2007 (providing details of the ATS).

23. See "Customs and Border Protection, On a Typical Day in Fiscal Year 2009, CBP. . .," http://www.cbp.gov/xp/cgov/about/accomplish/fy09_typical_day.xml.

24. See Scott Shane and Lowell Bergman, "Contained? Adding Up the Ounces of Prevention," *New York Times*, September 10, 2006, § 4, 1.

25. U.S. Customs and Border Protection, "CBP: Securing America's Borders" (September 2006), 4, http://www.customs.gov/linkhandler/cgov/newsroom/publications/mission/cbp_securing_borders.ctt/cbp_securing_borders.pdf.

26. See Shane and Bergman, "Contained?"

27. DHS Success Stories Case # 000016 (2005/03/01) (on file with author).

28. See Cam Simpson and Siobhan Gorman, "Terror Suspect Failed a Test," *Wall Street Journal*, December 9, 2009, A4.

29. For example, the Department of Justice's Motion for a Permanent Order of Detention cites CBP records of trips to Pakistan. Memorandum of Law in Support of the Government's Motion for a Permanent Order of Detention at 3–4, *United States v. Najibullah Zazi*, No. 09-CR-663 (RJD) (E.D.N.Y. September 24, 2009), http://www.justice.gov/opa/documents/zazi-detention-memo.pdf.

30. Umar Farouk Abdulmutallab, http://topics.nytimes.com/top/reference/timestopics/people/a/umar_farouk_abdulmutallab/index.html.

31. John F. Burns, "Britain Says Bomb Suspect Was Denied Visa Renewal," *New York Times*, December 29, 2009, A12.

32. See Ben Feller, "Obama: The Buck Stops with Me," *Huffington Post*, January 7, 2010, http://www.huffingtonpost.com/2010/01/07/obama-christmas-bomber-report_n_414309.html.

CHAPTER 10

1. See, e.g., *Gilmore v. Gonzalez*, 435 F.3d 1125 (9th Cir. 2006) (rejecting the claim of the right to fly without showing any identification).

2. 5 U.S.C. § 552a (2006).

3. There exist state-based statutory privacy protections and most state courts recognize a common law right to privacy of some form. See Samuel Warren and Louis D. Brandeis, "The Right to Privacy," *Harvard Law Review* 4 (1890): 193. Neither is an effective limitation on the action of the federal government.

4. 12 U.S.C. §§ 3401–3422 (2006).

5. Pub. L. No. 104–191, 110 Stat. 1936 (codified in scattered sections of 26, 29, and 42 U.S.C.).

6. The Foreign Intelligence Surveillance Act is a notable exception, governing the collection of the substance (as opposed to the call record data) of personal communications. See Foreign Intelligence Surveillance Act, 50 U.S.C. §§ 1801–1871 (2006).

7. See "Privacy Rights Clearinghouse, A Review of the Fair Information Principles: The Foundation of Privacy Public Policy," http://www.privacyrights.org/ar/fairinfo.htm.

8. See Privacy Act, 5 U.S.C. § 552a (2006); Council Directive 95/46/EC, 1995 O.J. (L281) 31, http://ec.europa.eu/justice_home/fsj/privacy/docs/95–46-ce/dir1995–46_part1_en.pdf.

9. See Fair Information Principles in note 7.

10. See U.S. Securities and Exchange Commission, *Privacy Impact Assessment (PIF) Guide* 4 (January 2007), www.sec.gov/about/privacy/piaguide.pdf.

11. Separately, the Privacy Act also affords individuals with the right to go to court to correct erroneous data collected about them. 5 U.S.C. § 552a(d) (2006). It is a never-ending source of friction with our international partners that this right extends only to the American citizens and legal residents.

12. See Newton N. Minow, "Seven Clicks Away," *Wall Street Journal*, June 3, 2004, A14; The Markle Foundation, *Protecting America's Freedom in the Information Age: A Report of the Markle Foundation Task Force* (2002), 28, http://www.markle.org/downloadable_assets/nstf_full.pdf.

13. I first outlined these ideas in Paul Rosenzweig, "Privacy and Consequences: Legal and Policy Structures for Implementing New Counter-Terrorism Technologies and Protecting Civil Liberty," in *Emergent Information Technologies and Enabling Policies for Counter-Terrorism*, ed. Robert L. Popp and John Yen (Wiley-IEEE Press, 2006), 421, 423–28.

14. This section is based in part on the essay Paul Rosenzweig, "The Changing Face of Privacy Policy and the New Policy-Technology Interface," *IEEE Intelligent Systems, Trends and Controversies* (September–October 2005): 84–86, www.dartmouth.edu/~humanterrain/papers/intelligent_systems.pdf.

15. See Homeland Security Act of 2002, Pub. L. No. 107–296 § 222 (2002).

16. See Intelligence Reform and Terrorism Prevention Act of 2004, Pub. L. No. 108–458, 118 Stat. 3638.

17. Implementing Recommendations of the 9/11 Commission Act of 2007, Pub. L. No. 110–53, § 1502, 121 Stat. 266, 424 (codified at 6 U.S.C.A. § 1152(g) (West 2008)).

18. The duties of Civil Liberties and Privacy Officer in the Office of the Director of National Intelligence are codified at 50 U.S.C. § 403–3d (2006). The Privacy and Civil Liberties Oversight Board is authorized by section 801 of the Implementing

Recommendations of the 9/11 Commission Act of 2007. In August 2012, the first four members of the Board were confirmed by the Senate.

19. Pub. L. No. 108–458, § 1016, 118 Stat. 3638.

20. See National Commission on Terrorist Attacks upon the United States, *The 9/11 Commission Report* (2004), 400–4406, http://www.9–11commission.gov/report/911Report.pdf; see generally "Task Force on National Security in the Information Age," in *Creating a Trusted Network for Homeland Security* (Markle Foundation, 2003), http://www.markletaskforce.org/.

21. See Intelligence Reform and Terrorism Prevention Act of 2004, § 1016, Pub. L. No. 108–458, 118 Stat. 3638.

22. Intelligence Reform and Terrorism Prevention Act of 2004, § 1016 (d)(2)(B).

23. See Helene Cooper, "Passport Files of 3 Hopefuls Are Pried Into," *New York Times,* March 22, 2008, A1.

24. Two contract employees were fired by the State Department in the Obama case and a third was disciplined (Cooper, "Passport Files of 3 Hopefuls Are Pried Into"). In the case of Joe Wurzelbacher ("Joe the Plumber"), whose tax records were disclosed, several Ohio state employees were identified and disciplined. See "Clerk Charged with Unlawful Search of Joe the Plumber," http://www.toledoonthemove.com/news/story.aspx?id=213580.

25. I first discussed the ideas in this section with my friend and colleague Kim Taipale of the Center for Advanced Studies. See also K.A. Taipale, *Play Room in the National Security State* (unpublished manuscript, on file with the author) (Center for Advanced Studies Working Paper Series No. 05:0515) (technological changes are transforming criminal justice system from one based on punishment and deterrence to one based on ubiquitous preventative surveillance and control through system constraints).

26. See, e.g., Kevin Courtney, "Red Light Cameras Work, But Are Fines Too High?" *Napa Valley Register,* February 14, 2010, http://www.napavalleyregister.com/news/local/article_1fbc2456–1932–11df-b32f-001cc4c03286.html.

27. Kevin J. O'Brien, "E.U. to Tighten Web Privacy Law, Risking Trans-Atlantic Dispute," *New York Times,* November 9, 2011, https://www.nytimes.com/2011/11/10/technology/eu-to-tighten-web-privacy-law-risking-trans-atlantic-dispute.html.

28. Ravi Mandalla, "New EU Data Protection Laws May Impose Big Fines," *ITProPortal.com,* December 7, 2012, http://www.itproportal.com/2011/12/07/new-eu-data-protection-laws-may-impose-big-fines/#ixzz1iiEFA89N.

CHAPTER 11

I have borrowed the title of this chapter from a wonderful ABA publication titled *No More Secrets: National Security Strategies for a Transparent World* (American Bar Association, Office of the National Counterintelligence Executive, and National Strategy Forum, March 2011), http://www.americanbar.org/content/dam/aba/migrated/2011_build/law_national_security/no_more_secrets_final_report.authcheckdam.pdf.

1. A more detailed description of how WikiLeaks achieves technical anonymity can be found at "About WikiLeaks," http://www.wikileaks.ch/About.html. WikiLeaks asserts that it does not solicit disclosures and declines to disclose details of its submission process in order to avoid compromise of the organization.

2. For an account of Wikileaks' association with the *New York Times*, see Bill Keller, "The Times's Dealings With Julian Assange," *New York Times*, January 30, 2011, http://www.nytimes.com/2011/01/30/magazine/30Wikileaks-t.html?ref=todays paper.

3. Mary Beth Sheridan, "Calderon: WikiLeaks Caused Severe Damage to U.S.-Mexico Relations," *Washington Post*, March 4, 2011, http://www.washingtonpost.com/wp-dyn/content/article/2011/03/03/AR2011030302853.html?wpisrc=nl_buzz.

4. David Smith, "Morgan Tsvangirai Faces Possible Zimbabwe Treason Charge," *Guardian* (London), December 27, 2010, http://www.guardian.co.uk/world/2010/dec/27/wikileaks-morgan-tsvangirai-zimbabwe-sanctions?CMP=twt_gu.

5. Keller, "The Times's Dealings with Julian Assange," 9.

6. Maha Azzam, "Opinion: How WikiLeaks Helped Fuel Tunisian Revolution," *CNN*, January 18, 2011, http://articles.cnn.com/2011–01–18/opinion/tunisia.wikileaks_1_tunisians-wikileaks-regime?_s=PM:OPINION.

7. Scott Shane, "Keeping Secrets WikiSafe," *New York Times*, December 11, 2010, http://www.nytimes.com/2010/12/12/weekinreview/12shane.html?_r=1&scp=5&sq=wikileaks&st=cse.

8. "Report of the Office of the Secretary of Defense Vietnam Task Force" (1967), http://www.archives.gov/research/pentagon-papers/

9. *No More Secrets*, 4.

10. As an interesting aside, the Israeli's are reported to have tracked al-Mabhouh to Dubai using a keystroke logger program that gave them his flight arrival information. Kim Zetter, "Dubai Assassination Followed Failed Attempt by Same Team," *Wired.com*, January 3, 2012, http://www.wired.com/threatlevel/2011/01/dubai-assassination/?utm_source=feedburner&utm_medium=feed&utm_campaign=Feed%3A+wired27b+%28Blog+-+27B+Stroke+6+%28Threat+Level%29%29.

11. The details here are taken from the excellent work by Ronen Bergman, "The Dubai Job," *GQ*, January 2011, http://www.gq.com/news-politics/big-issues/201101/the-dubai-job-mossad-assassination-hamas.

12. The Dubai police released a 27-minute video compilation. A shortened version of it was broadcast on television: "The Murder of Mahmoud al-Mabhouh," February 2010, http://video.gulfnews.com/services/player/bcpid4267205001?bckey=AQ~~,AAAAAFv9650~,tQKIhooE6H7bm0EXwcdF0fKpVqjAui-a&bctid=66672644001.

13. "Spy Craft: A Tide Turns," *The Economist*, July 15, 2010, http://www.economist.com/node/16590867.

14. This short section is derived from a blog post: Paul Rosenzweig and Charles Stimson, "WikiLeaks and Julian Assange: Time to Update U.S. Espionage Laws," *The Foundry*, December 8, 2010 (Heritage Foundation), http://www.heritage.org/research/reports/2010/12/wikileaks-and-julian-assange-time-to-update-us-espionage-laws.

15. 18 U.S.C. § 793(e).

16. Stephen I. Vladeck, "The Espionage Statutes: A Look Back and a Look Forward," testimony before Subcommittee on Terrorism and Homeland Security, Judiciary Committee, U.S. Senate, May 12, 2010, http://judiciary.senate.gov/pdf/10–05–12VladecksTestimony.pdf.

17. Joel Brenner, *America the Vulnerable: Inside the New Threat Matrix of Digital Espionage, Crime and Warfare* (Penguin Press, 2011), 208–9.

CHAPTER 12

Portions of the chapter appeared, initially in Paul Rosenzweig, "The Evolution of Wiretapping," *Engage* 12, no. 2 (Federalist Society, September 2011): 83–87.

1. Vikas Bajaj, "India May Be Near Resolution of BlackBerry Dispute," *New York Times,* August 17, 2010, http://www.nytimes.com/2010/08/18/business/global/18rim.html.

2. Charlie Savage, "U.S. Wants to Make It Easier to Wiretap the Internet," *New York Times,* September 27, 2010, http://www.nytimes.com/2010/09/27/us/27wiretap.html?_r=2&hp. Lately some companies have begun to share more data with the government. Craig Timberg and Elle Nakashima, "Skype Makes Chats and User Data More Available to Police," *Washington Post,* July 26, 2012, http://www.washingtonpost.com/business/economy/skype-makes-chats-and-user-data-more-available-to-police/2012/07/25/gJQAobI39W_story.html?hpid=z1.

3. This story is told, in greater detail, in Simon Singh, *The Code Book* (Doubleday, 1999), 4–5.

4. Singh, *The Code Book*, 11–12.

5. Ibraham A. Al-Kadi, "The Origins of Cryptology: The Arab Contributions," *Cryptologia* 16, no. 2 (April 1992): 97–126.

6. This very short summary has not done the math any justice at all. A good layman's summary of how this works can be found at Martin Gardner, "A New Kind of Cipher that Would Take Millions of Years to Break," *Scientific American* 237 (August 1997): 120–24.

7. Indeed, even if private keys are still used, the size of the keys has become almost impossible to decrypt. Current standard encryption algorithms commonly use anywhere from 128 to 1,024 bit keys, meaning the key is up to 1,024 bits long. At this length, brute force decryption becomes practically impossible. For a 128 bit length key, there are 339,000,000,000,000,000,000,000,000,000,000,000,000 possible keys. The number of possible keys for a 1,024 bit key is much, much larger—it would take millions of years, given today's computing power to try every possible key.

8. Because of its founders' notoriety, RSA is famous and was thought to be the strongest encryption security company in the country. Until, that is, they made an obscure announcement in the press alluding to the exploitation of some unidentified security vulnerability that degraded the effectiveness of their encryption product. "Open Letter to RSA Customers," March 21, 2011, http://www.rsa.com/node.aspx?id=3872.

9. Christopher Drew and John Markoff, "SecurID Breach Suggested in Hacking Attempt at Lockheed," *New York Times,* May 27, 2011, http://www.nytimes.com/2011/05/28/business/28hack.html?_r=1&scp=2&sq=rsa%20lockheed&st=cse.

10. See Whitfield Diffie and Susan Landau, "The Export of Cryptography in the 20th Century and the 21st," in *Sun Microsys Labs: The First Ten Years 1991–2001,* Sun Labs Perspectives Essay Series, ed. Jeanie Treichel and Mary Holzer (2001), 210–15, http://research.sun.com/techrep/Perspectives/PS-01–5.pdf.

11. Department of Commerce, Bureau of Export Administration, 15 C.F.R. Parts 734, 740, 742, 770, and 772, Docket No. RIN: 0694-AC11, effective January 14, 2000.

12. "Not Even the FBI Was Able to Decrypt files of Daniel Dantas," June 2010, http://www.webcitation.org/query?url=g1.globo.com/English/noticia/2010/06/not-even-fbi-can-de-crypt-files-daniel-dantas.html.

13. Jeffrey Yeates, "CALEA and the RIPA: The U.S. and the U.K. Responses to Wiretapping in an Increasingly Wireless World," *Albany Law Journal of Science and Technology* 12 (2001): 125, 135–36.

14. The list of communications technologies here is derived from a research paper written by Andrew Blair, a law student at George Washington University who submitted the paper for my Cybersecurity Law and Policy class in Fall 2010. I am also indebted to Mr. Blair for some of the research references on which I rely in this chapter. See Andrew Blair, "CALEA 2.0—Legal And Policy Considerations in Amending the Communications Assistance for Law Enforcement Act" (2010) (on file with author).

15. In the 2009 film *He's Just Not That Into You* (New Line Cinema), one of the characters, Mary (played by Drew Barrymore), bemoans the proliferation of communications methods: "I had this guy leave me a voice mail at work, so I called him at home, and then he e-mailed me to my BlackBerry, and so I texted to his cell, and now you just have to go around checking all these different portals just to get rejected by seven different technologies."

16. "IETF Policy on Wiretapping," May 2000, http://www.ietf.org/rfc/rfc2804.txt.

17. 389 U.S. 347 (1967).

18. Title III is now codified in the United States Code at 18 U.S.C. §§ 2510–22.

19. Electronic Communications Privacy Act of 1986, Pub. L. No. 99–508, 100 Stat. 1848 (1986), 18 U.S.C. § 2510.

20. "Probable cause" is a familiar criminal standard and is used in the Fourth Amendment to define the showing necessary for the issuance of a search warrant. It is a higher standard than "reasonable suspicion" but less than the standard needed to, say, convict at a criminal trial. One common definition is "information sufficient to warrant a prudent person's belief that the wanted individual had committed a crime (for an arrest warrant) or that evidence of a crime or contraband would be found in a search (for a search warrant)."

21. The list of offenses can be found at 18 U.S.C. § 2516.

22. The law makes clear that U.S. citizens cannot be targeted solely on the basis of their lawful business or political relationships with foreign governments or organizations, or on the basis of other activities protected by the First Amendment.

23. Communications Assistance for Law Enforcement Act, Pub. L. No. 102–414, 108 Stat. 4279 (1994), now codified at 47 U.S.C. § 1001–1021.

24. Dan Eggen and Jonathan Krim, "Easier Internet Wiretaps Sought; Justice Dept., FBI Want Consumers to Pay the Cost," *Washington Post,* March 13, 2004, A01; Marcia Coyle, "Wiretaps Coming to Internet; Critics Considering Legal Challenges," *National Law Journal* (2005): P1.

25. Initially, Voice over IP (VoIP) services (i.e., telephone-type connections using the web instead of phone lines for the connection) were excluded from CALEA. In 2006, interconnected VoIP services (i.e., any service where a portion of the call was connected to a PTSN, like the service provided by Vonage) were included under CALEA. See *In re Commc'ns Assistance for Law Enforcement Act & Broadband Access & Servs.*, 20 F.C.C.R. 14989, 9–37 (2005).

26. Savage, "U.S. Wants to Make It Easier to Wiretap the Internet."

27. Napster, for example was the first peer-to-peer network used for large-scale music sharing. Grokster, LimeWire, KaZaa, and the Pirate Bay have followed in a neverending succession of file sharing programs.

28. For example, Ubuntu Linux and World of Warcraft patches are distributed using the BitTorrent protocol. See Blair, "CALEA 2.0."

29. John C.K. Daly, "Echelon—the Ultimate Spy Network?" *United Press International*, March 1, 2004, http://slickmisc.spunge.org/list/200403/msg00006.html.

30. Duncan Campbell, "Inside Echelon: The History, Structure and Function of the Global Surveillance System Known as Echelon," *Echelon On Line*, July 25, 2000, http://echelononline.free.fr/dc/insideechelon.htm.

31. James Risen and Eric Lichtblau, "Bush Lets US Spy on Callers Without Courts," *New York Times*, December 16, 2005, A1.

32. Daly, "Echelon."

33. Savage, "U.S. Wants to Make It Easier to Wiretap the Internet."

34. The contrasting formulations were posited as useful analogies in *Doe v. United States*, 487 U.S. 201 (1988). In *Doe*, the signing of a blank bank consent form was considered more like the production of a physical object. By contrast, in *Hubbell v. United States*, 530 U.S. 27 (2000), the documents produced by the defendant in response to a subpoena were organized and selected through his own mental analysis and thus protected from disclosure. Few court cases have addressed the encryption question directly: two early cases, *United States v. Rogozin*, 2010 WL 4628520 (W.D.N.Y. Nov. 16. 2010) and *United States v. Kirschner*, 2010 WL 1257355 (E.D. Mich. March 30, 2010) thought that the password could not be compelled, while another, *In re Boucher*, 2009 WL 424718, *1 (D. Vt. 2009), http://federalevidence.com/pdf/2009/03-March/Inre-BoucherII.pdf, was decided on the technicality that Boucher had already given the government access to his computer once, so he could not object to doing so a second time and disclosing his encryption key. Most recently, in *United States v. Friscou*, Cr. No. 10–509 (D. Colo. 2012), http://www.wired.com/images_blogs/threatlevel/2012/01/decrypt.pdf, the court concluded that a password was more like the key to a lock and that a defendant could be compelled to disclose a password on pain of contempt for refusing to do so. The most recent, and perhaps most definitive case, *In Re: Grand Jury Subpoena Duces Tecum*, No. 11–12268 (11th Cir. 2012), http://www.ca11.uscourts.gov/opinions/ops/201112268.pdf, reflecting the first appellate court decision on the issue determined that compelled decryption was unconstitutional. Suffice to say, the final resolution of this question lies in the future.

35. Report of the Director of the Administrative Office of the United States Courts on Applications for Order Authorizing or Approving the Interception of Wire, Oral, or Electronic Communications for 2010 (June 2011), http://www.uscourts.gov/uscourts/Statistics/WiretapReports/2010/2010WireTapReport.pdf.

36. See FBI and Department of Justice, *Communications Assistance for Law Enforcement Act (CALEA) Implementation Plan*, Part V, March 3, 1997, http://www.cdt.org/digi_tele/CALEA_plan.html#five.

37. When the Clipper chip was first introduced, flaws in it were quickly found. See Matt Blaze, "Protocol Failure in the Escrowed Encryption Standard," August 20, 1994, http://www.crypto.com/papers/eesproto.pdf. More recently, Greek official communications were intercepted illegally through a security flaw created by the inclusion of built-in interception feature. See "Vodafone Greece Rogue Phone Taps: Details at Last," *The H Security*, http://www.h-online.com/security/news/item/Vodafone-Greece-rogue-phone-taps-details-at-last-733244.html.

38. In addition to the Indian example mentioned at the outset, the United Arab Emirates is seeking similar access. See "UAE Crackdown on BlackBerry Services to Extend to Foreign Visitors," *Washington Post*, August 3, 2010, http://www.washingtonpost.com/wp-dyn/content/article/2010/08/02/AR2010080204752.html.

39. Hillary Clinton, "Remarks on Internet Freedom," January 21, 2010, http://www.state.gov/secretary/rm/2010/01/135519.htm.

40. Jay Wack, personal interview with the author, February 2012.

41. Riva Richmond, "Attack on Comodo Sheds Light on Internet Security Holes," *New York Times*, April 6, 2011, http://www.nytimes.com/2011/04/07/technology/07hack.html?_r=1&scp=1&sq=comodo&st=cse.

CHAPTER 13

1. Gus W. Weiss, "The Farewell Dossier: Duping the Soviets," *Studies in Intelligence* (CIA 1996), https://www.cia.gov/library/center-for-the-study-of-intelligence/csi-publications/csi-studies/studies/96unclass/farewell.htm.

2. Thomas Reed, *At the Abyss: An Insiders History of the Cold War* (Presidio Press, 2004).

3. John Pomfret "History of Telecom Company Illustrates Lack of Strategic Trust between U.S., China," *Washington Post*, October 7, 2010, http://www.washingtonpost.com/wp-dyn/content/article/2010/10/07/AR2010100707210.html?hpid=topnews.

4. David Barboza, "Huawei Seeks a U.S. Inquiry to Clear Its Name," *New York Times*, February 25, 2011, http://www.nytimes.com/2011/02/26/technology/26huawei.html?_r=1&scp=1&sq=huawei%20open%20letter&st=cse.

5. Neal Ungerleider, "DHS: Imported Consumer Tech Contains Hidden Hacker Attack Tools," July 8, 2011, http://www.fastcompany.com/1765855/dhs-someones-spiking-our-imported-tech-with-attack-tools.

6. Cyber Space Policy Review (May 29, 2009), 34, http://www.whitehouse.gov/assets/documents/Cyberspace_Policy_Review_final.pdf.

7. Report of the Defense Science Board, "Mission Impact of Foreign Influence on DoD Software," September 2007, vi, http://www.acq.osd.mil/dsb/reports/ADA486949.pdf.

8. *Comprehensive National Cybersecurity Initiative* (May 2010), http://www.whitehouse.gov/sites/default/files/cybersecurity.pdf.

9. Kim Zetter, "Equipment Maker Caught Installing Backdoor Account in Control System Code," *Wired,* http://www.wired.com/threatlevel/2012/04/ruggedcombackdoor/.

10. CFIUS operates pursuant to section 721 of the Defense Production Act of 1950, as amended by the Foreign Investment and National Security Act of 2007 (section 721) and as implemented by Executive Order 11858, as amended, and regulations at 31 C.F.R. Part 800. The DNI is tasked with conducting an intelligence assessment of the risks posed by certain transactions and reporting to the committee on his findings. His representative sits, ex officio, on the committee and brings a counter-intelligence perspective to its deliberations where appropriate.

11. See James Jackson, "The Committee on Foreign Investments in the United States (CFIUS)" (Congressional Research Service, February 4, 2010), 9 (reporting that the Israeli firm Check Point Software Technologies decided to call off its proposed $225 million acquisition of Sourcefire, a U.S. firm specializing in security appliances for protecting a corporation's internal computer networks, because of a CFIUS inquiry). The author is personally aware of several similar transactions, the details of which are protected by the confidentiality rules that apply to CFIUS activities.

12. One other, rarely used, mechanism is section 232 of the Trade Expansion Act of 1962 (19 U.S.C. § 1862). Section 232 authorizes the Department of Commerce, in consultation with DoD and other appropriate agencies, see 15 CFR Part 705, to block the importation of goods that would displace domestically produced materials essential to the defense industrial base. Given the infrequency of its application, section 232 is of little practical import.

13. See Michael Aisenberg, "The Information Technology Supply Chain: Survey and Forecast of Emerging Obligations for Industrial Vendors," *ABA Info Sec. Quarterly* (Spring 2010): 1 and n.3, 6–8 (copy on file with author). I am indebted to Michael Aisenberg of MITRE, whose comments on the initial draft allowed the development of the analysis in this section.

14. The report is summarized in a useful briefing, www.combatcounterfeits.com/files/bis-counterfeit-briefing.ppt.

15. Aisenberg, "Information Technology Supply Chain," 10.

16. The observation as to the prioritization of threats was made by a participant at a conference on National Security Threats in Cyberspace whose comments were subject to Chatham House rules. They were for the public record but not for direct attribution.

17. A Collective Security Approach to Protecting the Global Critical Infrastructure (ITU Workshop on Creating Trust in Critical Network Infrastructures, Document CNI/09, May 2002), 13 n14.

18. It is true that all operating systems necessarily have vulnerabilities, and that would be true of government systems that run on ADA, or Windows, or Linux. The degree of comparative vulnerability of these operating systems is hotly debated. See, e.g., Geer et al., "Cyber*In*security: The Costs of Monopoly," http://cryptome.org/cyberinsecurity.htm (arguing that monoculture of Microsoft Windows increases vulnerability).

The point here is a much more limited one: when the operating system is constructed exclusively by the government, then the government has much greater control against the deliberate insertion of vulnerabilities and it will tend to minimize the extent to which it is subject to nonpurposeful malware attacks.

19. DoD has reported finding counterfeit hardware in systems that the Pentagon has purchased. See Ellen Nakashima, "Defense Official Discloses Cyberattack," *Washington Post,* August 24. 2010, http://www.washingtonpost.com/wp-dyn/content/article/2010/08/24/AR2010082406154.html?hpid=topnews. The Army's concept of cyber operations for the future recognizes the need to address hardware vulnerabilities. See TRADOC PAM 515-7-8, 12.

20. William J. Lynn III, "Defending a New Domain: The Pentagon's Cyberstrategy," *Foreign Affairs* (September/October 2010): 97, 101 (hardware tampering is "almost impossible to detect and ever harder to eradicate").

21. CNCI Initiative #11.

22. Report of the Defense Science Board, "Mission Impact of Foreign Influence," 51.

23. Report of the Defense Science Board, "Mission Impact of Foreign Influence," 51–68.

24. Department of Commerce, "Defense Industrial Base Assessment: Counterfeit Electronics" (January 2010), 208–11, http://www.bis.doc.gov/defenseindustrialbase programs/osies/defmarketresearchrpts/final_counterfeit_electronics_report.pdf.

25. Department of Commerce, "Defense Industrial Base," 211.

26. I first wrote about these in "The Organization of the United States Government and Private Sector for Achieving Cyber Deterrence" in *Proceedings of a Workshop on Deterring Cyber Attacks: Informing Strategies and Developing Options for U.S. Policy* (National Academy of Sciences2010).

27. The author pretends no expertise in the epidemiology of herd immunity. What little understanding he possesses comes from a few useful review articles. For example, P. Fine, "Herd Immunity: History, Theory, Practice" *Epidemiologic Reviews* 15, no. 2 (1993): 265–302. Notably, adoption of this approach is consistent with recent conceptual thinking suggesting that cybersecurity issues are analytically akin to public health problems. For example, IBM, *Meeting the Cybersecurity Challenge: Empowering Stakeholders and Ensuring Coordination* (February 2010), 11–23; K.A. Taipale, *Cyberdeterrence* (January 2009), http://papers.ssrn.com/sol3/papers.cfm?abstract_id=1336045.

CHAPTER 14

Portions of this chapter and the next first appeared as "Cybersecurity, and Public Goods: The Public/Private 'Partnership'" (Task Force on National Security and Law, The Hoover Institution, 2011).

1. Michael Arrington, "Google Defends against Large-Scale Chinese Cyber Attack," *TechCrunch,* January 12, 2010, http://techcrunch.com/2010/01/12/google-china-attacks/.

2. Ellen Nakashima, "Chinese Leaders Ordered Google Hack, U.S. Was Told," *Washington Post,* December 5, 2010, http://www.washingtonpost.com/wp-dyn/content/

article/2010/12/04/AR2010120403347.html. The author of this article has an active security clearance and has, therefore, been directed to treat the released cables as remaining classified. In repeating here this public report of the alleged contents of the WikiLeaks cables, he has neither examined the cable itself nor visited the WikiLeaks site.

3. Ellen Nakashima, "Google to Enlist NSA to Help It Ward off Cyberattacks," *Washington Post,* February 3, 2010, http://www.washingtonpost.com/wp-dyn/content/ article/2010/02/03/AR2010020304057.html?hpid=topnews.

4. In 2011, when the author was touring the cybersecurity operations center of a major U.S. systems integrator, he was confidently told that "we have everything the government has and more." Sadly, this same integrator has been in the news recently for having suffered a significant intrusion.

5. Typical is the statement of Senator Diane Feinstein at a Senate Judiciary Hearing in 2004: "I would also note that 85 to 90 percent of our nation's cyber-infrastructure remains under the control of the private sector," http://feinstein.senate.gov/04Releases/r-cyberterror.pdf. Likewise, Mishel Kwon, the former Director of the U.S. Computer Emergency Response Team (U.S.-CERT) has repeated this figure, noting in an interview "the high level of private ownership of critical infrastructure (between 85–90 percent),"http://blog.executivebiz.com/2010/02/mischel-kwon-cybersecurity-is-many-problems-on-many-different-levels/. Perhaps, we should accept this assertion since so many with responsibility in the area offer it as fact, but it has a bit of the air of an urban legend about it and no comprehensive survey documenting the figure appears to exist.

6. Thanks to Mr. Joshua House, a student in my Fall 2010 seminar on Cybersecurity Law and Policy at George Washington University, for an excellent research paper on which this chapter has relied for many of the sources in this analysis. See Joshua House, "Private Good, Public Good, or No Good?: The Law and Economics of Cybersecurity Policy" (December 2010) (on file with author).

7. See, generally, Paul Samuelson, "The Pure Theory of Public Expenditure," *Review of Economics and Statistics* 36, no. 4 (1954): 387–89; David Schmidtz, *The Limits of Government: An Essay on the Public Goods Argument* (Westview Press, 1991).

8. Eric A. Fisher, *Creating a National Framework for Cybersecurity: An Analysis of Issues and Opinions* (Nova Science Publishers, 2009), 7.

9. Benjamin Powell, "Is Cybersecurity a Public Good? Evidence from the Financial Services Industry," *Journal of Law, Economics, and Policy* 1 (2005): 497, 498.

10. Bruce H. Kobayashi, "Private Versus Social Incentives in Cybersecurity: Law and Economics," in *The Law and Economics of Cybersecurity,* ed. Mark F. Grady and Francesco Parisi (Cambridge University Press, 2006), 16. The assumption, here, is that information is a good. Some have argued that in the absence of artificial intellectual property protections, information is not a traditional economic good. For example, Murray N. Rothbard, *Man, Economy, and State: A Treatise on Economic Principles,* 2nd ed. (Ludwig von Mises Institute, 2009), 1033.

11. E. Gal-Or and A. Ghose, "The Economic Incentives for Sharing Security Information," *Information Systems Research* 16, no. 2 (2005): 186–208.

12. See Roy E. Cordato, *Welfare Economics and Externalities in an Open Ended Universe: A Modern Austrian Perspective* (Kluwer Academic Publishers, 1992), 2.

13. Markets in zero-day exploits are discussed in Charlie Miller, *The Legitimate Vulnerability Market: Inside the Secretive World of 0-day Exploit Sales* (Independent Security Evaluators, 2007), http://weis2007.econinfosec.org/papers/29.pdf.

14. See Christopher J. Coyne, "Who's to Protect Cyberspace?" *Journal of Law, Economics, and Policy* 1 (2005): 473, 475–76.

15. Kobayashi, "Private Versus Social Incentives." Less persuasively, Neal Katyal has argued that purchases of private security goods spread fear, thereby potentially increasing the crime rate. See Neal K. Katyal, "The Dark Side of Private Ordering: The Network/Community Harm of Crime," in *Law and Economics of Cybersecurity*, 202 (Cambridge University Press, 2006).

16. A useful summary is Gordon Tullock, "Public Choice," in *The New Palgrave Dictionary of Economics Online*, 2nd ed. (2008), http://www.dictionaryofeconomics.com/article?id=pde2008_P000240&q=rational%20choice&topicid=&result_number=10.

17. "White House Cybersecurity Plan Feared Inadequate By Experts, Could Violate Privacy," *E-Commerce Alert*, May 17, 2011 (quoting Josh Corman, Research Director, 451 Group), http://www.e-commercealert.com/article1067.shtml.

18. I am indebted to Professor Harvey Rishikof, Chair of the American Bar Association Standing Committee on Law and National Security, for this wonderful image. Quoting him also illustrates the proposition in a self-referential way. Like many in Washington, Professor Rishikof also has a government affiliation. If I had wanted to identify him by that affiliation, he would have required a week or more to get the requisite clearances from other officials. As a private sector actor, he authorized reliance on his imagery immediately.

19. See Joseph S. Nye Jr., *Cyber Power* (Harvard Belfer Center, 2010), 15, http://belfercenter.ksg.harvard.edu/files/cyber-power.pdf.

20. We see this type of argument made in the current disputes over net neutrality. Net neutrality refers to the requirement that ISPs be neutral in the way they treat content going across their networks. One objection to the neutrality requirement is that large-scale users (like those who provide streaming video) may crowd out smaller users (who, say, are just sending text emails) because of limited bandwidth. For this reason, some argue that a break from strict neutrality is necessary to more accurately distribute costs among users.

21. The classic exposition of this idea is Elinor Ostrom, *Governing the Commons: The Evolution of Institutions for Collective Action* (Cambridge University Press, 1990); see also Elinor Ostrom, "A General Framework for Analyzing Sustainability of Social-Ecological Systems," *Science* 325 (July 2009).

22. See James M. Acheson, *The Lobster Gangs of Maine* (1988); Pammela Quinn Saunders, "A Sea Change off the Coast of Maine: Common Pool Resources as Cultural Property," *Emory Law Journal* 60 (2011), http://papers.ssrn.com/sol3/papers.cfm?abstract_id=1701225.

23. For one example of such a success, see William Jackson, "Working Group Finds a Way to Thwart Conficker Worm, with Little Help from Federal Agencies," *Government Computer News*, January 26, 2011, http://gcn.com/articles/2011/01/26/conficker-working-group-lessons.aspx.

24. Wicked problems are problems of social policy that are complex and interdependent. Because they come with incomplete and contradictory information and often changing solution requirements, they are typically thought of as impossible to solve. The classic description is Horst Rittel and Melvin Webber, "Dilemmas in a General Theory of Planning," *Policy Sciences* 4 (Elsevier Scientific Publishing Company, 1973), 155–69, reprinted in *Developments in Design Methodology,* ed. N. Cross (John Wiley & Sons, 1984), 135–44, http://www.uctc.net/mwebber/Rittel+Webber+Dilemmas+General_Theory_of_Planning.pdf.

CHAPTER 15

1. Network traffic information can be information relating to suspicious packets, including ports, protocols, and routing information; specific virus/other malware signatures; IP addresses; and the identification of particularly suspect domains or servers. Personally Identifiable Information (PII) includes more person-specific types of information, such as identifying websites accessed, times and locations of logins/account access, discrepancies in user names, or content of communications, and is, more typically, related to a specific malfeasant activity (such as an attempted fraud, identify theft, or the transfer of terrorist finances).

2. One important caveat is in order at the outset: information sharing is no panacea. It can, and will, help in preventing attacks where the threat signatures are known. It is ineffective, however, in preventing zero-day attacks—that is, attacks that are effective on the zeroth day because nobody knows about them. In many ways, the problem is very much like the problem with preventing disease, and information sharing is like widely distributing a known, effective vaccine. But, no amount of information sharing (or vaccination) can protect you against a brand new virus.

3. Ellen Nakashima, "NSA Allies with Internet Carriers to Thwart Cyber Attacks against Defense Firms," *Washington Post,* June 17, 2011, http://www.washingtonpost.com/national/major-Internet-service-providers-cooperating-with-nsa-on-monitoring-traffic/2011/06/07/AG2dukXH_story.html. The regulations implementing this program were published in May 2012. DoD-DIB Voluntary Cyber Security and Information Assurance, 77 Fed. Reg. 27615 (May 11, 2012), http://www.gpo.gov/fdsys/pkg/FR-2012-05-11/pdf/2012-10651.pdf.

4. As discussed in Chapter 8, however, it does so at a significant cost. Because of privacy and civil liberties concerns, the private sector will not share the malicious code that it captures and interdicts with the NSA or DHS, thereby diminishing the government's ability to truly develop security information as a public good.

5. The draft provisions of the "Department of Homeland Security Cybersecurity Authority and Information Sharing Act of 2011" are in the May 2011 draft, 20–30, http://www.whitehouse.gov/sites/default/files/omb/legislative/letters/Law-Enforcement-Provisions-Related-to-Computer-Security-Full-Bill.pdf.

6. Pub. L. 99–508, Oct. 21, 1986, 100 Stat. 1848.

7. Title I is codified at 18 U.S.C. § 2510 *et seq.* The original Wiretap Act was passed in 1968 as Title III of the Omnibus Crime Control Act.

8. Title II is codified at 18 U.S.C. § 2701 *et seq.*

9. As a Department of Justice manual details, the provider exception to the Wiretap Act:

> grants providers the right "to intercept and monitor [communications] placed over their facilities in order to combat fraud and theft of service." United States v. Villanueva, 32 F. Supp. 2d 635, 639 (S.D.N.Y. 1998). . . .The exception also permits providers to monitor misuse of a system in order to protect the system from damage or invasions of privacy. For example, system administrators can track intruders within their networks in order to prevent further damage. See [United States v.] Mullins, 992 F.2d [1472,] 1478 [9th Cir. 1993] (need to monitor misuse of computer system justified interception of electronic communications pursuant to § 2511(2)(a)(i)). . . . .
>
> [P]roviders investigating unauthorized use of their systems have broad authority to monitor and disclose evidence of unauthorized use under § 2511(2)(a)(i), but should attempt to tailor their monitoring and disclosure to that which is reasonably related to the purpose of the monitoring. See, *e.g.,* United States v. Freeman, 524 F.2d 337, 341 (7th Cir. 1975) (phone company investigating use of illegal devices designed to steal long-distance service acted permissibly under § 2511(2)(a)(i) when it intercepted the first two minutes of every illegal conversation but did not intercept legitimately authorized communications).

Searching and Seizing Computers and Obtaining Electronic Evidence Manual, 3rd ed. (September 2009), ch. 4, http://www.cybercrime.gov/ssmanual/04ssma.html.

10. See *Department of Defense Strategy for Operating in Cyberspace,* July 2011, 12, http://www.defense.gov/news/d20110714cyber.pdf; William Lynn, "Defending a New Domain: The Pentagon's Cyberstrategy," *Foreign Affairs* (September/October 2010).

11. "US Govt Launches Pilot Cyber Defense Program with ISPs, Defense Firms," *International Business Times,* June 19, 2011, http://sanfrancisco.ibtimes.com/articles/165468/20110619/us-govt-launches-pilot-cyber-defense-program-with-isps-defense-firms-dib-cyber-pilot.htm.

12. By contrast, the government's inspection of packets arriving at its own portals is not Constitutionally problematic. See Department of Justice, Office of Legal Counsel, *Legality of Intrusion Detection System to Protect Unclassified Computer Networks in the Executive Branch,* August 2009, http://www.justice.gov/olc/2009/legality-of-e2.pdf.

13. Network traffic information is, almost certainly, analogous to telephone switching information. Because that sort of addressing information is publicly disclosed by the consumer (as a way of having his call completed or his e-mail delivered), the courts have concluded that the sender/receiver has no reasonable expectation of privacy and thus that the information is not subject to the Fourth Amendment's warrant requirement. See *Smith v. Maryland,* 442 U.S. 735 (1979).

14. The special needs doctrine has typically been applied in places (like schools) where the governmental authorities stand in a paternal relationship to their citizens. See *New Jersey v. T.L.O,* 469 U.S. 325 (1985) (allowing warrantless searches of a student for cigarettes and marijuana). It has also been used to authorize public safety drunk

driving checkpoints. *Michigan Dept. of State Police v. Sitz*, 496 U.S. 444 (1990). But, it is equally likely (if not more so) that the courts will look at government-operated Internet inspection systems as if they were police narcotics inspection checkpoints on the highway—a dragnet approach which is contrary to the Fourth Amendment. See *Indianapolis v. Edmond*, 531 U.S. 32 (2000).

15. The most notorious such program was John Poindexter's analytical system known as Total Information Awareness. Though little more than an experimental construct, the concept was eviscerated by public reaction. See William Safire, "You Are a Suspect," *New York Times*, November 14, 2002, http://www.nytimes.com/2002/11/14/opinion/you-are-a-suspect.html.

16. See generally, *National Security Threats in Cyberspace* (American Bar Association and National Strategy Forum, 2009), 8–9 (Rosenzweig, Workshop Rapporteur). The proposed Cybersecurity Act of 2012 (considered by Congress in August 2012 and rejected) would have provided an extensive regulatory structure for cybersecurity. See Paul Rosenzweig, "The Regulatory Provisions of the Cybersecurity Act of 2012," *Lawfare Blog* (February 19, 2012), http://www.lawfareblog.com/2012/02/the-regulatory-provisions-of-the-cybersecurity-act-of-2012/.

17. See Richard Thaler and Cass Sunstein, *Nudge: Improving Decisions about Health, Wealth, and Happiness* (Yale University Press, 2008).

18. The details of the proposal are contained in the "Cybersecurity Regulatory Framework for Covert Critical Infrastructure Act," which was part of the package submitted to Congress by the Administration on May 12, 2011, http://www.whitehouse.gov/sites/default/files/omb/legislative/letters/Law-Enforcement-Provisions-Related-to-Computer-Security-Full-Bill.pdf. Some of the analysis in this subsection originally appeared in Paul Rosenzweig, *Obama Cybersecurity Proposal Flawed, But Fixable*, The Heritage Foundation, Web Memo No. 3300 (June 2011).

19. This, of course, is a perfect expression of the irony posed by the balance between transparency and secrecy. On the one hand, few could doubt the good-government value of publicly naming sectors or companies that are performing poorly. On the other hand, in doing so, the government might as well paint a target on the figurative corporate forehead. The prospects are so disadvantageous that one suspects the authority to name will be useful mostly for its *in terrorem* effect of coercing behavior, rather than any practical value of disclosure.

20. Note that the limitation is of comparative efficiency. The author is well-aware of the literature relating to the excessive transaction costs that may be ascribed to the tort system of liability. For example, Lester Brickman, *Lawyer Barons: What Their Contingency Fees Really Cost America* (Cambridge University Press, 2011); Walter Olson, *The Rule of Lawyers: How the New Litigation Elite Threatens America's Rule of Law* (Truman Books, 2002). Nevertheless, in many respects, the tort system is more efficient than direct government regulation.

21. With one exception: There is a liability standard increasingly applicable to a limited class of cybersecurity cases in which the data integrity of customer information is breached. See 15 U.S.C. § 6801 and 16 C.F.R. § 314.4(a)-(c). But, this liability structure is not yet fully developed and applies to a problem—data and identity theft—which, while clearly troubling, may not rise to the level of a national security concern.

22. Nobody actually owns or operates the Internet itself. While private sector and government actors own pieces of the cyber domain (various routers and nodes, for example), the actual rules for how the cyber domain works are set by the IETF which is an "open international community of network designers, operators, vendors and researchers concerned with the evolution of the Internet architectures and the smooth operation of the Internet." See "Overview of the IETF," http://www.ietf.org/old/2009/overview.html. This community operates by the promulgation of technical standards which, in the end, become de facto operating requirements for any activity in cyberspace. Thus, some questions about cybersecurity necessarily require engagement with an engineering community that is both internationalist and consensus-oriented, characteristics that may be inconsistent with effective U.S. government action.

23. My friend, and former boss, Stewart A. Baker, is fond of this analogy and thinks it says much about how we should approach cybersecurity. For example, Baker, *Cyberwar*, presentation to Medill National Security Journalism Initiative (June 23, 2011).

CHAPTER 16

1. This story is told in: Matthew L. Wald, "As Wind Energy Use Grows, Utilities Seek to Stabilize Power Grid," *New York Times*, November 4, 2011, http://www.nytimes.com/2011/11/05/business/energy-environment/as-wind-energy-use-grows-utilities-seek-to-stabilize-power-grid.html.

2. "Staged Cyber Attack Reveals Vulnerability in Power Grid," http://www.youtube.com/watch?v=fJyWngDco3g.

3. Lisa Rein, "Power Grid Updates Left System Vulnerable to Cyberattacks, Auditors Say," *Washington Post*, February 8, 2012, http://www.washingtonpost.com/politics/power-grid-updates-left-system-vulnerable-to-cyberattacks-auditors-say/2012/02/07/gIQAMxBVxQ_story.html.

4. I am not, of course, the first to lay this out. An excellent treatment is given by Thomas H. Karas, Judy H. Moore, and Lori K. Parrot, *Metaphors for Cybersecurity* (Sandia National Laboratory, 2008), 30–34, http://evolutionofcomputing.org/Multicellular/Cyberfest%20Report.pdf.

5. This idea is developed, at length, in Scott Charney, *Collective Defense: Applying Public Health Models to the Internet* (Microsoft Corp., 2010), http://download.microsoft.com/download/7/F/B/7FB2F266–7914–4174-BBEF-2F5687882A93/Collective%20Defense%20-%20Applying%20Global%20Health%20Models%20to%20the%20Internet.pdf.

6. "The Hack on Stratfor," January 11, 2012, http://www.stratfor.com/weekly/hack-stratfor.

7. Franklin Kramer, *U.S. Should Aim for Cyber-Resilience*, January 19, 2011, http://www.acus.org/news/franklin-kramer-us-should-aim-cyber-resilience.

8. I am indebted to my former colleague at DHS, Adam Isles, whose thoughts on the idea of public–private partnership in a different context sparked this idea. More recently, this idea has been echoed in cybersecurity legislation proposed by Representative Dan Lungren (H.R. 3674, 112th Cong.).

9. This paper serves only as an outline of certain aspects of the CAC. The author acknowledges that significant further consideration and development of the idea are

necessary, but offers these preliminary thoughts for the purpose of generating discussion. Representative Lungren calls this the National Information Sharing Organization or NISO.

10. Appropriate legal structures might include mandatory reporting, anonymization of information given to the CAC, compartmentalization of information that cannot be anonymized, and the development of a penalty structure for the misappropriation of CAC-protected information.

11. For example, DARPA Network Challenge (also known as Red Balloon Challenge), as described at https://networkchallenge.darpa.mil/default.aspx.

12. Isabel Kershner, "Cyberattacks Temporarily Cripple 2 Israeli Web Sites," *New York Times,* January 16, 2012, https://www.nytimes.com/2012/01/17/world/middleeast/cyber-attacks-temporarily-cripple-2-israeli-web-sites.html?scp=1&sq=israle%20cyberwar&st=cse.

CHAPTER 17

This chapter is derived from Paul Rosenzweig, "The Organization of the United States Government and Private Sector for Achieving Cyber Deterrence," in *National Research Council, Proceedings of a Workshop on Deterring Cyber Attacks: Informing Strategies and Developing Options for U.S. Policy* (National Academies Press, 2010), and is reprinted with the kind permission of the Academy.

1. A honey pot is a website that is designed with features intended to lure and entice potential visitors, much as honey attracts bees, or Winnie the Pooh.

2. The details of this event were disclosed in Ellen Nakashima, "Dismantling of Saudi-CIA Web Site Illustrates Need for Clearer Cyberwar Policies," *Washington Post,* March 19, 2010, http://www.washingtonpost.com/wp-dyn/content/article/2010/03/18/AR2010031805464.html.

3. William Banks and Elizabeth Rindskopf-Parker, "Introduction," *Journal of National Security Law and Policy* 4 (2010): 1, 3.

4. PDD/NSC-63, Critical Infrastructure Protection, May 22, 1998, http://www.fas.org/irp/offdocs/pdd/pdd-63.pdf.

5. PDD/NSC-63 §8.

6. PDD/NSC-63, Annex A.

7. PDD/NSC-63 § VI.

8. For example, initially few, if any, private sector participants were routinely invited to the large-scale TOPOFF exercises in which U.S. government officials examine their response to predicted future terrorist incidents. See ISAC Council White Paper, "The Integration of ISACs in to Government and Department of Defense Homeland Security and Homeland Defense Exercises," January 2004, http://www.isaccouncil.org/whitepapers/files/Integration_of_ISACs_Into_Exercises_013104.pdf. Though this particular issue has been resolved in more recent exercises, it is emblematic of the challenges faced in integrating a public and private sector response.

9. There have been no significant recent studies of the effectiveness of ISACs by outside sources. A dated review, conducted by GAO in 2005, reports a number of breakdowns in information sharing. See "Critical Infrastructure Protection: Department of Homeland Security Faces Challenges in Fulfilling Cybersecurity Responsibilities"

(GAO-05-434, May 2005), 32. A slightly more recent study from 2006 found that successful integration varied widely across the ISAC sectors. See "Critical Infrastructure Protection: Progress Coordinating Government and Private Sector Efforts Varies by Sectors' Characteristics" (GAO-07-39, October 2006).

10. "The National Strategy to Secure Cyberspace" (February 2003), http://www.dhs.gov/xlibrary/assets/National_Cyberspace_Strategy.pdf.

11. "The National Strategy to Secure Cyberspace," 20–24.

12. Homeland Security Presidential Directive-7 (HSPD-7) (December 17, 2003).

13. HSPD-7 § 16.

14. Comprehensive National Cybersecurity Initiative (declassified version), http://www.whitehouse.gov/cybersecurity/comprehensive-national-cybersecurity-initiative. Three of the initiatives (calling for a cyber counter-intelligence policy, development of a deterrence strategy, and adoption of a supply change risk management strategy) have aspects of cyber defense or resilience to them, but more appropriately are characterized as policies of cyber assurance, cyber attack, or noncyber response. As with any taxonomy, the categorization of policies is indefinite at the margins and of utility only insofar as it aids analysis.

15. *Cyber Space Policy Review: Assuring a Trusted and Resilient Information and Communications Infrastructure* (May 2009).

16. *Cyber Space Policy Review*, 7 and also vi (recommendation #1, calls for appointment of NSC-level policy cyber coordinator).

17. *Cyber Space Policy Review*, 8.

18. TRADOC PAM 525–7-8, Cyberspace Operations Concept Capabilities Plan (February 2010), http://www.tradoc.army.mil/tpubs/pams/tp525-7-8.pdf.

19. "Navy Stands Up Fleet Cyber Command, Reestablishes U.S. 10th Fleet," January 29, 2010, http://www.navy.mil/search/display.asp?story_id=50954.

20. See "Memorandum for All Airmen, Air Force Cyberspace Mission Alignment" (August 20, 2009).

21. The new commander of Cyber Command is dual-hatted and also serves as the Director of the NSA. A useful summary of the political considerations that led to this unusual result can be found in Richard A. Clarke and Robert K. Knake, *Cyber War* (Harper Collins, 2010), 32–44.

22. Presumably this support to civil authorities will be provided consistent with existing military doctrine. DoD Directive 5111.13 (March 2009) defines Defense Support to Civil Authorities (DSCA) as: "Support provided by U.S. Federal military forces, National Guard forces performing duty in accordance with [Title 32, U.S. Code], DoD civilians, DoD contract personnel, and DoD component assets, in response to requests for assistance from civil authorities for special events, domestic emergencies, designated law enforcement support, and other domestic activities. Support provided by National Guard forces performing duty in accordance with [Title 32, U.S. Code] is considered DSCA, but is conducted as a State-directed action. Also known as civil support."

23. See generally, Unified Command Plan § 18.d(3); *Advanced Questions for Lieutenant General Keith Alexander*, USA Nominee for Commander, United States Cyber Command in Hearings before the United States Senate Armed Services Committee, April 13, 2010, http://www.washingtonpost.com/wp-srv/politics/documents/questions.pdf.

24. Department of Devense Strategy for Operating in Cyberspace, July 2011, http://www.defense.gov/news/d20110714cyber.pdf.

25. Andrea Shalai-Esa, "Ex-U.S. General Urges Frank Talk on Cyber Weapons," *Reuters*, November 6, 2011, http://uk.reuters.com/article/2011/11/06/us-cyber-cartwright-idUKTRE7A514C20111106.

26. Department of Defense Cyberspace Policy Report: A Report to Congress Pursuant to the National Defense Authorization Act for Fiscal Year 2011, Section 934, November 2011, http://www.defense.gov/home/features/2011/0411_cyberstrategy/docs/NDAA%20Section%20934%20Report_For%20webpage.pdf.

27. Department of Defense Cyberspace Policy Report, 4.

28. The Office of the President, "National Security Strategy," (May 2010), 49–53, http://www.whitehouse.gov/sites/default/files/rss_viewer/national_security_strategy.pdf; *Cyber Space Policy Review* (May 29, 2009), 20–21, http://www.whitehouse.gov/assets/documents/Cyberspace_Policy_Review_final.pdf; Center for Strategic and International Studies, *Securing Cyberspace for the 44th Presidency* (December 2008), 20–23, http://csis.org/files/media/csis/pubs/081208_securingcyberspace_44.pdf.

29. We also need structures to ensure that activities intended to prevent a successful cyber attack by U.S. opponents or to enable a successful cyber attack by our own government are pursued in conformance with the laws and policies of the United States. A number of potential activities in support of a cyber policy have significant privacy and civil liberties implications—concerns we have considered in earlier chapters. Putting the answer to those questions in different chapters is by no means a diminishment of their importance.

CHAPTER 18

1. This chapter, like the previous one, is based on an extended study done for the National Academy of Sciences—Paul Rosenzweig, "The Organization of the United States Government and Private Sector for Achieving Cyber Deterrence," in *National Research Council, Proceedings of a Workshop on Deterring Cyber Attacks: Informing Strategies and Developing Options for U.S. Policy* (National Academies Press, 2010)—and is reprinted with the kind permission of the Academy.

2. The military, alone, has over 15,000 networks and 7 million computing devices. Its systems are probed thousands of times and scanned millions of times each day. See William J. Lynn III, "Defending a New Domain: The Pentagon's Cyberstrategy," *Foreign Affairs* 97 (September/October 2010). Multiply that by the vulnerabilities in other federal departments (not to mention state, local, and private sector networks) and the scope of the problem becomes impossibly daunting.

3. Speech of Secretary of State Hillary Clinton (Washington, DC, January 21, 2010), http://www.state.gov/secretary/rm/2010/01/135519.htm.

4. GAO, "Cybersecurity: Progress Made but Challenges Remain in Defining and Coordinating the Comprehensive National Initiative" (GAO-10-338) (March 2010), 13.

5. Current conceptual thinking in conflict management broadly recognizes that soft power systems will often be effective supplements to the hard power of a kinetic response. For example, Joseph Nye, *Soft Power: The Means to Success in World Politics* (Public Affairs, 2004). Theorists characterize the panoply of soft power instruments

through the mnemonic MIDLIFE—that is Military, Intelligence, Diplomacy, Law enforcement, Information, Financial, and Economic instruments of power. All, conceiv-
ably, could be of use in deterring cyber attacks and intrusions.

6. GAO, "Cybersecurity," 2.

7. J. Nicholas Hoover, "NSA to Build $1.5 Billion Cybersecurity Data Cen-
ter," *Information Week,* October 29, 2009, http://www.informationweek.com/news/
government/security/showArticle.jhtml?articleID=221100260.

8. This book is neither the time, nor the place, to debate recent controversies over
NSA activities. Suffice it to say that the controversies are real, and the public confidence
in the NSA's rectitude comparatively diminished.

9. See "Letter from Rod Beckstrom to Janet Napolitano," March 5, 2009, http://
epic.org/linkedfiles/ncsc_directors_resignation1.pdf. Beckstrom resigned his position
as Director of the National Cybersecurity Center in part because of his perception that
the NSA was, inappropriately, "control[ing] DHS cybersecurity efforts."

10. Statement of Richard L. Skinner, Inspector General, Department of Homeland
Security, before the Committee on Homeland Security, U.S. House of Representatives
(June 16, 2010).

11. The existence of the Perfect Citizen program was disclosed in Siobhan Gorman,
"U.S. Plans Cyber Shield for Utilities, Companies," *Wall Street Journal,* July 8, 2010.

12. NSA has denied aspects of the initial report. See "NSA Launches Infrastructure Cybersecurity Program," *Information Week,* July 9, 2010, http://www.information
week.com/news/government/security/showArticle.jhtml?articleID=225702741&cid=
RSSfeed_IWK_News.

13. Ellen Nakashima, "White House, NSA Weigh Cybersecurity, Personal Privacy,"
Washington Post, February 7, 2012, http://www.washingtonpost.com/world/national-
security/white-house-nsa-weigh-cyber-security-personal-privacy/2012/02/07/gIQA
8HmKeR_story.html.

14. "Memorandum of Understanding Regarding Cybersecurity," October 10, 2010,
http://www.dhs.gov/xlibrary/assets/20101013-dod-dhs-cyber-moa.pdf.

15. Emblematic of the challenges faced by the cyber coordinator is the 2010 memorandum allocating responsibility between OMB and DHS for federal agency compliance with the requirement of the Federal Information Security Act of 2002 (FISMA).
See "Clarifying Cybersecurity Responsibilities and Activities," M-10-28, July 6, 2010,
http://www.whitehouse.gov/omb/assets/memoranda_2010/m10–28.pdf. Irrespective
of the merits of that allocation, the memorandum is notable for the fact that it was
co-signed by the cyber coordinator and the Director of OMB and issued on OMB
letterhead, reflecting the coordinator's lack of directive authority.

16. As I've said, this problem is common to many science and technology questions.
It may also, amusingly, arise in connection with more prosaic social phenomenon: "Fit-
ness fads change too quickly for anyone to keep up with all of them." NU FitRec at 2
(Spring–Summer 2011) (on file with author).

17. The Administrative Procedures Act requires new rules and regulations to be
subject to notice to the public and comment thereon. 5 U.S.C. § 551 *et. seq.*

18. This is, of course, just an estimate. One study, see Stuart Shapiro, *Explaining Ossification: An Examination of the Time to Finish Rulemakings,* August 11, 2009,
http://ssrn.com/abstract=1447337, estimated that the median time for completion of

a rule, from its first appearance in the Unified Agenda to promulgation was 618 days, while the mean was 831 (or 27+ months). If one counts from the date the rule is first formally proposed, the mean is only 324 days, but my own experience is that significant rules require substantial pre-proposal consideration and consultation. For complex rules, that will engender significant comment (as we can anticipate will be the case with cyber rules), my assumption is that longer periods of consideration will be necessary more frequently than shorter periods.

19. Though the rapidity of action in cyberspace greatly exacerbates the problems of hierarchy in our policy-making process, those problems are not limited to cyber issues. As the Project for National Security Reform put it in a recent report: "The legacy structures and processes of a national security system that is now more than 60 years old no longer help American leaders to formulate coherent national strategy.... As presently constituted, too, these structures and processes lack means to detect and remedy their own deficiencies." Project for National Security Reform, *Forging a New Shield* (November 2008), i, http://pnsr.org/data/files/pnsr_forging_a_new_shield_report.pdf.

20. Maggie Michael, "Egyptians Plan First Tunisian-Inspired Protests, Draw 80,000 Supporters on Facebook," January 24, 2011, http://www.startribune.com/world/114479579.html.

21. David D. Kirkpatrick and David E. Sanger, "Egyptians and Tunisians Collaborated to Shake Arab History," *New York Times,* February 13, 2011, http://www.nytimes.com/2011/02/14/world/middleeast/14egypt-tunisia-protests.html?_r=1&ref=todayspaper.

22. Christopher Rhoads and Geoffrey Fowler, "Egypt Shuts Down Internet, Cell Phone Service," *Wall Street Journal,* January 29, 2011, http://online.wsj.com/article/SB10001424052748703956604576110453371369740.html.

23. El Gazzar, "Government Restores Internet Service after a Weeklong Shutdown," *Wall Street Journal,* February 2, 2011, http://online.wsj.com/article/SB1000142405274870396080457611969051469244.6html.

24. Kirkpatrick and Sanger, "Egyptians and Tunisians Collaborated to Shake Arab History."

25. Literally dozens of articles could be cited for the proposition. For a relatively un-tendentious example, see Rachel Newcomb, "Why Obama's Position on Egypt's Mubarak Was Too Little, Too Late," *Christian Science Monitor,* February 2, 2011, http://www.csmonitor.com/Commentary/Opinion/2011/0202/Why-Obama-s-position-on-Egypt-s-Mubarak-was-too-little-too-late.

26. The text of this draft proposal, transmitted to Congress in May 2011, is available at http://www.whitehouse.gov/sites/default/files/omb/legislative/letters/Law-Enforcement-Provisions-Related-to-Computer-Security-Full-Bill.pdf.

27. Ibid. § 244, 24.

28. "White House Cybersecurity Plan Feared Inadequate by Experts, Could Violate Privacy," *E-Commerce Alert*, May 17, 2011 (quoting Josh Corman, Research Director, 451 Group), http://www.e-commercealert.com/article1067.shtml.

29. Professor Harvey Rishikof, Chair of the American Bar Association Law and National Security Advisory Committee and former Chair of the Standing Committee on Law and National Security.

CHAPTER 19

1. Chris Demchack and Peter Dombrowski, "Rise of a Cybered Westphalian Age," *Strategic Studies Quarterly* (Spring 2011), http://www.au.af.mil/au/ssq/2011/spring/demchak-dombrowski.pdf.

2. In 1648 the Peace of Westphalia ended the 30 Year War and established the modern system of national sovereignty. The Westphalian system is premised on the territoriality of states, and the principle of noninterference by one state in the internal affairs of another. That system has, more or less, controlled international affairs for over 450 years. The text of the treaty is available at http://avalon.law.yale.edu/17th_century/westphal.asp.

3. To "test any website and see real-time if it's censored in China," see Great Fire Wall of China, http://www.greatfirewallofchina.org/.

4. L. Gordon Crovitz, "Opinion: Dictators and Internet Double Standards," *Wall Street Journal,* March 7, 2011, http://online.wsj.com/article/SB1000142405274870358 0004576180662638333004.html.

5. Associated Press, "Australia Says Web Blacklist Combats Child Porn," March 27, 2009, http://www.physorg.com/news157371619.html.

6. "Belarus: Browsing Foreign Websites a Misdemeanor," December 30, 2011, http://www.loc.gov/lawweb/servlet/lloc_news?disp3_l205402929_text.

7. Demchack and Dombrowski, "Rise of a Cybered Westphalian Age," 35.

8. Vinton G. Cerf, "Internet Access Is Not a Human Right," *New York Times,* January 4, 2012, https://www.nytimes.com/2012/01/05/opinion/internet-access-is-not-a-human-right.html?_r=1&ref=todayspaper.

9. Report of the Special Rapporteur on the promotion and protection of the right to freedom of opinion and expression, 78, A/HRC/17/27, May 16, 2011, http://www2.ohchr.org/english/bodies/hrcouncil/docs/17session/A.HRC.17.27_en.pdf.

10. The problem is exacerbated if American government data were to be stored overseas, it would potentially be subject to the same sort of legal wrangle, with the cloud service providers caught in the middle. The problem is surely magnified when one thinks of the types of information that American governments collect and store. At the federal level, we store taxpayer information, procurement information, social security retirement information, Medicare and Medicaid health related information, and educational data (to name but a sampling). At the state or local level, we add real estate data, birth and death records, criminal records, and more detailed education records (again, this is but a small sample). At all levels of government, we store the working-day information that helps government function: e-mail exchanges, calendars, and the like. In short, the scope of our government's data holdings is as wide as the expanse of government and likely contains information that touches upon all aspects of American life.

11. "International Strategy for Cyberspace," May 2011, http://www.whitehouse.gov/sites/default/files/rss_viewer/international_strategy_for_cyberspace.pdf.

12. Art. 25, Hague Convention of 1899, http://www.icrc.org/ihl.nsf/FULL/150?OpenDocument.

13. Stewart Baker, "Denial of Service," *Foreign Policy* (September 30, 2011), http://www.foreignpolicy.com/articles/2011/09/30/denial_of_service?page=full.

14. John Markoff and Andrew E. Kramer, "In Shift, U.S. Talks to Russia on Internet Security," *New York Times,* December 13, 2009, http://www.nytimes.com/2009/12/13/ science/13cyber.html.

15. Jack Goldsmith, "Cybersecurity Treaties: A Skeptical View," in *Future Challenges in National Security and Law,* ed. Peter Berkowitz (February 2011), http://www.futu rechallengesessays.com.

16. Stewart Baker, Shaun Waterman, and George Ivanov, *In the Crossfire: Critical Infrastructure in the Age of Cyber War* (McAfee, 2010), 30.

17. "Agreement between the governments of the member states of the Shanghai Cooperation Organization on Cooperation in the field of International Information Security," www.sectsco.org/EN/show.asp?id=95; www.sectsco.org/EN/show. asp?id=224.

18. Speech of Secretary of State Hillary Clinton (Washington, DC, January 21, 2010), http://www.state.gov/secretary/rm/2010/01/135519.htm.

19. James Glanz and John Markoff, "U.S. Underwrites Internet Detour around Censors Abroad," *New York Times,* June 12, 2011, http://www.nytimes.com/2011/06/12/ world/12internet.html.

CHAPTER 20

1. Dan Gardner, *Future Babble: Why Expert Predictions Are Next to Worthless, and You Can Do Better* (Dutton, 2011).

2. A great example of the peril of prediction is told by Benjamin Wittes: "In 1914, in the wake of the assassination of the Archduke Franz Ferdinand, a foreign affairs writer named F. Cunliffe-Owen looked for the bright side. While 'it is only natural that one should be stricken with horror at the brutal and shocking assassination,' he wrote in the *New York Sun,* 'it is impossible to deny that [the archduke's] disappearance from the scene is calculated to diminish the tenseness of the [general European] situation and to make peace both within and without the dual Empire.' The archduke was so universally regarded as a 'disturbing factor and as committed to forceful and aggressive policies, that the news of his death is almost calculated to create a feeling of universal relief.'" Benjamin Wittes, "Notes on Global Security in the 21st Century" (Draft 2011) (on file with author) (citing F. Cunliffe-Owen, "Death of Francis Ferdinand Makes for Peace of Europe," *New York Sun,* June 29, 1914). Talk about wrong . . .

3. Vernor Vinge, *Marooned in Realtime* (Bluejay Books, 1986; reprinted by Tor Books, 2004). For those interested, this Singularity is viewed through the perspective of time travelers who have jumped beyond it, only to find the entire human race gone missing.

4. Vivek Kundera, *Federal Cloud Computing Strategy* (February 2011), 2, http:// www.cio.gov/documents/federal-cloud-computing-strategy.pdf.

5. Bob Brewin, "Congress Directs Defense to Use Commercial Data Centers," *Nextgov,* December 11, 2011, http://www.nextgov.com/nextgov/ng_20111219_7716.php.

6. The Communications Assistance for Law Enforcement Act (CALEA), Pub. L. No. 103–414 (1994) (codified at 47 U.S.C. §§ 1001–10) enhances the ability of law enforcement and intelligence agencies to conduct electronic surveillance by

requiring that telecommunications carriers and manufacturers of telecommunications equipment modify and design their equipment to ensure that they have built-in surveillance capabilities. Utilizing these capabilities, federal agencies may, when authorized by law, monitor all telephone, broadband Internet, and VoIP traffic in real-time.

7. Maple Story is a MMORPG (massively multiplayer online role-playing game) where the players take on powers as warriors, magicians, thieves, or the like and interact with each other while performing tasks within the virtual world. See http://www. maplestory.com/.

8. See "Real Taxes for Real Money Made by Online Game Players," *Wall Street Journal,* October 31, 2008, http://blogs.wsj.com/chinajournal/2008/10/31/real-taxes-for-real-money-made-by-online-game-players/.

9. In addition to China's recent move to regulate virtual currency, South Korea has a body of case law that applies to virtual activity. Applications of American law to the virtual word are sporadic and, as the MySpace suicide case discussed in Chapter 7 makes clear, fraught with difficulty.

10. Aliya Sternstein, "Fomer CIA Director: Build a New Internet to Improve Security," *NextGov,* July 6, 2011, http://www.nextgov.com/nextgov/ng_20110706_1137.php.

11. SIPRENET and JWICS are classified U.S. government systems handling, respectively, Secret and Top Secret level material. They are interconnected between government users but physically isolated from unclassified computers.

12. For an elegant story about quantum computing and one of its leading theorists, see David Deutsch and Rivka Galchen, "Dream Machine," *The New Yorker,* May 2, 2011.

13. John Markoff, "Moving toward Quantum Computing—Science in 2011," *New York Times,* November 8, 2010, http://www.nytimes.com/2010/11/09/science/09compute.html.

14. Rebecca Boyle, "Quantum Processor Calculates That 15 = 3x5 (With Almost 50% Accuracy!" *Popular Science,* August 20, 2012, http://www.popsci.com/science/article/2012-08/quantum-processor-calculates-15-3x5-about-half-time.

CHAPTER 21

1. This chapter is derived from Paul Rosenzweig, "10 Conservative Principles for Cybersecurity Policy," *Backgrounder* 2513 (January 2011) (The Heritage Foundation).

Glossary

Anonymous A loose collective group of cyber hackers who espouse Internet freedom and often attack websites that they consider symbols of authority.

Botnet A network of computers controlled by an outside actor who can give those computers orders to act in a coordinated manner, much like orders to a group of robots.

CNCI The Comprehensive National Cybersecurity Initiative is the broad federal strategy for fostering cybersecurity in America. When first drafted in 2008, it was classified. An unclassified version was publicly released in 2010.

Cyber Space Policy Review In May 2009 one of the first actions of the Obama Administration was the development of and release of a broad-based cyberspace policy review. This review has guided federal strategy since then.

Denial of Service Attack A denial of service attack is one where a malicious actor repeatedly sends thousands of connection requests to a website every second. The many malicious requests drown out the legitimate connection requests and prevent users from accessing the website.

Distributed Denial of Service A DDoS attack is related to a denial of service attack. The difference is that in a DDoS attack, the attacker uses more than one computer (often hundreds of distributed slave computers in a botnet) to conduct the attack.

DNSSEC The Domain Name System Security Extension is a proposed suite of security add-on functionalities that would become part of the accepted Internet Protocol. New security features will allow a user to confirm the origin authentication of DNS data, authenticate the denial or existence of a domain name, and assure the data integrity of the DNS.

Domain Name System The Domain Name System (or DNS) is the naming convention system that identifies the names of various servers and websites on the Internet.

In any web address, it is the portion of the address after http://www. One example would be microsoft.com.

Einstein   Intrusion detection and prevention systems operated by the federal government, principally to protect federal networks against malicious intrusions of malware.

Encryption   The act of concealing information by transforming it into a coded message.

Firewalls   Computer security systems designed to prevent intrusions, much like the walls of a house prevent entrance.

Hacktivist   A contraction of the two words, hacker and activists. The word denotes a hacker who purports to have a political or philosophical agenda and not be motivated by criminality.

IC3   The Internet Criminal Complaint Center (IC3) is a unit of the U.S. Department of Justice. It serves as a central collection point for complaints of criminal cyber activity and provides estimates of criminal effects.

ICANN   The Internet Corporation for Assigned Names and Numbers (ICANN) is a nonprofit organization that sets the rules for creating and distributing domain names. Originally charted by the U.S. government, it now operates on a multilateral basis from its headquarters in California.

IETF   The Internet Engineering Task Force (IETF) is a self-organized group of engineers who consider technical specifications for the Internet. IETF sets voluntary standards for Internet engineering and also identifies best current practices. Though it has no enforcement mechanism, IETF standards are the default for all technical Internet requirements.

Intrusion Detection System   Computer security systems that detect and report when intrusions have occurred and a firewall has been breached.

IP Address   An Internet Protocol address is the numeric address (typically it looks like this: 172.16.254.1) that identifies a website on the cyber network. Using the IP address, information can be communicated from one server to another. One of the critical functions of the domain name system is to translate domain names (that appear in the English language) into numerical IP addresses.

ISAC   Information Sharing and Analysis Center. A cooperative institution chartered by the federal government that brings together sector-specific private sector actors to share threat and vulnerability information. There are ISACs for the financial sector, the chemical industry, the IT sector, and most other major private sector groups.

ISC   The Internet Systems Consortium is a nonprofit 501(c)(3) corporation that produces open source software to support the infrastructure of the Internet. Its work is intended to develop and maintain maintaining core production quality software, protocols, and operations.

Keylogger   As the name implies, a keylogger program is one that records all of the keystrokes entered on a keyboard (like a password, say) and then reports those keystrokes to whoever installed the program.

Letters Rogatory   Formal letters of request for legal assistance from the government of one country to the courts of a foreign country. This is the mechanism by which Mutual Legal Assistance Treaties are implemented.

Logic Bomb   A program that tells a computer to execute a certain set of instructions at a particular signal (a date, or an order from outside, for example). Like many bombs or mines, the logic bomb can remain unexploded and buried for quite some time.

Malware   Short for malicious software. A general term describing any software program intended to do harm.

Microblogs   Systems, like Twitter, that allow blogging on the Internet but only on a micro scale. Twitter, for example, is limited to 140 characters per post.

MLAT   Mutual Legal Assistance Treaties are agreements between nations to exchange information in support of investigations of violations of criminal law or public law.

NCIX   The National Counterintelligence Executive (NCIX) is part of the Office of the Director of National Intelligence. Its mission is the defensive flip-side of our own espionage efforts. The NCIX is charged with attempting to prevent successful espionage against the United States by our adversaries.

Peer-to-Peer   Most Internet transmissions involve some routing by intermediate servers that serve a controlling function. Peer-to-peer (P2P) systems, as the name implies, enable direct communications between two (or more) end points without the need for intermediate routing and with no centralized or privileged intermediate.

Phishing   Phishing is a cyber tactic that involves dangling bait in front of an unsuspecting user of the Internet. Typical is an e-mail with an attractive link to click on that takes the unwary user to a malicious site.

SCADA   Supervisory Control and Data Acquisition system. SCADA systems are used to control industrial processes like the manufacture of a car. They can be, but are not necessarily, controlled by other computer operating systems.

Spear Phishing   A phishing attack that is targeted at a particular, specific recipient, much like using a spear to try to catch a particular fish.

Trojan Horse   As the name implies, this is a computer program or message that, on the outside looks like an innocent piece of code. Contained within the code, however, is a malicious piece of software.

US-CERT   The United States Computer Emergency Readiness Team is a component of the Department of Homeland Security. Its mission is to serve as a central clearinghouse for information concerning cyber threats, vulnerabilities, and attacks—collecting information from government and private sector sources and then widely disseminating that information to all concerned actors.

Virus   A piece of code that infects a program, much like a virus infects a person, and replicates itself.

WikiLeaks   WikiLeaks is a website founded by Julian Assange. It accepts anonymous leaks of classified, secret, and confidential information and then posts it to the website as an effort in transparency. Controversial in operation, their most famous leak was of 250,000 U.S. State Department classified cables.

Wiretapping   The interception of a message in transit by someone who is not the intended recipient. It gets its name from the practice of attaching two clips to a copper telephone wire to intercept a phone call.

Worm   A worm is a standalone program that replicates itself. It often hides by burrowing in and concealing itself amongst other program code, like a worm in dirt.

Zero Day Exploit   A zero-day exploit is a vulnerability in a software program that has never previously been used or discovered. Since most vulnerabilities are quickly patched after they become known, zero-day exploits, which are not yet patched, are very valuable. They are intrusions that will be successful on the zeroth day.

Bibliography

This bibliography is arranged by general topic area of interest for greater ease of research.

COMPUTERS AND THE INTERNET: GENERALLY

Gleick, James. *The Information: A History, A Theory, A Flood.* Pantheon, 2011.

Goldsmith, Jack, and Tim Wu. *Who Controls the Internet? Illusions of a Borderless World.* Oxford University Press, 2006.

Lessig, Lawrence. *Code Version 2.0.* Basic Books, 2006.

Morozov, Evgeny. *The Net Delusion: The Dark Side of Internet Freedom.* Public Affairs, 2011.

Post, David G. *In Search of Jefferson's Moose: Notes on the State of Cyberspace.* Oxford University Press, 2009.

Reid, T. R. *How Two Americans Invented the Microchip and Launched a Revolution.* Random House, 2001.

Zittrain, Jonathan. *The Future of the Internet and How to Stop It.* Yale University Press, 2008.

COUNTER-TERRORISM

Baer, Martha, Katrina Heron, Oliver Morton, and Evan Ratliff. *Safe: The Race to Protect Ourselves in a Newly Dangerous World.* HarperCollins, 2005.

Baker, Stewart. *Skating on Stilts: Why We Aren't Stopping Tomorrow's Terrorism.* Hoover Institute, 2010.

Chesney, Robert. "Military-Intelligence Convergence and the Law of the Title 10/Title 50 Debate." *Journal of National Security Law and Policy* 5 (2012): 539.

George, Roger Z., and Harvey Rishikof, eds. *The National Security Enterprise: Navigating the Labyrinth.* Georgetown University Press, 2011.

Schmitt, Eric, and Thom Shanker. *Counterstrike: The Untold Story of America's Secret Campaign against Al-Qaeda.* Macmillan, 2011.

CYBERSECURITY: GENERALLY

Charney, Scott. *Collective Defense: Applying Public Health Models to the Internet.* Microsoft Corp., 2010.

"Cybersecurity Symposium." *Journal of National Security Law and Policy* 4, no. 1 (2010).

Department of Justice, Office of Legal Counsel. *Legality of Intrusion Detection System to Protect Unclassified Computer Networks in the Executive Branch.* August 2009.

Department of Justice, Office of Legal Counsel. *Legal Issues Relating to the Testing, Use, and Deployment of an Intrusion Detection System (Einstein 2.0) to Protect Unclassified Computer Networks in the Executive Branch.* January 2009.

Executive Office of the President, *National Strategy for Trusted Identities in Cyberspace.* April 2011.

Karas, Thomas, Judy Moore, and Lori Parrot. *Metaphors for Cybersecurity.* Sandia National Laboratory, 2008.

DATAMINING AND GOVERNMENT DATABASES

Bailey, Dennis. *The Open Society Paradox: Why the 21st Century Calls for More Openness—Not Less.* Brassey's, 2004.

Harris, Shane. *The Watchers: The Rise of America's Surveillance State.* Penguin Press, 2010.

The Markle Foundation. *Protecting America's Freedom in the Information Age: A Report of the Markle Foundation Task Force.* 2002. The Markle Foundation.

The Markle Foundation. *Creating a Trusted Network for Homeland Security.* 2003.

O'Harrow, Robert, Jr. *No Place to Hide.* Free Press, 2005, The Markle Foundation.

Smith, Derek V. *Risk Revolution: The Threats Facing America and Technology's Promise for a Safer Tomorrow.* Longstreet Press, 2004.

ECONOMICS

Fisher, Eric A. *Creating a National Framework for Cybersecurity: An Analysis of Issues and Opinions.* Nova Science Publishers, 2009.

Grady, Mark F., and Francesco Paris, eds. *The Law and Economics of Cybersecurity.* Cambridge University Press, 2006.

Ostrom, Elinor. *Governing the Commons: The Evolution of Institutions for Collective Action.* Cambridge University Press, 1990.

Powell, Benjamin. "Is Cybersecurity a Public Good? Evidence from the Financial Services Industry." *Journal of Law, Economics and Policy* 1 (2005): 497.

Thaler, Richard, and Cass Sunstein. *Nudge: Improving Decisions about Health, Wealth, and Happiness.* Yale University Press, 2008.

ENCRYPTION AND WIRETAPPOING

Al-Kadi, Ibraham A. "The Origins of Cryptology: The Arab Contributions." *Cryptologia* 16, no. 2 (April 1992).

Gardner, Martin. "A New Kind of Cipher that Would Take Millions of Years to Break." *Scientific American* 237 (August 1997).

Landau, Susan. *Surveillance or Security: The Risks Posed by New Wiretapping Technologies*. MIT Press, 2011.

Levy, Steven. *Crypto: How the Code Rebels Beat the Government, Saving Privacy in the Digital Age*. Penguin Press, 2001.

Singh, Simon. *The Code Book*. Doubleday, 1999.

ESPIONAGE AND CRIME

Brenner, Joel. *America the Vulnerable: Inside the New Threat Matrix of Digital Espionage, Crime and Warfare*. Penguin Press, 2011.

Office of the National Counterintelligence Executive. *Foreign Spies Stealing US Economic Secrets in Cyberspace*. October 2011.

U.S.–China Economic and Security Review Commission. *Report to Congress*. November 2010.

VeriSign. *The Russian Bussiness Network: Rise and Fall of a Criminal ISP*. March 2008.

THE FUTURE

Garnder, Dan. *Future Babble: Why Expert Predictions are Next to Worthless, and You Can do Better*. Dutton, 2011.

Hawkins, Jeff. *On Intelligence: How a New Understanding of the Brain Will Lead to the Creation of Truly Intelligent Machines*. Owl Books, 2004.

Taleb, Nassim. *Black Swan: The Impact of the Highly Improbable*. Random House, 2007.

GOVERNMENT ORGANIZATION

Center for Strategic and International Studies. *Securing Cyberspace for the 44th Presidency*. December 2008.

Department of Homeland Security and National Security Agency. *Memorandum of Understanding Regarding Cybersecurity*. October 10, 2010.

Executive Office of the President. *Cyber Space Policy Review: Assuring a Trusted and Resilient Information and Communications Infrastructure*. May 29, 2009.

Executive Office of the President. *Comprehensive National Cybersecurity Initiative*. 2010 (declassified version).

HARDWARE PROBLEMS

Department of Commerce. *Defense Industrial Base Assessment: Counterfeit Electronics*. January 2010.

Report of the Defense Science Board. *Mission Impact of Foreign Influence on DoD Software*. September 2007.

INTERNATIONAL CYBERSECURITY

Demchack, Chris, and Peter Dombrowski. "Rise of a Cybered Westphalian Age." *Strategic Studies Quarterly* (Spring 2011).

Executive Office of the President. *International Strategy for Cyberspace.* May 2011.
Goldsmith, Jack. "Cybersecurity Treaties: A Skeptical View," in *Future Challenges in National Security and Law*, edited by Peter Berkowitz (Hoover Institution, 2011).

MALWARE
Alperovitch, Dmitri. *Revealed: Operation Shady RAT.* McAfee, August 2011.
Bowden, Mark. *Worm: The First Digital World War.* Atlantic Monthly Press, 2011.
Combating Robot Networks and Their Controllers: A Study for the Public Security and Technical Program (unclassified version 2.0, May 6, 2010).
Symantec. W32.Stuxnet Dossier (February 2011).
"Tracking GhostNet: Investigating a Cyber Espionage Network." *Information Warfare Monitor* (March 29, 2009).

PRIVACY AND SECRECY
Mayer-Schoenberger, Victor. *Delete: The Virtue of Forgetting in the Digital Age.* Princeton University Press, 2009.
No More Secrets: National Security Strategies for a Transparent World. American Bar Association, Office of the National Counterintelligence Executive and National Strategy Forum (March 2011).
Raul, Alan Charles. *Privacy and the Digital State: Balancing Public Information and Personal Privacy.* Kluwer Academic Publishers, 2002.
Rosen, Jeffrey. *The Naked Crowd: Reclaiming Security and Freedom in an Anxious Age.* Random House, 2004.
Solove, Daniel J., and Paul M. Schwartz. *Privacy, Information and Tehcnology,* 2nd ed. Wolters Kluer, 2009.

WARFARE
Carr, Jeffrey. *Inside Cyber Warfare.* O'Reilly, 2010.
Clarke, Richard A., and Robert K. Knake. *Cyber War: The Next Threat to National Security and What to Do About It.* HarperCollins, 2010.
Department of Defense. *Strategy for Operating in Cyberspace.* July 2011.
Department of Defense. *Cyberspace Policy Report.* November 2011.
Government Accountability Office. *Defense Department Cyber Efforts.* May 2011.
Kramer, Franklin, Stuart Starr, and Larry Wentz, eds. *Cyberpower and National Security.* National Defense University, 2009.
Libicki, Martin. *Cyberdeterrence and Cyberwar.* RAND, 2009.
Lynn, William J., III. "Defending a New Domain: The Pentagon's Cyberstrategy." *Foreign Affairs* 97 (September/October 2010).
Nye, Joseph S., Jr. *Cyber Power.* Harvard Belfer Center, 2010.
Nye, Joseph. *Soft Power: The Means to Success in World Politics.* Public Affairs, 2004.

Owens, William, Kenneth Dam, and Herbert Lin, eds. *Technology, Policy, Law, and Ethics Regarding U.S. Acquisition and Use of Cyber Attack Capabilities.* National Academies Press, 2009.

Proceedings of a Workshop on Deterring Cyberattacks: Informing Strategies and Developing Options for U.S. Policy. National Academies Press, 2010.

Rattray, George J. *Strategic Warfare in Cyberspace.* MIT Press, 2001.

Index

About the Author

PAUL ROSENZWEIG is the founder of Red Branch Consulting PLLC, a homeland security consulting company, and a senior advisor to The Chertoff Group. Rosenzweig formerly served as Deputy Assistant Secretary for Policy in the Department of Homeland Security. He also serves as a professorial lecturer in law at George Washington University, a senior editor of the *Journal of National Security Law & Policy,* and a visiting fellow at The Heritage Foundation. In 2011 he was a Carnegie Visiting Fellow at the Medill School of Journalism, Northwestern University.